RAJA RAMMOHUN ROY

RAJA RAMMOHUN ROY

Edited by

Dr. Shiv Gajrani

Dr. S. Ram

Commonwealth

Raja Rammohun Roy

First Published : **2012**

ISBN 81-311-0012-X

Published by :

Ajay Verma
For COMMONWEALTH PUBLISHERS
4831/24, Prahlad Street,
Ansari Road, Darya Ganj,
New Delhi - 110002
Ph. : 23272541, 23257835
Fax : 91- 011- 23257835
e-mail : campusbooks@hotmail.com

Typesetting by :

Arjun Computers
Delhi - 110051

Printed at :

Roshan Offset Printers
Delhi

PREFACE

In the category of social reformers, the name of Raja Rammohun Roy is most significant in the annals of Indian sub-continent. A contemporary of Lord William Bentinck, an enlightened Governor-General of India, he showed much interest and took up several measures having deep bearing on the social life of common people. The evils of social ills like sati, infanticide, widow remarriage and others were taken up quite seriously for their eradication from their routes. He had to face criticism from the orthodox elements of our society. But his firm resolve and disciplined work did pay him as well as the Indian society rich dividends.

Thus he was the pioneer in the social reform movement. And after a few decades, other social reformers representing various organisations, began to work on the lines and way of life shown by Raja Rammohun Roy. This volume, therefore, covers several aspects of social reforms which proved useful for a common Indian.

We have collected the material from several academic institutions and research centres. These are the Nehru Memorial Museum and Library, Sapru House Library, Central Secretariat Library, Jawaharlal Nehru University Library, Indian Council of Historical Research Library and Delhi University Library and feel much beholden to the members of the staff of these institutions for their help during my researches. We are grateful to the several eminent authors whose writings have been used in this volume.

Dr. Shiv Gajrani
Dr. S. Ram

CONTENTS

1 THE CAREER

Rammohun lived and led an active life in this city for only fifteen years, from 1815 to 1830. He left for England on November 15, 1830, reached there on April 8, 1831 and died there on September 27, 1833 after having lived and worked there for about two years and a half. How he engaged himself these seventeen years and odd and what he strove to do to bring about a social, religious and intellectual transformation towards modernization in the life of his countryman, is more or less well-known. The essays that follow in this book happen to be attempts to interpret his life and work of these seventeen years in the main. One need not, therefore, try to repeat the same or even summarise the main trends and emphases of these essay. But one may attempt to draw attention to certain broad features of Rammohun's activities during the last seventeen years of his life in the context of his own times as much as in that of what happened in the history of our land people in the century and a half that followed after his death.

One of Rammohun's unique contributions to the Hinduism of his times was to give back to it its own essence, and make it stand on its own fundamental truth, namely, the Upanishadic Brahman as the one and only object of devotion and adoration. This essentially intellectual concept of godhead had become obscured by layer upon layer of false, irrelevant and irrational ideas, myths and legends which has led to the worship of a countless number of gods and goddesses in their anthropomorphic or theriomorphic forms, complex rites and rituals of doubtful significance and meaningless, sometimes even inhuman, practices and observation. All that Rammohun essayed to do was to rid the religion of these accretions and make known to his knowledgeable countrymen that they had a higher, nobler and a more intellectual concept of godhead and a much simpler and more straight forward form of devotion and adoration.

But what is more significant is that he sought to establish this position with full knowledge of the relevant scriptural texts in this regard, in original Sanskrit, and by and through a close comparative study of the texts, tenets and behavioural practices of other religions, namely, Islam and Christianity. In presenting his case he appealed to man's reason and intellect and to nothing else; indeed his method was always rational, critical and analytical, logical argument being his tool. How different this method was and what it meant, should be clear when it is realised that in the past, in traditional dialogues and disputations in regard to religion, the reasoning at the final analysis rested on the authority of scriptural texts, revealed, quasi-revealed or otherwise, and not on human reasoning. Rammohun was thus the first in contemporary Indian to break away form this tradition and take his stand on the rational functioning of the mind and the intellect, a gift which he had readily accepted from the contemporary Western intellectual tradition. He had also accepted, equally readily, the comparative method in the study of religion and the analytical tool of textual criticism, both as gifts from the same Western intellectual tradition. Insofar as India was concerned he was thus the pioneer in introducing into the intellectual life of the land, modern attitudes and approaches and modern tools and techniques in regard to the study and understanding or religion, be it Hindu-Brahmanism or Islam or Christianity. It is immature understanding or obstinate orthodoxy to bring in for comparison other contemporary personalities in this regard; they all belonged to the older tradition of reasoning on scriptural authority and had hardly any knowledge and experience of what Rammohun was seeking to do and with what tools and techniques. Rammohun was indeed trying to modernise the intellectual life of India while others were trying to perpetuate the tradition in the name of *sastriya* authority. Indeed, none in the then Bengal could appreciate Rammohun properly before men like Akshay Kumar Datta and

Isvarchandra Vidyasagar, who had the same rational and intellectual approach to religion, took up once more the work which Rammohun had begun.

The same rational and intellectual approach marked whatever Rammohun did in regard to the eradication of certain inhuman practices that obtained in Hindu-Brahmanical society of contemporary Bengal, the practice of Sati, for instance. He was as vehemently opposed to this practice as a few others were. But he was somewhat and somehow reluctant to have the practice abolished by and through legislation enacted by a foreign colonial political authority. His method was to have the inhuman evil wiped out through educating and rousing public opinion against the practice, and he wrote and argued ceaselessly towards that objective. He knew that legislation by a foreign authority would drive the practice underground, which it actually did, in Bengal as elsewhere, for quite some time. But if a strong, knowledgeable public opinion could be created against the practice, for which the time was ripe, it could be wiped out altogether. Later Indian history has proved how right Rammohun was in this regard. Isvarchandra Vidyasagar had a legislation enacted in favour of allowing Hindu widows to remarry and lead normal married life. Since then there has been no bar to widows marrying for the second or more times. But even to this day traditional Hindu-Brahman society has not been able to reconcile itself to the marriage of its widows. Harbilas Sard's Act, promulgated in pre-Independent India, prohibiting child marriage, has also met with the same fate. The practice of child marriage is still almost a normal practice in the lower orders of Hindu society. The argument boils down to this that any step to be taken in matters social, which affects society in its socio-religious beliefs and practices as much as they do in regard to economic interests, the society concerned has to be educated in regard to any reform measure to be undertaken and a public opinion created. One may or may not agree with this reasoning, but this seems to have been the argument that prevailed with Rammohun, and he may not have been altogether wrong.

But a much more significant reform measure which Rammohun was interested in and pleaded for, was the right to property for Hindu women, an item of activity in his life which has not received a attention it deserved at the hands of scholars and intellectuals. He was first to draw the attention of his countrymen in this regard, but not until Independence the voice of Rammohun did have a sound hearing and no attention was paid to this pitiable, helpless situation of Hindu women. His soul must have felt pleased when Independent India chose to extend to them the right that Rammohun had pleaded for more than a century and a half before!

But much more than social reform Rammohun was deeply interested in those area of contemporary life where he though, he should be able to bring about a transformation in the direction of modernization of the intellectual life of his contemporary countrymen. Unerringly did he realise that the main instrument in this regard was at that time the English language and through the doors and windows of this language, the free and uninhibited flow of contemporary Western ideas and institutions and Western sciences. To that end he worked and wrote incessantly, not for gaining any immediate practical worldly advantage for his countrymen but with a view to liberate their minds from medieval orthodoxy and obscurantism. He therefore did all that he could to further the interest of the introduction of the Western system of education through the medium of English. Whether his name appears among the signatories who appealed for the foundation of the Hindu College or not—it is common knowledge why it does not-is a somewhat irrelevant question in this regard, since any student of history of the period knows that there was no better and no more active protagonist and fighter for this cause among Indians than Rammohun himself. His was the vision of an India coming out of the closed shell of mediaevalism and crossing the threshold of the modern world with the aid of what the English people had brought to the doors of India. The principal signatories to the appeal for the foundation of the Hindu College had no such vision and no imagination to understand what

Rammohun was struggling for; what interested others were certain immediate practical, worldly ends.

To what extent Rammohun was committed to the Western idea of progress and of modernisation through Western learning and science, would be evident from one simple fact of his life in Calcutta. In 1831 when Parliament renewed the Company's Charter for the third time, it directed the Government of India to spend not less than a lakh of rupees every year towards "the revival and improvement of [Indian] literature and the encouragement and promotion of a knowledge of the science among the British territories of India". But nothing was done in this regard for a number of years. Then in 1823 Lord Amherst's Government decided, mainly at the persistent behest of the Sanskritist, Colebrooke, to spend this amount, or a considerable part of it, towards the foundation and maintainenance of a Sanskrit College in Calcutta. Rammohun self somewhat disturbed and wrote a long letter to Amherst detailing his opinion in regard to what he though, should be the policy of the Government of India in respect of education and learning in this country. He argued that Europe and England had found it worthiest to give up the system of education which had been made current by the medieval School men, that is by the scholastic clericals, and to replace it by a different system dominated by Bacon's idea of knowledge and learning, and that this new system was instrumental in bringing about the great transformation from the darkness of medieval ignorance, orthodoxy and superstition to the light and knowledge, the power and progress which characterised modern European civilization. The remedy in India, he argued, should not be different. He argued further that if it was the intention of Government to keep India immersed in the mediaeval darkness of ignorance, orthodoxy and superstition, there was certainly no better way than to persist in the system of education and learning through Sanskrit, just as mediaeval Europe had done through Latin. He suggested instead that the Government should adopt a liberal, modern and progressive policy in India through the establishment of a college given to the British system of education through the medium of the English language, employment of a few "European Gentlemen of talents and education to instruct the natives of India in Mathematics, Natural Philosophy, Chemistry, Anatomy and other useful sciences, which the nations of Europe have carried to a degree of perfection that has raised them above the inhabitants of other parts of the world". He also pleaded for the rearing up of libraries and laboratories with necessary equipments in the same institution. He though that he spending of Government funds in this regard would be much more fruitful than doing so in perpetuation an old system of education which would only mean perpetuation of the mediaeval scholastic tradition.

Rammohun himself, even his antagonists of today would admit, was a great Sanskrit scholar, one who has rad the *sastras* as any scholastic would and knew what mediaeval scholastic learning meant and was intended for. Therefore when he was speaking against its perpetuation, he was fully conscious of what he was doing. It was not for nothing that he referred to Bacon in this regard; he could have referred to others as well. But symbolically and ideologically speaking, Bacon was enough for his purpose. Clearly and unequivocally, Rammohun was looking forward to a social transformation in India from mediaeval scholasticism which was another world for scriptural and priestly authoritarianism, obscurantism and orthodoxy, to the modern world of reason, of science and of the modern idea of progress. It is a sort of intellectual obtuseness to interpret Rammohun's attitude in this regard as his opposition to Sanskrit as such, as some have done; what he was opposed to was the perpetuation of the traditional form of Sanskrit education and mediaeval scholastic learning. How true Rammohun's vision and attitude were has been amply proved by the persistence even to this day, of forces which are backward-looking, orthodox and conservative, and even when knowledgeable at their best, closed, narrow and scholastic, and all this in the name of India's priestly Brahmanical tradition. This has been very largely due to the mediaeval scholastic tradition and approach which still obtain in that are concerned with teaching and research in the so-called Oriental and Indological studies.

The same attitude characterised Rammohun's activities in regard to adaptation, translation and interpretation of Sanskrit scriptural text in Bengali, an item of work which invited the positive wrath of all traditionalists in the country. Evidently Rammohun wanted to draw the *sastras* out of the monopolistic control of the priestly and scholastic communities who had thereby created large vested interests in the contemporary Hindu social order, by making them available and interpreting their contents of knowledge to more and more people. Despite opposition by the traditionalists, Rammohun's idea and the example set by him caught on, and it was not long before it began to be emulated first by the Christian missionaries and then by the Bengali intellectuals themselves. One may not forget that this is exactly what happened in Europe when Martin Luther and the Reformation movement initiated by him released the Bible from the bondage to Latin and to the mediaeval scholastic tradition, and made it available in the regional languages. Not a little of the success of the Reformation movement was due to this one single measure.

Equally significant was Rammohun's support to and utilisation of the opportunities thrown open by the new technology of printing, an innovation that has considerably helped and accelerated the pace of progress of the Reformation movement in Europe for centuries earlier. Rammohun seems to have welcomed this innovation and utilised it as much and as best as he could towards the furtherance of his idea of progress and his immediate objective which was not very different from that of the European Reformation movement. Any attack on the freedom that this technology had brought about, any curtailment of the opportunities opened up by it, Rammohun resisted and fought against as much as he could. He was actively associated for most of the year he was in Calcutta, with a number of newspapers and periodicals in Persian, Urdu, English and Bengali, directly as editor and writer, or indirectly as patron, policy-maker and occasional contributor. Newspapers and periodicals, he recognised at once, were major instruments of his times for the modernization and liberalization of the mind which he was fighting for all the time. An analysis of the news and views of the journals of the time would show that Rammohun's association lay with those alone which were liberal and forward-looking in their outlook and were prepared to uphold the causes with which he had identified himself. When therefore in April 1823 John Adams, the Acting Governor General, took away the freedom of the newspapers and periodicals to articulate whatever news and views they wanted to, Rammohun was the first and perhaps the only one to draw up and address a memorandum to the authorities criticising the Government action and strongly upholding the freedom of the newspapers and periodical. But not until two years after his death was this freedom restored (May 18, 1935).

Even in his youth Rammohun was drawn to Islam because of the absolute unitariness of its godhead and its egalitarianism. He studied Islam and its scriptures as closely as he did Brahmanical Hinduism and its sastras, both from the point of view of its doctrines and its behavioural manifestations. Later in life, when in Calcutta, he was also deeply attracted towards Christianity; the life of Christ and his precepts of morality and peace had made a deep impression on him. He therefore studied the Bible and the origin and evolution of its textual versions and of Christianity, as closely as a student of Divinity would but also as critically and analytically as a student of comparative religion would. He entered into long polemics with Christian missionaries some of whom he knew very closely, and placed himself in close comradeship with the Unitarian Christians and their church. But ultimately, he drew himself away from both Islam and Christianity. In both he found prejudices and superstitions, bigotry and narrow-mindedness and apocryphal beliefs and practices clouding heavily the pristine purity of the respective faiths and blocking the clear passage of rational thought and practice. Besides, he came to dislike Islam for the Muslim intolerance of other religions, and Christianity became distasteful to him because of the "unscripturablity and unreasonableness of the doctrine of Trinity" prevalent among the Christians, the doctrine being not only apocryphal but also obscurantist. He had also observed that even the missionaries of the Christian Church did not care much for the religious and moral precepts of Jesus Christ.

Equally had he drawn himself away from the prejudices, superstitions, apocryphal and irrational beliefs, immoral practices, multiplicity of gods and goddesses and the rites and rituals that attended their worship, etc. which have been obtaining for centuries in the religion to which he was born. Indeed, he came to believe in nothing which did not stand the test of human reasoning. He was convinced "that in point of vices the Hindus were not worse than the generality of Christian in Europe and America", but defended the fundamentals of Hinduism again and again against the ignorant and malafide attacks of Christian missionaries. More than this; he found in Hinduism that it had a hard, solid core in the intellectual concept of Brahma, the one absolute godhead, which would be sustained rationally and to whom adoration could be made and devotion paid without taking recourse to any irrational faith or myth or apocryphal legned or meaningless religious rites and observances. He also thought that here was a concept which agreed with the fundamental concepts of both Islam and Christianity, and which could therefore form the basis of his vision of a universal religion. Indeed, it was this vision or dream that seems to have led him to the establishment of the Brahmasabha where he introduced a faith and a mode of worship sought to integrated the fundamentals of Hinduism, Islam and Christianity and quite a few of the practices of all the three major religions of India. A universal religion for mankind is still a dream or vision of all sensitive souls, which may or may not ever be achieved; like peace and harmony among the peoples of the world, this vision to eludes mankind from one failure to the next. Yet it is there and perhaps will ever be, and there will be sentinels to remind humanity and make them conscious of the needs of such a vision and of human efforts to that end. In his time Rammohun was that sentinel, one and the only one perhaps in the warring world of the nineteenth century.

But Rammohun was far from being a dreamer and a visionary; indeed, he was a very practical man of human affairs and never lost his touch with actual life. With him religion was also a social institution with a social purpose. He felt convinced that the Hinduism that he saw practised before his eyes by the Hindus was "not well calculated to promote their political interests. The distinction of castes, introducing innumerable divisions and sub-divisions among them has entirely deprived them of any patriotic feeling, and the multitude of religious rites and ceremonies and the laws of purification have totally disqualified them from undertaking any difficult enterprise.. It is, I think, necessary that some change should take place in their religion, at least for the sake of their political advantage and social comfort." There was not another man in India or Rammohun's time to have an understanding of this kind and to speak in this language.

Rammohun's intellectual quest led him beyond the frontiers of the "great tradition" of the three formal religions—Brahmanical Hinduism, Islam and Christianity—to certain "little traditions" of Indian religions and religious practices which were of a certain protestant character. His close association with the *avadhut* Hariharananda Swami is more or less well-known. Equally well-known is his interest is his interest in certain elements of contemporary Tantrik faith and practice and his regard for the *Mahanirvanatantra* in particular. This Tantrik text, everybody knows, is not one of the classical ones; indeed, it is recognised as a very late text, and I for one would not feel surprised if one day it is found that Rammohun himself was its compiler. But be that as it may, the fact remains that he was drawn to these faiths and practices just as he was to another contemporary Bengali cult, that of the Kartabhajas. It will be noticed that there is one lowest common denominator which characterises all these cults and sects. First, these cults and sects were all protestant in their attitudes and approaches towards Brahmanical Hinduism and its system of caste and practice of icon-worship. Secondly, the followers of these cults were all believers in the unitariness of godhead. It is no wonder therefore that Rammohun would seek to find an argument or two in his favour from among these sects and cults also a sort of support in favour of his personal stand. That the esoterism of these sects could not have beguiled a rational mind like that of Rammohun's, one may perhaps assert with some amount of certainty.

In that dark, narrow-visioned and ossified India of the late eighteen and early nineteenth century, Rammohun's was the only vision and voice which held India as one cultural and political entity despite her caste system, multiplicity of religions and religious sects, of languages, customs and behaviour patterns and not the lest, narrow local and regional prides and prejudices. Whether he was speaking of Buddhism and Sikhism, or pleading for a piece of political or economic reform, or enganging himself in polemics with the Christian missionaries, he always held up before his minds eye the vision and image of the totality of India. This one cannot help perceiving that here was something which he left as a legacy to those of his successors who took upon themselves the task of modernizing the country.

Enough has gone into the essays that constitute this small book, to show that Rammohun besides being a patriot and nationalist, albeit the first of the kind in India, was also a political and economic thinker, his ideas being basically derived from the latest in progressive political and economic thought of the West, but articulated in down to earth, practical terms in the contemporary context of India's needs and requirements which he seems to have known so well. But more than this, he was a humanist, a cosmopolitan and universalist, one who has indeed drawn the whole world unto him and had acquired a world-view of things. And by himself being so in word and deed, he was able to give a new direction to the contemporary and future culture of India. One may not forget for centuries in the past this had not happened in India.

At the time of the first death-centenary of Rammohun, in

a public meeting in Calcutta (1933) Rabindranath Tagore described Rammohun as the path-finder of modern India. What the poet said was just a statement of fact which is widely recognised by his grateful countrymen. The present esay has been written to show that in all matters in which he engaged himself—and he did so practically in everything that concerned contemporary life, thought and action as none else among his contemporaries and very few of his nineteenth century successors did—he brought to bear upon each one of them a new idea and vision and a new technique of thought, his attitude and approach to men and things being rational and intellectual from beginning to end. His interests and knowledge too, were encyclopaedic in form character, encompassing religion and philosophy, language and literature, politics and economics, society and education, science and technology and public affairs of contemporary life of his own countrymen as much as of those of the wide world outside.

Rationalism, encyclopaedism, nationalism, humanism, cosmopolitanism, a critical and analytical, intellectual and comparative outlook, acceptance of science and technology as direct major tools for social transformation—these are the elements which constituted what one calls the modern world, at any rate of the late eighteenth, nineteenth and a good part of the twentieth century. Insofar as India was concerned Rammohun was the first, and for quite some time after, the only one to commit himself to and take a leading part in all these elements, and do so consistently, tenaciously and with firm intellectual conviction. By being the first active and consistent spokesman and upholder of these elements which had brought about and sustained and modern civilized world. Rammohun proved himself to be the first great moderniser of India and India's first great intellectual to have a vision and image of India forging ahead to play one day meaningful role in the history of the world.

In a context of this nature it is idle if not meaningless historical inquiry which tries to prove, for instance, that Rammohun was no inquiry which tries to prove, for instance, that Rammohun was no signatory to appeal for the foundation of the Hindu College, thereby implying what, one does not known, or that he opposed the spending of public money for the establishment of the Sanskrit College, ostensibly towards the perpetuation of traditional priestly and scholastic education, or that he was opposed to legislation by a foreign colonial power towards the abolition of the inhuman custom of Sati, or that Mrityunjay Vidayalankar was an earlier and better writer of Bengali prose than Rammohun. If Rammohun was no signatory to the Hindu College appeal, the reason is quite well-known why he was not. Besides, does it prove that Rammohun was no protagonist of the modern system of English education and that he did not work actively and ceaselessly towards its introduction in the country? Or, does it prove that Radhakanta Deb and others who were signatories were greater protagonists of the modern English system of education than Rammohun was? Motivations apart, available evidence is overwhelmingly against both these assumptions. Secondary, Rammohun made no secret of the fact that he was decidedly against the perpetuation of the traditional system of scholastic learning which the proposed Sanskrit college was going to do, and publicly did he oppose the move. This does not prove that Rammohun was against Sanskrit and its great linguistic, literary and cultural heritage as such. In fact, none in his times seems to have imbibed its essence more than he had done. Thirdly, Rammohun was convinced that legal and police powers already available in the hands cf Government were more than enough to cope with the Sati evil, if they really wanted to, but they did not, since, they were afraid of orthodox public opinion voiced by men like Radhakanta Deb, Bhavanicharan Bandhyopadhyay, Tarinicharan Mitra and others. Rammohun therefore bent all his energies towards combating this orthodox opinion by articulating himself publicly through all sorts of public media available at that time. His opposition to further legislation by a foreign colonial power, with which one may agree or not, does not therefore prove that he was opposed to the eradication of the inhuman and immoral custom, and did not work ceaselessly to that end. Fourthly, Mrityunjay

Vidyalankar was certainly an earlier writer of Bengali prose, and a fine writer indeed. But he wrote text-books of stories, fables and anecdotes, including a popular history of India, for the students of the Fort William College, mainly at the behest of William Carey, and this in a style which was easy, lucid and freely flowing. He never made any attempt to write *intellectual* Bengali prose, as Rammohun did for the better part of his life, except in his voluminous *Vedantachandrika* written as a venomous polemics in bad taste and directed against Rammohun and his stand on the *Vedanta*. The Bengali prose of Mrityunjay's *Vedanta-chandrika* is however neither earlier nor better than that evolved by Rammohun for discussion and interpretation of the Hindu-Brahmanical *sastras*. This is not the place for a discussion of the evolution of Rammohun's prose style, but one may note in passing that when discussing or interpreting the *sastras* he chose to write in a style which was very close to that of the Sanskrit commentators, since on such occasions he was addressing his words to the traditional Sanskrit *pandits* and school men and trying to meet them on their own terms. But when he was writing for the knowledgeable general public on matters other than sastric, he chose to write in a different style which was clear, lucid and easily intelligible and yet intellectual and all the time.

Be that as it may, some of our scholars, even the more mature and senior ones, who have worked on Rammohun and his times, seem to think that all "facts" are equally meaningful and relevant. That "fact" and truth in history are synonymous, that "facts" can be looked at and interpreted in isolation from the total context of a given situation and away from their inter-relation with other relevant "facts", and that acts of omission and commission of an individual or a group can be interpreted and judged without reference to recorded motivations which prompted those acts. Or, otherwise they would not have spent time and energy to prove certain factual point which have very little meaning or relevance in the total context of Rammohun's encyclopaedic life and activities. Besides, they would not have arrived at the conclusions which they did if they would have looked at their "facts" and interpreted them in the light of and in association with Rammohun's other activities in the same and allied fields along with the recorded motivations thereof. If they did so they would have realised that even if what they had arrived at, were absolute as "facts", these would not much affect even the relevant areas of Rammohun's life, far less his total contribution to modern Indian culture and his image as the first modernizer in this part of the world. Once this is realised, there would be, one hopes, a further realisation that even their so-called "proven" facts are just like small slippery plants in a huge, sprawling and majestic forest.

But the real meaning of such attempts at clouding the image of Rammohun and confusing the causes that he stood for, seems to me to lie elsewhere. This meaning is, to my mind, historically and culturally so significant that even at the risk of trying the patience of my readers I would try to explain what I mean.

Even during his life-time Rammohun had to encounter strong opposition from many powerful adversaries, and in respect of practically every single item of social change which he stood for. Forces of tradition, of orthodoxy and conservatism were very strong and their activist spokesman included some of the leading and powerful members of the Hindu gentry of Calcutta. In regard to matters social and religious their attitude and approach, out and out priestly and scholastic, were clearly and straight forwardly in favour of the perpetuation of the traditional system in every respect, including the custom of *Sati* even, not to speak of the mediaveval social order and its behaviour pattern. In regard to the Western system of education in the English medium, their attitude was somewhat ambivalent; they did not like or welcome it, but since it was fast becoming a practical necessity because of the historical situation, they were being obliged to its acceptance. Of political and economic issues raised by the changing historical situation, they did not have much of an awareness, far less any active interest. Insulated from what was happening in the wide world outside, they had no interest in science and technology and their attitude towards other religions and cultures than their own was somewhat characterized by racial prejudice, if not positive race hatred. Their world view was thus altogether different from that of Rammohun; the difference was indeed of a polar nature.

The history of this subcontinent for the last well-high one hundred and fifty years has shown, very clearly and manifestly, that the mainstream of Indian public life and culture, at any rate of its knowledgeable and dominant minority that has been providing the leadership, has been flowing, by the large along the channel dug by Rammohun. A forward-looking, rational and intellectual outlook, an active interest in social, political and economic reform and regeneration, increasing modernization of our life and thought by opening ourselves up to Western education and learning, ideas and institutions and to science and technology and yet at the same time trying to articulate ourselves, both creatively and intellectually, more and more in our regional languages, and retain some of those values of our past culture which are still potent-these have been the features which have in general characterised our public life and activities. Confining oneself to Bengal alone for a moment one may say that men like Devendranath Tagore, Akshay Kumar Dutta, Isvarchandra Vidyasagar, Michael Madhusudan Datta, Rajnarayan Basu, Bipinchandra Pal and Rabindranath Tagore, for instance, were all as much products as moulders of this culture to which Rammohun had given the original drive and direction.

But there is no reason to assume that the forces of tradition, of orthodoxy and conservatism and of priestly scholasticism had lost their hold altogether, that the breed of Radhakanta Deb and Bhabanicharan Bandyopadhyay, for instance, had become extinct. No, by no means. In fact, these forces, howsoever, dim and dormant at times, always remained as an undercurrent of the mainstream, strong enough from time to time to slow down the pace of the latter or/and to twist and torment it and create thereby fissures, confusions and contradictions in the contemporary body politic as much as in its cultural and intellectual articulation. It was this undercurrent that caused confusion in even such a creative intellectual and forceful personality as that of Bankimchandra Chattopadhyay in his later days.

These forces are at work even to this day, in our won times, and make themselves manifest in our contemporary political and socio-economic life; indeed, there are political parties which are fed and nourished by the under current of these forces. It is no wonder that these forces should be at work among a few of our historians as well. One does not find it difficult to see why the image of Rammohun should disturb them.

Rammohun worked within the limitations of a society which was not of his choice but to which he came to belong. The vast masses of this society were not only illiterate but also uneducated and totally unconscious of their rights and privileges. Leading a life of precarious existence and oppressed by local landed interests and an insensate priesthood, they had lost all initiative and enterprise and had been reduced to creatures of destiny. The social strata which Rammohun belonged to, took virtually no notice of these vast masses. The time was not just yet ripe; the social climate was altogether different, Besides, Rammohun chose to speak a language of reason which was altogether unintelligible to them; he also chose tools and techniques of social transformation, which were not designed to build a bridge by which he could reach a wider people. His approach was too rational and too intellectual and sophisticated from them. The issues too, with which he concerned himself all his life, were relatively far away from their lives. Rammohun worked within these sovereign social limitations, the reason why Gandhi while once referring to Rammohun made a casual remark that compared to personalities like Sri Chaitanyadeva Rammohun was a pigmy. Whether one agrees with Gandhi in this regard or not is a different matter, but one does not find any difficulty to understand why Gandhi said what he did. Chaitanya chose to speak a language which the common man could easily follow and respond to; by the tools and techniques he chose he could build a bridge to reach them, and he chose issues which found a ready response in their hearts. Thus did Chaitanya become one of them, their leader and spokesman, and acquire the power and prestige which enabled him to bring about social transformation of the kind he wanted. Rammohun did not have Chaitanya's broad sway over multitudes of men and women.

Indeed, Rammohun's area of functioning was a limited one, not necessarily in a geographical sense alone, but more in a social sense. His language was the language of the *elite* of all persuasions and profession; his tools, techniques and issues were all such as could interest and affect the mind and behaviour pattern of the newly forming urban, educated or semi-educated and intelligent upper and middle classes alone. His words and action were all directed towards them, for their consumption alone. Not that he said so but he seems to have worked all his life towards the creation of a small urban, educated, intelligent, well-informed and professional middle class which could provide leadership to the people of India. That this leadership should be rational and intellectual, forward-looking, open to the world outside and committed to modernisation in all walks of our life, thought and action, was *albeit* the direction of whatever he said and did.

History helped him and he seems to have been eminently successful in bringing about the class he presumably had in view. Like Rammohun, this class too came to suffer from the same limitations as he himself did. For long, indeed, not until Gandhi made his appearance on the Indian scene, this class did not know how to speak the language of the people nor try to build a bridge to reach them in any other manner. This limitation has given to modern Indian culture, despite all its achievements, a somewhat shoddy and unreal character which we have not yet been able to get rid of altogether.

2 SOCIAL IDEOLOGY

CONTEMPORARIES WHOM RAMMOHUN MET

1. Fanny Parks, author of Wanderings of a Pilgrim based on experiences of her 24 years of stay in the East, knew Rammohun intimately in his early life in Calcutta.
2. William Rathbone of Liverpool.
3. Spurzheim, the phrenologist, of Liverpool.
4. William Roscoe, a versatile scholar and author or *Life of Lorenzo de Medici and Christian Morality as Contained in the Precepts of New Testament in the Language of Jesus Christ.*
5. Jeremy Bentham, the renowned philosopher of the time. He proposed Rammohun's name for the British Parliament.
6. Joanna Baillie (1762-1831), Scottish poet and dramatist, whom Wordsworth held up as a model of English womanhood.
7. John Bowring (1792-1872), friend and biographer of Jeremy Bentham.
8. Lucy Aikin, daughter of Dr. John Aikin, Editor of *Atheneum.*
9. Ann Letitia De Breton, niece of Lucy Aikin, author of Memories of Seventy Years which contains a profile of Rammohun. She was John-Hare's neighbour.
10. Miss Kiddell of Stapleton Grove who took charge of Rammohun during his illness. Rajaram stayed with her for some time.

11. David Hare, educationist and philanthropist of Calcutta, who was Rammohun's intimate friend.
12. John Hare James Hare, Miss Hare in whose London house Rammohun stayed as guest.
13. Miss Castle, the Carpenters, the Estlines of Bristol who nursed Rammohun during his illness.
14. James Sutherland, who was with Rammohun in the same boat. He late become principal, Hooghly College.
15. H.T. Colebrooke, James Princep, H.T. Princep, H.H. Wilson, all renowned orientalists.
16. Alexander Duff. William Woodford, John Digby, Sandford Arnot, Buckingham, Middleton, Bryce.
17. Harriet Martineau (1802-76), an English advocate of Unitarianism and translator of Comte.
18. RobertOwen (1774-1858), socialist and father of Robert Dale Owen.
19. Robert Aspland, Editor of Monthy Repository.
20. Basil Montagu (1770-1851), an intimate friend of Words worth and Coleridge.
21. Rev. W.J. Fox, foreign secretary to the British and Foreign Unitarian Association.
22. John Towill Rutt, author of a biography of Priestley which he dedicated to Rammohun.
23. Fanny Kemble, actress, singer, poet and author of Record of a Girlhood.
24. Dr. Chalmers (1780-1847) of Edinburgh, introduced to Rammohun by Duff in Calcutta.
25. Thomas Moore, poet who met Rammohun at a dinner and became intimate with him.
26. Thomas Campbell, who wanted Rammohun to go to Parliament and seconded Bentham's proposal.

27. J.W. Hobhouse, President, Board of Control, who presented Rammohun to the King of England.
28. Duke of Cumberland (King's brother) who introduced Rammohun to the House of Lords.
29. Lord Brougham to whom Rammohun was introduced by Roscoe.
30. C.W. Wynn, President, Board of Control.
31. Charles Grant(jr.), President, Board of Control.
32. Abbe Gregoire, Bishop of Blois (France).
33. Victor Jacquemont, French naturalist and traveller.
34. Garcin De Tassy, orientalist and author of *Rudiments de la langue Hindi,* which contains a letter from Rammohun.
35. Burnouf (1801-1852), French Indologist.
36. Dowager Duchess of Cork, a celebrated hostess.
37. Rev. Dr. Kenny, Vicar of St. Olave.
38. Bishop Heber.

ENGAGEMENTS RAMMOHUN ATTENDED IN ENGLAND AND FRANCE

Within three or four months of his arrival in England, Rammohun started a round of parties and very soon in some of These he was the central figure. The important one's are given below :

1. Evening parties and dinners at Liverpool besides visits to churches of different denominations.
2. Parties at Manchester and meeting with William Roscoe.
3. Arrival in London and a visit to Jeremy Bentham at his house, the latter having called on Rammohun the previous night at his hotel.

4. Parties in London extending over one and a half months.
5. Visit to churches of different denominations in London.
6. East India Company's dinner City of London Tavern on July 6, 1831, attended by many prominent persons, including some retired Governors-General.
7. Reception in his honour at the Unitarian Association of England in May 1831.
8. Audience with King William IV at St. Jame's Palace on September 7, 1831, presented by Sir J.W. Hobhouse, President Board of Control.
9. King William's banquet at the opening of the London Bridge.
10. Coronation ceremony of King William where he was seated with the Ambassadors of other countries of Europe.
11. Unitarian Anniversary Divine service on February 8, 1832.
12. Select Committee of the House of Commons on Indian Reforms where Report was submitted in August, 1832.
13. Audience with King Louis Philip of France on October 14, 1832, followed by participation at the Banquet.
14. Second audience with the King of France and dinner with him.
15. Reception at Societe Asiatique of Paris for Conferment of diploma of its Honorary Membership in 1832. Rammohun had been elected a member of the Society on July 5, 1824.
16. Meeting with Robert Owen in the middle of April, 1833.
17. Rammohun's successful representation on behalf of the Emperor of Delhi to the King of England through the Board of Control.

18. Tenth Annual meeting of the Royal Society of Great Britain and Ireland on may, 11, 1833 as honoured guests.
19. Rammohun was present when the Privy Council rejected the appeal of the orthodox Hindus against the Regulation made by Bentinck in 1829.

A. LETTERS FROM RAMMOHUN TO AMERICANS.

1. To "A gentleman in Boston". This gentlemen had met Rammohun in Calcutta (published in *Christian Register*, February 1821).
2. To David Reed, Editor, Christian Register of Boston (published in Christian Register December 1821).
3. To "A gentlemen in Baltimore" October 1882.
4. To "A gentleman in Baltimore" December 1882.
5. To David Reed, written on January 13, 1824 in reply three specific question put to him by reed (published in *Christian Register* May 1824).
6. To W. Ward, February 1824.
7. To Rev. Henry Ware, written on Feburary 2, 1824, with a set of questions concerning prospects of Christianity in India (published in Christian Register 1824).
8. To "A gentlemen" in this country, December 1824.
9. To the Boston India Association, December 1825.
10. To William Alexander (from Regent's Park London address) July 1831.
11. To Joseph Tuckerman, Not dated.
12. Correspondence between Rammohun and Ellery Channing. Not yet traced.

B. LETTERS ABOUT, OR REFERENCES TO, RAMMOHUN ROY BY AMERICANS

1. W. Adam to Dr. J. Tuckerman 1826

2.	W. Adam to Rev. Gannett, Boston	1826
3.	W. Adam to Dr. J. Tuckerman	1827
4.	W. Adam to Rev. W.J. Fox	1827
5.	W. Adam to Dr. J. Tuckerman	1827
6.	W. Adam to Dr. J. Tuckerman	1828
7.	Dr. Tuckerman to the Unitarian Association	1828
8.	Lucy Aikin to Channing	1831
9.	Dr. Tuckerman to Lant Carpenter	1833
10.	Lucy Aikin to Channing	1833
11.	Unitarian Clergyman of Rammohun	Not dated
12.	English Unitarian Association in Morning Chronicale	Not dated.

C. LETTERS FROM RAMMOHUN

1. To John Digby, England (late 1816 or early 1817)

I take this opportunity of giving you a summary account of my proceedings since the period of your departure from India.

The consequences of my long and uninterrupted researches into religious truth has been I have found the doctrines of Christ more conducive to moral principles, and better adopted for the use of rational beings, than any others which have come to my knowledge; and have also found Hindus in general more superstitious and miserable, both in performance of their religious rites and in their domestic concerns, than the rest of the known nations on the earth; I therefore, with a view to making them happy and comfortable both here and hereafter, not only employed verbal arguments against the absurdities of the idolatry practised by them, but also translated their most revered theological work, namely Vedant, into Bengali and Hindustani, and also several chapters of the Ved, in order to convince them, that the unity of God, and absurdity of idolatry, are evidently pointed out by their own Scriptures. I, however; in the beginning of my pursuits, met with the greatest opposition from their self-interested leaders, the Brahmins, and was deserted by my nearest relations; I consequently felt extremely melancholy, in that critical situation, the only comfort that I had was the consoling and rational conversation of my European friends, specially those of Scotland and England.

I, now with the greatest pleasure inform you that several my countrymen have risen superior to their prejudices, many are inclined to seek for the truth, and a great number of those who dissented from me have now coincided with me in opinion. This engagement has prevented me from proceeding to Europe as soon as I could. But you may depend upon my setting off for England within a short period of time; and if you do not return to India before October next, you will most probably receive a letter from me, informing you of the exact time of my departure for England, and of the name of the vessel on which I shall embark.

The above latter appears in the preface to the London edition of Abridgement of Vedanta and Kenopanished, published by Digby in 1817.

2. To Rev. Thomas Belsham, London (1821)

As Mr. Roberts, who is about to leave India for England, has kindly offered to take charge of any letter or parcel that I might wish to send to Europe, I embrace this opportunity of expressing the gratitude I have felt for your kind notice of me and of rendering you my sincere thanks for the encouraging letter which I had the honour of receiving from you a few months ago. I at the same time should consider myself guilty of ingratitude if I neglect to offer you my warmest acknowledgements for the numerous essential benefits I have derived from that most valuable production for 'Improved Version'; it is unquestionably the best of all the versions that have hitherto appeared in English, and it is read before the Unitarian Society in Calcutta at their times of worship by its Minister Revd. Mr. Adam whose abilities and acquirements joined with his piety, sincerity, zeal and diligence had rendered him a real I honour to our community. Since my compiling and publishing the 'Precepts of the New Testament' I have been under the necessity of defending myself against the attacks of the Baptists and other Missionaries, although it was my wish to avoid as much as possible any ground of disputation with so many worthy characters. These persons are not destitute of zeal, but appear in common with a grater number of their fellow believers deficient in discretion, for they know or ought to know, that the more they employ their ingenuity in support of the idea of a Triune God the more they expose Christianity to the objections of the intelligent among both Hindus and Mussalmans and the further they drive away from all attention to their doctrines such Christians as, besides having been so brought up can think for themselves and have sincerity enough to preserve a correspondence between their sentiments and professions.

From the annexed quotations No. 1 and No. 2 from missionary works lately a published you will perceive that these Gentlemen are obliged to make the confession that in religious discussions they have little or no chance of a firm stand against those Hindus who have rejected idolatry and whom they consider imbued with Socinean principle.

This is one circumstance which has for a long time perplexed me and I still feel myself unable to understand. It is that a body of such honourable and earned men as is formed by the Dignitaries and common clergy of the Church of England should so uniformly continue during their lives to manifest their adherence to those 39 articles faith which they so solemnly subscribed to on first assuming the duties of their office, notwithstanding the fluctuations of opinion, to which their mind might naturally be supposed subject, from now arguments under perpetually changing circumstances continually presenting in the course of studies or communications with persons of a different mode of thinking. Were the doctrines contained in the articles alluded to such in order to secure immediate assent from any person of plain understanding. I could comprehend the existence of such conviction of their truth, as no argument however subtle should able to shake but as it is notorious on the contrary that many of the doctrines they contain are prescribed solely as articles of faith, deduced from authority which it is impious to dispute, though avowedly incomprehensible to human reason it is to me most surprising that arguments coming in aid of the understanding and reconciliation to reason the sacred authority deduced as they are from a variety of at least plausible sources should so very seldom seem to weigh at all in the minds of any individual members of so numerous a body. It might be unfair to doubt their sincerity yet how else to account for such an uniformity of opinion amongst so many men studying those subjects during their whole lives, I must confess myself quite at a loss.

If providence permit my visiting England, one of the greatest pleasures, I promise myself is the enjoyment and benefit of your company. I am glad to inform you that the Revd. Mr. Fox has been kind enough to send to Mr. Adam your excellent commentaries on the Epistles of St. Paul, for which we are all thankful. I am inclined to think those are the works of yours which that your intention to send me. With my sincere whishes that you may enjoy health and happiness in your declining years. (Modern Review 1932).

3. To Sir Bowring, London, (September 15, 1822). For Text Seep. 307, of My Earlier Work on Raja Rammohun Roy

4. To Dr. T. Rees, London (1824)

Reverend Sir.... I received your letter of the 16th June last., accompanied by a parcel of books to my address, with feelings of peculiar gratification. I cannot but be proud of the honour which the Committee have conferred upon me in reprinting my compilation of 'The Precepts of Jesus' and the two Appeals in its defence. I beg you will oblige me by communicating to the members my warm acknowledgement for so distinguished a mark of their approbation. I also beg you will accept my best thanks for you valuable present of the Racovian Catechism, which I shall not fail to read with due attention.

I have no language to express the happiness I derive from

the idea that so many friends of truth, both in England and America, are engaged in attempting to free originally pure, simple and practical religion of Christ from the healthenish doctrines and absurd notions gradually introduced under the Roman power, and I sincerely pray that the success of those gentlemen may be as great (if not greater than) that of Luther and others, to whom the religious world is indebted for laying the first stone of religious reformation, and having recommended the system of distinguishing divine authority from human creeds, and the practice of benevolence from ridiculous outward observances...

5. To J.B. Estlin of Bristol, Calcutta (1827)

Dear Sir,.... Mrs, Matthew being about to depart for Europe, has kindly offered to take charge of any latter of pamphlet that I may address to you. I embrace this opportunity of acknowledging the receipt of your letter and of the books, your excellent father's Lectures on Moral Philosophy, & c., which I had the honour to receive through Mrs. Matthew upwards of two years ago, and apologizing you for the delay which has unavoidably taken place in answering your kind communication. For a period of more than two years, owing to the most affecting circumstances arising from the hostile feelings of some individuals towards my family, I found myself unable to pursue any undertaking or carry on correspondence, even with those whom I sincerely loved and revered, either residing in this country or in any other part of the globe. As I intend to lay those circumstances before the public within a short period in the form of pamphet, I refrain from detailing them at present. I however trust that in consideration of the accident alluded to, you will kindly excuse the apparent neglect of which I confess I am guilty, and for which I have no other apology to offer....

6. To C.W. Wynn (1827)

....Allow me to return the volume containing the evidence on the state of Ireland, which you so very kindly lent me. It is, I presume, impossible for an uninterested person to peruse it as it is, and not come to a determination to second the cause of Catholic emancipation; I content myself with an appeal to your humanity and good sense, I regret very much that I, who am heartily anxious to co-operate with you on all religious and secular matters, should be compelled to differ so widely from you in this single but important point. As there is, I fear, no chance of any change in our respective opinions on this subject, I hasten to conclude this with my fervent wishes for your health and success in all your view and undertakings in India."

7. To J. Crawford (1882)

In the famous Jury Bill, Mr. Wynn, the late President of the Board of Control...This is the sum total of Mr. Wynn's Jury Bill, of which we bitterly complain.

Supposing that some 100 years hence the Native character becomes elevated from constant intercourse with Europeans and the Acquirements of general and political knowledge as well as of modern arts and sciences, is it possible that they will not have the spirit as well as the inclination to resist any unjust and oppressive measures.....

In common with those who seem partial to the British rule from the expectation of future benefits, arising out of the connection, I necessarily feel extremely grieved in often witnessing Acts and Requisitions passed by Government without consulting or seeming to understand the feelings of its Indian subjects and without considering that these people have had for more than half a century the advantage of being ruled by and associated with an enlightened nation, advocates of liberty and promoters of knowledge.

8. To the Governor-General, Calcutta (1830)

From the kindness....to take some interest. Having at length surmounted all the obstacles of a domestic nature... I am now resolved to proceed to that land of liberty...I have determined not to appear there as the Envoy of His Majesty Akbar the second, but as a private individual.. Chance of success may be improved.

9. Translation of a Letter to the Heir Apparent to the Emperor of Delhi (1830)

My representation is that in obedience to the orders of His Majesty, having attentively pursued the treaty between the Hon'ble Company and his late father with other papers relating thereto, I found His Majesty's right to the revenue of the territories West to the Jumna amounting to upwards of 30 Lakhs of Rupees clearly and incontestably established by those documents, notwithstanding which the Hon'ble Company pay him only 12 lakhs. As His Majesty...cannot comprehend the good or evil of others...

10. To the Governor-General, Calcutta (1830)

I beg leave to your Lordship that some months ago I was informed by His Majesty Abu-nasar Muin-ud-din Muhammad Akbar Badshah that His Majesty has apprized you Lordship of my appointment as his Elichi (Envoy) to the Court of Great Britain, and of the having been pleased to invest me as His Majesty's servant with the title of Rajah in consideration of the respectability attached to that situation. Not being anxious for titular distinction, I have hitherto to refrained from availing myself of the honour conferred on me by His Majesty.

His Majesty, however, being of opinion that it is essentially necessary for the dignity of his Royal House, that I, as the representative there of to the most powerful monarch in Europe, and Agent for the settlement of His Majesty's affairs........ should be invested with the title above-mentioned, has graciously forwarded to me a seal engraved for the purpose at Delhi. I , therefore , take the liberty of laying the subject before your Lordship, hoping that you will be pleased to sanction my adoption of such title......

11. To A. Stirling, Secretary, Political Department, Government of India, Calcutta (March 7, 1830)

It having been brought to my notice by a friend that the John Bull newspaper of the 25 Ultimo has amongst a issue of other falsehoods and misrepresentations connected my name with the charge of having obtained certain Papers by bribery, I think it but due to myself as well as to the individuals in the employment of Government who may be supposed implicated in such a charge, to deny the allegation.

All the papers alluded to were sent to me from His Majesty the king of Delhi, many of them he must have had in his own possession as having been publicly addressed to his Predecessors or himself, and other may have been procured by private favour from Functionaries who were above the reach of bribery...that however this may be I beg distinctly of indirectly concerned, the charge of bribery is absolutely false and unfounded. I beg leave to submit for your satisfaction a letter of old date from His Majesty who will confirm what I have now stated. The hand writing you write readily recognize as that of the Moonshee usually employed by him, so as to leave in you mind no doubt of its authenticity.

12. To Chairman and Dy. Chairman of the East India Company, London (1831)

I have the honour ..... principal object of my visiting England is to lay before the British authorities..... with which I am charged from His Majesty, King of Delhi..... not being attended with success. I would beg to state on the present occasion what I possess full and unlimited powers from His Majesty to negotiate and agree to the final settlement.....to be his fair and equiable claims of the Company..... As from the printed statement you will perceive that this claim regarding His Majesty's stipend was brought before and decide upon by Lord Amherst's Government, the present local Government of India could not reverse the decision passed by their predecessors......

13. To Chairman and Dy. Chairman of the East India Company, London (1831)

In continuation of my former address....of the authorities in England, I beg in the first place to bring to your notice the Minute of the Government of Lod Minto...an appeal to the authorities in England...records of your Hon'ble Court.

14. To Sir Charles Grant (1831), Followed by Two More Letters

15. To Hyde Villiers, London (1831) Followed by Three More Letters

16. To Jeremy Bentham, London (1831)

17. To Dr. Lant Carpenter, London (May 7, 1841)

......I indeed congratulate myself and you on the glorious prospects that are at present opening upon this country and all the countries depending upon it, nay on the world itself, from most important, wise and salutary political reforms now in progress....

18. To Garcin De Tassy, in Persian Language from England and (August 1, 1831)

Your blessed letter has reached me; it fills your servant with joy and honour. May the omnipotent condescend to keep you in good health. I shall wait for the day of meeting in accordance with the wish expressed in this letter. For more than three months, your servant is in England. If God wishes he shall soon have the honour to be present at Paris and through your introduction he wishes to see Mr. Chezy. Your humble servant is very grateful for the attentions you have promised him, and he wishes to thank you from the bottom of his heart. A longer letter will exceed the bounds of politeness.

19. To Prinetalleyrand, Minister for Foreign Affairs, France

Ist. To the Minister of Foreign Affairs of France, Paris, Sir, you may be surprised at receiving a letter from a Foreigner, the Native of a country situated many thousand miles from France and I assuredly would not now have tresspassed on your attention, were I not induced by a sense of what I consider due to myself and by the respect I feel towards a country standing in the foremost rank of free and civilised nations.

2nd. For twelve years past I have entertained a wish (as noticed, I think, in several French and English periodicals) to visit a country so favoured by nature and so richly adorned by the cultivation of arts and sciences, and above all blessed by the possession of a free constitution. After surmounting many difficulties interposed by religious and national distinctions and other circumstances, I am at last opposite you coast, where however, I am informed that I must not place my foot on your territory unless I previously solicit and obtain an express permission for my entrance from the Ambassador or Minister of France in England.

3rd. Such a requisition in quite unknown even among the Nations of Asia (though extremely hostile to each other from religious prejudices and political dissensions, with the exception of China, a country noted for its extreme jealousy of foreigners and apprehensions of the introduction of new customs and ideas. I am, therefore, quite at a loss to conceive how it should exist among a people so famed as the French are for courtesy and liberality in all other matters.

4th. It is now generally admitted that not religion only but unbiased commonsense as well as the acute deductions of scientific research lead to the conclusion that all mankind are one great family of which numerous nations and tribes existing are only various branches, hence enlightened men in all countries must feel a wish to encourage and facilitate human intercourse in every manner by removing as far as possible all impediments to it in order to promote the reciprocal advantage and enjoyment of the whole human race.

5th. It may perhaps be urged that during the existence of war and hostile feelings between any two nations (arising probably from their not understanding their real interests), policy required of them to adopt those precautions against each other. This, however, only applies to a state of warfare. If France, therefore, were at war with surrounding nations or regarded their people as dangerous, the notice of the such an extraordinary precaution might have been conceived.

6th. But as a general place has existed in Europe for many years, and there is more particularly so harmonious an under standing between the peoples of France and England and even between their present Governments, I am utterly at a loss to discover the case of a regulation which manifests, to say the least, a want of cordiality and confidence on the part of France.

7th. Even during peace the following excuses might perhaps be offered for the continuance of such restrictions, though in my humble opinion they cannot stand a fair examination.

First : If it be said that persons of bad character should not be allowed to enter France, still it might I presume, be answered that the granting of passports by French Ambassador here is not usually founded on certificate of character or investigation into the conduct of individuals. Therefore, it does not provide a remedy for that supposed evil.

Secondly : If it be intended to present felons escaping from justice, this case seems well-provided for by the treaties between different nations for the surrender of all criminals.

Thirdly : If it be meant to obstruct the flight of debtors from their creditors, in this respect likewise it appears superfluous, as the bankrupt laws themselves after a short imprisonment set the debtor free even in his own country, therefore, voluntary exile from his own country would be, I conceive, a greater punishment.

Fourthly : If it be intended to apply to political matters, it is in the first place not applicable to my case. But on general grounds I beg to observe that it appears to me, the ends of constitutional Government might be better attained by submitting every matter of political difference between two countries to Congress composed of an equal number from the parliament of each, the decision of the majority to be acquiesced in by both nations and the Chairman to be chosen by each Nation alternately, for one year, and the place of meeting to be one year within the limits of one country and next within those of other, such as Dover and Calais for England and France.

8th. By such a Congress all matters of difference, whether political or commercial, affecting the nations of any two civilised countries with constitutional Governments, might be settled amicable and just to the satisfaction of both and profound peace and friendly feeling might be preserved between them from generation to generation.

9th. I do not dwell on the inconvenience which the system of passports imposes in urgent matters of business and in cases of domestic affection. But I may be permitted to observe that the mere circumstance of applying for passport seems a tacit admission that the character of the applicant stands in need of such a certificate of testimonial before he can be permitted to pass unquestioned. Therefore, any one may feel some delivacy in exposing himself to the possibility of refusal which would lead to aninference unfavourable to his character as a peaceable citizen.

My desire, however, to visit that country is so great that I shall conform to such conditions as are imposed on me, if the French Government , after taking the subject into consideration, judge it proper and expedient to continue restrictions, contrived for different state of things, but to which they may have become reconciled by long habit, as I should be sorry to set up my opinion against that of the present enlightened Government of France.

20. To Mrs. S.C. Belnos, London (March 5, 1832)

Madam, I have with great pleasure looked over your drawing, and read your descriptions of them, and I now have the satisfaction to inform you, that they tare true, representations of nature, so much so, that they have served to bring to my recollection, the real scenes alluded to, of that unhappy country.

The drawing are so expressive of themselves, that the description, however excellent, are scarcely necessary to any one acquainted with India.

I have retained the copy handed over to me, and wishing you every success in your present undertaking (published by Prof. Suniti K. Chatterjee in *Prabasi,* Calcutta Kartick 1939).

21. To William Rathbone, London (1832)

My Dear Sir... I am now happy to find myself fully justified in congratulating you and my other friends at Liverpool on the complete success of the Reform Bills, notwithstanding the violent opposition and want of political principle on the part of the aristocrats. The nation can no longer be a prey of the few who used to fill their purses. As I publicly avowed that in the event of the Reform Bill being defeated I would renounce my connection with the country, I refrained from writing to you or any other friend in Liverpool until I knew the result. Thank heaven I can now feel proud of being one of your fellow-subjects, and heartily rejoice that I have had the infinite happiness of witnessing the salvation of the nation, nay of the whole world.

22. To Wood Ford of Brighton, (1833)

.......I rejoice to observe that the translation of the Vedas, etc..., which I presented to Mrs. W. before my departure for the continent of Europe, has proved interesting to her and to yourself. I am now confirmed in the opinion, that her good sense and her national devotion to religion will not induce her to reject any....reasonable sentiments, on the ground that they are not found in this book, or in that volume.

I was detained in France too late to proceed to Italy last year, besides, without a knowledge of French, I found myself totally, unable to carry on communication with foreigners, with my degree of facility. Hence I thought I would not avail myself of my travels through Italy and Austria to my own satisfaction. I have been studying French with a French gentleman who accompanied me to London, and now is living with me.....

23. To the Court of Directors, London (1833)

In answer to your Secretary's letter of the 27th ultimo I beg leave to state that in consequence of the suspense of payment by the House of Messrs. Richards Machintosh & Co., my Agents in London, and the failure of Messrs. Machintosh & Co., in Calcutta, who were my Agents as well in general pecuniary transactions as in receiving my rents and managing my landed property, I found myself rather embarrassed and on the 8th of May last to the liberty of addressing you for a loan of money to enable me to proceed to India to manage my affairs there in person.

Being requested by you on the....security I intended to offer. Since my last letter to your Secretary... could not expect a speedy supply from that quarter.

To relieve myself from the present want, I as a Native of India, naturally first look up to you in difficulty and feel less reluctance in applying to you than to others. Should you think it proper to afford me you assistance with a loan of £ 2,00 on my personal security, I shall gratefully repay the sum either within a year in this country or within three years in India from the day of receipt of it.

24. To Woodford, London (August 22, 1833)

"....I was glad to hear from Mr. Carey some time ago, that you and Mrs. W. were in good health when he saw you last and Sir Henry Strachey, whom I had that pleasure of seeing about three weeks ago, has confirmed the same information. He is indeed an extraordinary man and I feel I delighted whenever I have an opportunity of conversing with that philosopher. I have been rather poorly for some days past, I am now getting better, and entertained a hope of proceeding to the country in a few days when I will endeavour to pay you a visit in Taunton. The reformed Parliament has disappointed the people of England, the minister may perhaps redeem their pledge during next session. The failure of several mercantile houses in Calcutta has produced much distrust, both in India and England. The news from Portugal is highly gratifying though another struggle is still expected. I hope you will oblige me by presenting to Mrs. W. with my best respects, the accompanying copy of a translation giving an account of the system of religion which prevailed in Central India at the time of the invasion of that country by Alexander the Great."

25. To Wood Ford, London (August 22, 1833)

"...As every person of a reflecting turn of mind feels interested about antiquities, I have the pleasure of sending the accompanying translatin which gives an account of the system of religion prevailing in Central India at the time of Alexander the Great and beg your acceptance of it. My health has been rather indifferent; I therefore intend to proceed to Wales through Bristol by Thursday next. I hope you will present my best regards to your worthy parents...."

This above letter does not disclose the identity of the addressee but the contents bear a very close resemblance to those of the letter written by Rammohun to Woodford (with whom Digby worked for sometime at Murshidabad etc.). The "translation" referred to above, took place... was presumably from Greek and possibly by Rammohun himself.

26. About A Dozen Short Letters to Miss Kiddell and Miss Castle About His Intended Visit to Bristol

Rammohun's Works

A. In Persian and Arabic

1. *Tuhfat-ul-Muwahhiddin* (1803-04). The text is in Persian and the foreword in Arabic. Tuhfat-ul-Muwahhiddin was translated into English by Moulvi Obaidullah El Obaide and published by the Adi Brahmo Samaj, Calcutta, in 1884. A Bengali translation from the original Arabic-Persian text was published by Girish Chandra Sen, the well known missionary of the Bharatvarshiya Brahmo Samaj and an eminent scholar of Islamic theology. The only Bengali translation extant to-day was published by J.N. Das, Secretary, Sadharan Brahmo Samaj, Calcutta.

2. *Manazarat-ul-Adyan.* No copy of the book has as yet been fond, but Rammohun makes a clear reference to it at the *Tuhfat.* Kazi Abdul Wodood however thinks that it must have been circulated either in printed or in manuscript form.

3. *Javav-i-Tuhfat-ul-Muwahhidin* (1820). An anonymous Persian booklet written in defence of Rammohun's *Tuhfat* against the attacks of the Zoroastrians, now in

the British Museum, London. Some scholars hold that it was written by Rammohun himself.

B. In Bengali and Sanskrit

1. *Vedanta-Grantha* (1815).
2. *Vedantasara* (1815).
3. *Talabakaropanishador Kenopanishad* (1816). Bengali translation based on Samkara-charya's gloss.
4. *Isopanishad* (1816). Bengali translation based on Samkara charya's gloss.
5. *Utsabanda Vidyavagiser Sahit Bichar.* Sastric disputation with Utsabananda (Vidyavagis). Under this head, Rammohun wrote three pamphlets in Sanskrit (1816-17) Utsabananda, who was an orthodox pandit, eventually accepted Rammohun's position and is said to have joined the Brahmo Samaj when that organisation came into being in 1820.
6. *Bhattacharyer Sahib Bichar* (1817). Sastric disputation with Mrityunjoy Bhattacharya (Vidyalankar). It is a reply in Bengali to the criticisms of Rammohun's Vedanta Granta Grantha, as embodied in Mrityunjoy's Vedanta Chandrika published in 1817.
7. *Mandyukyopanishad* (1817). Bengali translation according to the gloss of Samkaracharya.
8. *Kathopanishad* (1817). Bengali translation according to Samkarcharya's gloss.
9. *Goswamir Sahit Bichar* (1818). Sastric disputation with Goswami. It is a reply in Bengali to the criticisms of the Vaishnavite.
10. *Sahamaran Vishaya Pravartak-O-Nibartaker Sambad* (1818). Which in literal translation meant a conference between an advocate and an Opponent of the Custom of *Sati.* This was Rammohun's first Bengali tract on *Sati.*

11. *Gayatrir Artha* (1818), an elucidation in Bengali of the most respected Gayatrimantra of the Rig-Veda.

12. *Mundakopanishad* (1819), Bengali translation according to the gloss of Samkaracharya.

13. *Atmanatma—Viveka* of Samakaracharya with Bengali translation (1819).

14. *Sahamaran Vishaye Pravartak Nivartaker Dwitta Samvad* (1819), a second Coference between an Advocated and an Opponent of the Custom of *Sati*. This was Rammohun's Second Bengali tract on Sati, in replay to the criticisms of his first Bengali tract by Pandit Kashinath Tarkavagis in his Vidhayak Nishedhaker Sambad, published with an English translation earlier in 1819.

15. *Kavitakarer Sahit Bichar* (1820), Sastric disputation with the author. A tract in Bengali in reply to an anonymous opponent who has been mentioned as Kavitakar or "composer of verse".

16. *Subrahmanya Sastrir Sahit Bichar* (1820). Sastric disputation with Subrahmanya Sastri. This was published simultaneously in four languages Sanskrit, Bengali, Hindi and English. The third annual report of the School Book Society mentions a tract by Rammohun Roy under the litle "Reply to the Observation of Sobha Sastree". No separate work of that name, however, has come to light as yet. Evidently it is a slip. Subra (abbreviation of Subrahmanyam) not Sobha.

17. A Bengali tract called *Brahmo-Puttalika Samvad* (1920), mentioned by Rev. Long (Cataloguep. 103) to have been a work of Rammohun Roy under a pseudonym.

18. *Brahman Sevadhi* : Brahmana-O-Missionary Samvad (Numbers 1,2 & 3) (1821). A general defence of Brahmanical Hinduism against the attacks of the Christian missionaries. The first three numbers of Brahman Sevadhi were published together with their

English translations under the title *The Brahmanical Magazine : The Missionary and the Brahman.*

19. *Chari Prasner Utter* (1822). The tract contains Rammohun's reply to four questions asked by an orthodox opponent in the columns of the *Samachar Darpan* April6, 1822, under the name *Dharma-Samathapanakamkhi* (one wishing to establish supremacy of religion).

20. Prarthana-patra (1823) published with an English version entitled *Humble Suggestions to his countrymen who believe in the One True God.*

21. *Pedri-O-Sisya Semvad* (1823). It criticises Trinitarianism in the shape of an imaginary dialogue between a Trinitarian and three Chinese convert to Trinitarian Christianity. Its English version "Dialogue between a Trinitarian Missionary and three Chinese Converts" was published in 1823, and the Bengali version must have been a little earlier.

22. *Gurupadhuka* (1923). The book has not been traced but has been mentioned in Rev. Longs Catalogue of Bengali Books (Calcutta 1855). It must be a small tract written in reply to an anonymous attack (entitled Jnananjanasalaka) on Rammohun.

23. Pathya-pradan or Medicine for the Sick (1823). A reply to Pandit Kashinath Tarkapanchanan's Pashanada Pirana.

24. *Brahmanishtha Grihasther Lakshan* (1826). It discusses the essentials of a householder who is truly devoted to Brahman.

25. Kayasther Sahit Madyapan Vishayak Bichar: A Sastric Disputation with a gentleman of the Kayastha Caste, on the question of drinking of wine. In 1826 this track was published under the name *Ramchandra Das.*

26. *Vajrasuchi* (1827), a Sanskrit text and Bengali translation of the Vajrasuchi Upanished, a Mahayana Buddhist text which criticises Brahmanical caste system.

27. *Gayatry Paramopasana-vidhanam* (1827). A Sanskrit-Bengali tract on the mode of worshipping the Absolute through the Gayatri Mantra. Its English translation also appeared in the same year.
28. *Brahmopasana* (1828). It is a tract on Divine Worship.
29. *Brahmasangit* (1828). A Book of Bengali devotional hymns containing compositions of Rammohun Roy.
30. *Anusthan* (1829). A Bengali tract which, under the form of a dialogue between a master (Achraya) and his disciple (Sisya), discusses Rammohun's concept of Upasana (divine worship) and its method.
31. *Sahamaran Vishaya* (1829). This is Rammohun's last Bengali tract on *Sati* published as a reply to the attacks of two orthodox opponents who wrote under the names of "Vipra" and "Mughabodha-chhatra".
32. *Kshudra Patri.* This leaflet contains two Upanishadic verses and two elegant hymns composed by Rammohun. It was published apparently before Rammohun had sailed for England.
33. *Gaudiya Vyakaran* (1833). It is a grammar of the Bengal language written on the model of Rammohun's earlier work in English on the same subject in 1826. The text was published by the Calcutta School Book Society, when Rammohun was in England.

C. In Hindi

1. *Vedanta-Grantha* (1815). Hindi translation from the Bengali original.
2. *Vedantasara* (1815). Hindi translation from the Bengali original. The above two books have not been traced. Rammohun refers to these two Hindi publications in the preface to *An Abridgement* (Calcutta, 1816). See Nag and Burman : English Works of Raja Rammohun Roy, Part II. pp. 59-60)
3. Subrahmanyan Sastrir Sahit Vichar (1820).

D. In English (Published in Calcutta)

1. Translation of an *Abridgement of the Vedanta* (1816). A sacred book on Hindu Theology which dwells on the unity of Godhead.
2. Translations of the *Cena* (*Kena*) *Upanishad* (1816). A sacred book on Hindu Theology which, according to the gloss of the celebrated Samkaracharya, established the unity and the omnipotence of the Supreme being.
3. *Translation of the Ishopanishad* (1816). Covers one of the chapters of the Yajur Ved which, according to Samkaracharya's gloss, established with the greatest stress the concept Advaitism.
4. *A Defence of Hindu The is min* reply to the attack (from Madras) of an Advocate of idolatry (Samkar Sastry).
5. *A Second Defence of the Monotheristical system of the Vedas* (1817) in reply to "an Apology for the Present State of Hindu worship" of Mrityunjaya Vidyalamakara.
6. *Counter-Petition of an orthodox section at Hindu inhabitants of Calcutta against Sati* (1818).
7. Translation from the Bengali of a *Conference between an Advocate and for and an Opponent of the Practice of Burning Widows Alive* (1818).
8. Translation of the Moonduck-Upanishad (1819), according to the gloss of Samkaracharya.
9. Translation of the Kuthopunishad (1819) according to the gloss of Samkaracharya.
10. *An Apology for the Pursuit of Final Beatitude* (1820). It is the English version of Rammohun's disputation with Pandit Subrahmanyam Sastri.
11. *A Second Conference* (1820) *between an advocate for, and an Opponent of, the practice of Burning Widows alive.*

12. The Precepts of Jesus, the Guide to Peace and Happiness based on the New Testament ascribed to the four Evangelists (1820).

13. *An Appeal to the Christian public in defence of the "Precepts of Jesus"*, by a Friend to Truth (1820).

14. Second Appeal to the Christian Public in defence of the "Precepts of Jesus" (1821).

15. *The Brahmanical Magazine or* the Missionary and the Brahman, being a vindication of the Hindu religion against the attack of Christian Missionaries (1821).

16. *Brief Remarks regarding Modern Encroachments on the Ancient a Right of Females* according to the Hindu Law of Inheritance (1822).

17. *The Brahmanical Magazine* or the Missionary and The Brahman, No. IV (1823).

18. *Final Appeal to the Christian Public in Defence of the "Precepts of Jesus"* (1823).

19. *Humble Suggestion to his Countrymen who believe in One* True God (1823), published in the name of Prasanna Kumar Tagore.

20. Petitions against the Press Regulations :

    (a) Memorial to the Supreme Court (1823)

    (b) Appeal to the King in Council (1823)

21. A few queries for the serious Consideration of Trinitarians Part I & II (1823).

22. *A Dialogue between a Missionary and three Chinese Converts* (1823).

23. *A vindication of the carnation of the deity as the common basis of Hinduism (1823) published under the pseudonym Ram Doss.*

24. *An Appeal to Lord Amherst on Western Education* (December 2, 1823).

25. *A letter to Rev. Henry Ware on the Prospects of Christianity in India* (1824).
26. *Translation of a Sanskrit tract in English on Different Modes of Worship* (1825), (published under the signature "By a friend of the Author")
27. Bengali Garammar in English Language (1826).
28. Translation into English of a Sanskrit Tract on the Divine worship of the Supreme Being as revealed in the Vedas.
29. Answer of a Hindu to question, "Why do you frequent Unitarian place of worship instead of the numerously attended Established Churches?" This tract was published in the name of Chandra Sekhar Dev (1827).
30. *Symbol of the Trinity* (1828).
31. *The Universal Religion* : Religion Instructions founded on a Sacred Authorities (1829).
32. *Petition to the Government against* Regulation lll of 1828 for the resumption of Lakheraj Lands (1829).
33. *Petition to the Padishah* (Akbar II) *of Delhi to King* George IV of England (1829).
34. *Address to Lord William Bentinck, Governor*-General of India upon the passing of the Act for the abolition on the Sati (1830).
35. *Essay on the Rights of Hindus over Ancestral Property* according to the Law of Bengal (1830).
36. *Letters of Hindu Law of Inheritance* (1830).
37. *Abstract of Arguments regarding* the Burning of widows considered a Religious Rite (1830).
38. *Counter-Petition to the House of Commons* with regard to the Memorial of the advocates of the *Sati* (1830).
39. *Authorities of Hindu Religion* in favour of slaying the cow and eating its flesh (unpublished).

E. In English (Published in England)

1. *Abridgement of the Vedanta* and the English translation of the Kenopanishad (reprinted 1817) with A prefeace by John Digby.
2. *The Precepts of Jesus* together with the First and Second Appeal to the Christian Public (1823) with a preface by Thomas Rees, published by the Unitarian Society.
3. *Final Appeal* to the Chirstian Public in defence of the Precepts of Jesus (1823).
4. *Answer to Queries by Rev. H. Ware of Cambridge (U.S.)* Printed in "Correspondence relative to the Prospects of Christianity and the means of Promoting its Reception in India" (1823).
5. *Treaty* with the king of Delhi. Decision thereon by the Governor-General of India; Reports of the British Resident and Political agent at Delhi.
6. *Some Remarks* in vindication of the Resolution passed by the Government of Bengal in 1829 abolishing the practice of female sacrifices in India, (1823). This tract does not form part of Nag and Burman publications. A Copy of it was discovered by Prof. U.N. Ball in the library of the Foreman Christian College, Lahore. It will be found in the Modern Review March, 1934.
7. *Essay on the Right of Hindus over Ancestral Property* according to Law of Bengal with an Appendix containing Letters on the Hindu Law Inheritance (1832).
8. *Exposition of the Practical Operation of the Judicial and Revenue system of India* and of the general character and condition its Natice Inhabitants, as submitted in Evidence to the Authorities in England.
9. *Answer of Rammohun to the Queries on the Salt Monopoly* (March 19, 1832), reprinted in the Modern Review, May, 1934.

10. Translation of Several *Principal Books, Passages and Texts of the Vedas,* and of some Controversial Works in Brahmanical Theology.

This collection includes the following Tracts :

(a) Translation of Abridgement of the Vedant.

(b) Translation of the Moonduk-upanishud.

(c) Translation of the Kena Upanishud.

(d) Translation of the Katha-upanishud.

(e) Translation of the Ishopanishud.

(f) A Translation into English of a Sanskrit Tract inculcating the Divine Worship, etc.

(g) A defence of Hindu Theism.

(h) Second Defence of the Monotheistical System of the Vedas etc.

(i) An apology for the pursuit of Final Beatitude, independently of the Brahminical Observances.

(j) Translation of a Conference between an Adovcate for, and an Opponent of, the practice of burning widows alive.

(k) A Second Conference between an Advocated for, and an Opponent of, the practice of burning widows alive.

(l) Abstract of Arguments regarding the burning of widows, considered as a Religious Rite.

(m) Brief Remarks regarding Modern Encroachments on the Ancient Right of Female according to the Hindoo Law of inheritance.

11. *Appeal to the British Nation against a violation of common justice and breachof public faith by the Supreme Government of India with the native inhabitance* (1823. A copy of the tract is available at the

Library of the Foremer Christian College, Lahore. The Government of India in September, 1829 rejected the appeal which Rammohun submitted on behalf of the landholders of Bengal, Bihar and Orissa against Regulation lll of 1828 for the resumption of Lakheraj lands. Rammohun while in England preferred an appeal on the matter to the Board of Control in the name of his companion, Ramratan Mukherjee. Even this failed to produce any satisfactory result and he then published the above booklet in the name of the same Ramratan Mukherjee. The *Times* of London in its issue of April 6, and 13, 1833 made some adverse remarks on the action of the Government regarding this particular issue.

12. Translation of the Creed maintained by the Ancient Brahmins as founded on the Sacred Authorities (1833).

13. *The Autobiographical letter (Sketch)*. It was published by Sandford Arnot in the Athenaeum of October 5, 1833.

F. Works Published in America

1. *Correspondence Relative to the Prospects of Christianity and the Means of Promoting its Reception in India* (Cambridge University Press, 1824).

2. *The Precepts of Jesus* to together with the First, and the Second Appeals to the Christian Public (B Bates, New York 1825).

3. Appeal to the Christian Public in Defence of the Precepts of Jesus Boston Christian Register Office about April, 1826, Miss Adrienne Moore is not certain whether it was really an American edition of any of the Appeals or merely an advertisement by the Christian Register Office of the 1825 London edition of the Final Appeal.

4. *The Precepts of Jesus* together with the First, Second and the Final Appeals to the Christian public, Parts. I &II (*Christian Register* Office, Bosten 1828).

5. A Vindication of the Incarnation of the Deity as a Common Basis of Hinduism and Christianity. (Salem, Massachusetts, 1828).
6. Brief Extracts from Rammohun Roy's Appeals, (Philadelphia Unitarian Association Publication. Miss Moore adds the following comment : "This is possibly an excerpt torn from some publication").
7. Miss Moore mentions in appendix to her list of Publication entitled : Address to the Members of Congress on the Abolition of Slavery.

G. In German

Translation of the *Abridgement of the Vedanta.*

H. In Dutch

Translation of the collection entitled *Translation of Several Principal Books, Passages and Texts of the Vedas* Published in London in 1832.

3 RELIGIOUS BELIEFS

As stated earlier, on September 11, 1833, Rammohun had prolonged discussions with the Rev John Foster. It is said that on that day :

> "That Rajah avowed unequivocally his belief in the resurrection of Christ and in the Christian miracles generally. As the same time, he said that the internal evidence of Christianity had been the most decisive of this conviction". Mr. Esttin's Diary for the 11th attest that the Rajah gave an account of the process which he went through in arriving as his present religious conclusions : "his belief in the Resurrection of Christ, as the foundation of his faith in the general resurrection, he firmly declared."

A corroboration came from another eminent man, Rev. William Jay Bath, whose impression was like wise. More than a year earlier, on June 17, 1832, Jay had delivered a sermon in Rowland Hill's Chapel and among those present had been Rammohun and the Lord Mayor of London. Rammohun had been so impressed by Jay's Speech that he wanted to have it circulated at his own expense, as is borne out by the following extract written long after (in 1843) :

When the service was over the Rajah came into the chapel house and pressed for leave, at his own expense, to print the sermon for distribution among his friends....The author, with regard to this very extraordinary man, cannot help remarking that not only from the circumstances of his exposing this sermon (which, through not highly doctrinal, has allusions and intimations which would not accord with some theology), but from subsequent intercourse, as also, from the testimony of others, he is persuaded that though at his first embracing

Christianity he was Unitarian in his views, he was after he came to this country as sincere and earnest enquirer after evangelical truth, and would have professed his adoption of it has he not been prematurely removed by death.

Following this Rowland Hill meeting, Jay and another colleague of his, the Rev. Warner, has long talks with Rammohun, It was claimed by them that they found him a signal convert to Evangelical religion. Foster was even of the view that Rammohun, towards the close of his life, had come to accept the divinity of Jesus, to which of course Estlin joined issue by asserting that what Rammohun meant was that Christ had a divine mission. But Estlin ageed with Foster that so far as Resurrection was concerned, Rammohun had eventually accepted it. Neither the Rev. Sutherland nor Sandford Arnot (who knew him more intimately) could, however, agree with the above conclusion. As Sutherland explained in *India Gazette* of February 1834 :

On questions of religious faith, Rammohun Roy was in general too pliant, perhaps from his excessive fear of giving offence or wounding the feelings of anybody which accounts for the controversy which has arisen about religious opinions. In fact, no matter what the creed of the parties with whom he conversed on such a subject, he was sure to impress them with an idea, either that he was of their peculiar faith, or that they had converted him to it. A lady once observed to me that the was rejoiced to find that he was sincere Trinitarian, and that he merely gone to Unitarian places of worship from curiosity, as he has attended Quakes meeting, the Jewish Synagogue, etc.

Despite these conflicting views regarding Resurrection, Divinity, etc. his passionate attachment to Christianity was clear upto the end of his life. At one time Rammohun had been so moved by its precepts and ethical teachings that he was thought many to be on the verge of conversion. In the later years in London, his daily life was marked by the same attachment to Christianity. Mrs. Estlin (Estlin's mother) recorded her diary :

The Raja read the Scriptures daily in Hebrew and Greek-Miss Hare often read them to his also—this was never omitted.

For all this we have to depend, however, on Sandford Arnot's considered opinion since he was the closest to him in England. Arnot forfeited the general sympathy of people around him by his weakness about money matters, but in respect of other things, particularly Rammohun's views on religious experiences, he continued to be trusted by unbiased persons like Sutherland, Estline, Carpenter, etc. When therefore Arnot dismissed as wrong the impression that Rammohun was moving more and more towards Christianity or that he believed in the divinity of Christ, it proved to be the end of the Controversy. Rammohun, Arnot explained, was a mun of large sympathies and soft nature an that is why his easy not or courtesy acquiescence in whatever was pressed before him during the time he was ıying in physically low spirit, was often misunderstood. Still, even Arnot thought, he could detect an appreciable mental uneasiness in Rammohun in his attitude towards strictest Unitarianism. The point will be clear from the following :

He evidently now began to suspect that the Unitarian form of Christianity was too much rationalised (or sophisticated, perhaps, I may say) to be suitable to human nature. He remarked in the Unitarians want of that fevour of Zeal and devotion found among other sects, and felt doubts whether a system appealing to reason only was calculated by produce a permanent influence on mankind.

UNITARIANISM

It however does not mean that Unitarianism is not the highest concept towards which humanity should be drawn. It only means that this concept has to be fully sought keeping life's lighter side of joy in ethical work. The adherents should maintain the dance and rhythm of life which concentrating on the Supreme.

According to Arnot, the Saint of Change came in Rammohun towards the end of his life. Rammohun felt pained at any neglect of Ethical life but equally at the unreasonable emphasis on reason, for both would tend would tend towards unbalanced growth.

He perceived the same defect in the Unitarian philosophy, and ridiculed the notion that man, a being governed by three powers.... reason, imagination and passion could be directed by those who addressed themselves only or chiefly to the first of these powers, over-looking the importance of the two other elements of human nature, which must continue to exert an everlasting influence.

Long ago when writing and preface to the English translation of Kenopanished, Rammohun had urged that only with reason and tradition as living force, could there be a balanced growth in man. After he saw European life so openly, he changed a little and felt that society's external glamour was so tempting as to make conscious ethical life precarious. He also could discern amongst the Unitarians a greater dryness and scholasticism in all matters. There is no doubt that much too-much brain-taxing matter came upon him and he must have realised a greater need for joy and relaxation. He began to feel the need of combining the quiet worshipful attitude of Hinduism with Christian piety and Muslim fraternity. This was the indication of Universal Worship.

UNIVERSAL WORSHIP

When Brohmo Sabha (a church of liberal Hinduism) was founded (in 1829 under the name Brahmo Samaj), with the objective of preaching and encouraging non-idolatrous worship of Brohmo, it was thought that not only the enlightened Hindus would find in it the fulfilment of their inner carvings but also the liberal and thoughtful people of all faiths would be attracted. It is true that the number of adherents grew but they were largely form the upper layers of society. The upper strata easily felt a real call to develop a higher form of worship. Within a short time, king of Universal form of worship developed which did appeal to different sections of Indian people. But in its effort to include many others, it fell short by the fact that it was based on Hindu scriptures.

RELIGIOUS LIFE IN ENGLAND

Rammohun was in the midst of intense religious life of the

Christians (Baptists, Anbaptists, Anglicans, Presbyterians, Catholics, Unitarians etc.), their ethical propensities and their mechanical teachings in the new English surroundings. Rammohun's alert mind could easily distinguish the true and abiding from the transient and fleeting in European life. This formed the common substratum of different denominations. The following will show Rammohun's all-embracing Catholicism :

His defence of Christianity against Hinduism, and of Hinduism against Christianity, can be easily explained on this basis, though they have been stumbling blocks to some. More wonderful still, he defends Christianity as he conceived it against unreservedly the authority of the Christian Scriptures. He accepts what authority is claimed in and for the Christian Bible as God's own truth; he argues as a Christian, and by collation of texts and the application of the acknowledged canons of spiritual interpretation, he finds the purest Universal Religion as the precious truth taught in these Scriptures. So with Islam, so with the Hindu sastras, and so would he have done doubtless with the Buddhism and Jainism. And yet in playing as many parts he kept his personality intact and integral.

In his Rammohun painfully realized how in the Indian society Hindus, Muslims and Christians were growing in closed compartments without any mutual exchange. The petrified forces of tradition and unbridled religious passions and prejudices prevailed over rationality. Rammohun struggled against these incessantly by writing and whenever possible by advocating. Towards the latter half of his life, those who had glimpse of his mental make-up saw in him a synthesis of the three cultures. This would entitle him, as a universal man who had adopted the best of other religions, to be called a man of universal religion.

UNIVERSAL RELIGION

B.N. Seal given succinctly an idea of what its contents are :

... All religions, ethnic or credal , all religions by which masses of men have lived as social aggregated, must be recognised as moving along their own lines of historic tradition to a universal ideal or centre of convergence. That ideal is the ideal of Universal Religion. To put the Raja's implications in the terms of our own age this is not a static ideal, but a developing ideal, and as the different religions in the course of their own forward march approach one another and approach the common centre more an more, the centre of convergence itself shifts or moves forward; so that the ideal always remains an ideal, beckoning ever forward and upwards to the infinitudes of God.

....He could combine in his personal religion the fundamentals of Hindu, Christian and Islamic experiences. He transvalued all these values, and he made them integral to his own valuation of life. In truth, he practised the discipline of Yoga, the discipline of the Christian Saint. Thus he was multipersonal in all true sense of the term. These historic cults and cultures had been fused in one discipline of Universal humanity in his soul....

....Every sphere of human interest, all the sciences and arts must be autonomous, and as such ruled only by the natural laws pertaining to their respective domains. And religion will be there only to coordinate these various spheres and activities by its own guiding principles and goal, Lokasreyas, or the Universal good. The progressive convergence of the national religions is possible only on this fundamental assumption and Hindu Smriti, Moslem Shariat, and Christian Canonical Law must, in fulfilments of their own basic religious principles, adapt themselves to the revelation of God's own truth in science and the Laws of Nature and Society.

The true and abiding verities as indicated above existed as much in Christianity as in Islam and Hinduism. It flashed in Rammohun's mind that these verities should be the nucleus of a Universal Religion as our ideal. Rammohun gave serious thought to the bast in Hindu, Muslim and Christian scriptures and he realised that this would widen the Indian's vision.

Rammohun's mind was alert, self-critical and progressive. He watched with interest how much Christian virtues were reflected in the habits and behviour of the English, how much of their daily life was actuated by material considerations and how much by religion. Rammohun's vitality for evaluation new elements in the social life around him as remarkable. His mind did not stagnate anywhere. It was a veritable cauldron of heterogeneous trends and passions, of traditionalism and rationalism, intellectualism and humanism. What emerged did not do fully either Islam. Christianity, Hinduism or any established religion. His restless mind sought realisation in a Universal Religion. But it remained confined to a very few.

His firm stand on Unitarianism in the controversy which lasted over three years, after it became known in Europe and America through his writings, drew a profound response from all quarters. His strenuous efforts seemed to indicate that he had found in Unitarianism the guide to lead men the way he desired. It is true Unitarianism took him a long way, but a time came when he found it inadequate. Soon it became plain to him that he had outgrown the phase when he wrote the preface to the English translation of *Kenopanishad*. While he viewed the balanced growth of man on the basis of Unitarianism and reason, he now felt that there was a need to give a greater role to "tradition".

This weightage on tradition religious life with a diminishing stress on intellectualism and rationality, with a growing conviction that men's perversity increased as rationality became a fetish, impressed him more and more clearly during his stay in England. Comparing Rammohun's earlier years in Calcutta, Arnot noted :

As he advanced in age, he became more strongly impressed with the importance of religion to the welfare of society, and the pernicious effects of skepticism. In his younger years, his mind had been deeply struck with the evils of believing too much, and against that he directed all his energies; but in his later days, he began to fell that there was as much, if not greater, danger in the tendency to believe too little.

4 POLITICAL AND ECONOMIC THOUGHT

The main ingredients of Rammohun Roy's political thought seem to have been derived from the anti-mediaevalist composition of his general philosophy of life. He did not subscribe to that part of popular Vedantism which lent itself to the projection of abstract universalism. What appealed to him was the aspect of Vedantic thought which comprehended the Brahman through *Tatastha lakshanam*—the Brahman's relation to the universe—in terms of which he is recognised both in his transcendent and immanent qualities. This was how Rammohun Roy arrived at a philosophy of world-affirmation. He derived a system of social ethics, according to which individualistic ethics was tempered by the principle of *loka-sreya*—service of humanity. In economics and politics, while he recognised the autonomy of the sphere of either, he also emphasised the role of religion as a rational regulative principle of both economics and politics and as an instrument for creating an ideal state. But while religion has its proper domain, the problems of political economy have to be solved by methods relevant to it along their 'natural' and 'rational' lines of solution. He thought that there are laws of politics and government, in accordance with which the State must solve its financial and political problems.

Rammohun Roy's rational social philosophy (including his basic political philosophy) was not moulded into shape by the impact of Western thought alone. Indeed, to begin with, as a young man of thirty, he was influenced by certain elements of the rationalist categories of thought contained in Arabic and Persian literature. Later he was deeply stirred by his study of the *Upanishads* and of the *Mimamsa* philosophy, particularly the *Purva Mimasmsa*, which coloured his social philosophy.

The rationalist mould of his social philosophy had been cast before he learned the English language and came in contact with Western thought. In his most perceptive essay, *Rammohun, the Universal Man*, the eminent Indian savant, Brajendranath Seal, says "Rammohun seems to have studied the writings of the Rationalists and Freethinkers, certainly the Mujahhidins, the Sufis and the Mutazilas, and, perhaps, also the speculations of Hume, Voltaire Volney." The influence of Locke and Hume was evident in his analysis of superstition, and particularly of its underlying psychological causes. But Seal very rightly stresses the fact that Rammohun Roy drew a great deal of his rationalist inspiration from the Darsanas, especially the *Purva Mimamsa*.

Rammohun Roy thus clearly was his way to the path of rational enquiry, to a 'world-view' based on the primacy of human experience gained through the medium of the senses, of the mind and intelligence and empirical experience. He thus seems to have started a movement of return to nature, to objective existence and objective laws, a sense of which was lost through the ages in our preoccupation with mediaeval subjective idealism. He instinctively recognised that this was essential for India's social, economic and political modernisation. In the course of his famous letter on education addressed to Lord Amherst in 1824, he pleaded for the teaching of Western literature and science in the educational institutions run by the Government. Rammohun Roy's writings served the same purpose as Baconian philosophy did in Europe at one time. He preached against idolatry flowing from subjective idealism of the mediaeval type, against asceticism as a general social practice. While he pleaded for the sanctity of human desires, sensibilities and instincts, he took care to say that they had to be regulated by divine laws as revealed through the laws of society. This was a kind of hegelianism in politics and economics, minus, of course, its pure transcendentalism.

Rammohun Roy's species of rationalism could not be identified with the French rationalism of the 18th century which created an intellectual and social ferment in the generation of educated Indians that followed his generation. It was fused with a deep humanist concern for religion. Rammohun Roy thought that religion (in its humanist content) is a social need, because it emphasises the sanctity of human relations, of humane economic and political institutions based on justice and benevolence. There is not doubt that he imbibed the current notions of 'natural rights' and 'natural liberties'; but materialistic hedonism, devoid of a humanistic ethics derived from spirituality, was foreign to the basic premises of his social and political philosophy. He sought a synthesis between the spirit of the Eastern culture and the ethos of Western culture insofar as he avoided the exaggerations of both materialism and absolute idealism. Rammohun Roy's genius lies in the fact that he realised the necessity for obviating the clash of Eastern and Western cultures earlier than the actual impact of Western learning and the clash of cultures that followed in its wake-a conflict situation which he had not himself experienced but had clearly foreseen.

Rammohun Roy's political thought can be understood correctly if we bear in mind his role as great synthesizer. In the field of social ethics, he tried to harmonise social authority-the static aspect of social and civic life-with individual freedom, the dynamic factor, thus trying to reconcile order with progress. According to him, individual progress is the criterion of social progress, but individual progress is impossible unless the conditions of social progress are created and sustained by social action. He believed in the individual's 'natural rights', including the right to life, the right to property, the right of free speech and the right of free association-the fundamental 'human rights' as understood in the modern world. Nevertheless, his ethical sheet-anchor was the Benthamite principle of the 'greatest happiness of greatest number'—*loka-sreya* (common good)—which, philosophically speaking, clears the way to social-economic reforms. Moreover he understood that 'natural rights' did not imply any possibility of the violation of the equal rights of others.

Rammohun Roy had a synthetic view of a rational and

humane socio-political order. He respected different types of culture, and varieties of social structure and ethos, as revealed in history. These divergent types of culture existed not only in the different countries of the world but also in India itself, which was as microcosm of cultural diversity. Rammohun Roy thought that this diversity has to be respected and cherished, but it must transcend itself to reach out towards universal humanity. Thus he commended a different process of nation-building, unlike what had characterised the West, as the result of which nationalism would be consistent with true internationalism and cosmopolitanism. What could be this process? Let the Hindu and the Muslim retain each his own identity and develop as authentic cultural types; but they must transcend this narrowness by being universalists and cosmopolitans. Rammohun Roy's Brahma Sabha, the real object of which has been much misunderstood, was designed to be a forum for such emancipated spirits of all faiths and persuasions, not a sanctuary of new religion. Rammohun Roy perceived that such a process of emancipation will, on the one hand, rid nations and peoples of their chauvinistic exclusiveness and even violence, and, on the other hand, form the basic of true secularism within national boundaries.

Rammohun Roy's conception of real secularism deserves particular attention today, because historical forces seem to have projected secularism as a principle of political ethics and practice in a dramatic manner in our part of the world, unfortunately through an unparalleled process of bloody attrition.

Rammohun Roy realised that India is as diverse as humanity itself—a scene of commingling of many languages, religions, customs and social practices, diverse sub-cultures and varieties of experience of many levels. If India had to become a great nation, the nation-building process must not imply obliteration of this diversity. He perceived that India must have a modern secular state and a modern economy. But this does not mean secularism in the sense of preoccupation of the state and the individual with materialistic self-interest unconcerned with religion. Rammohun Roy thought that in a country like India in which religion pervades diverse cultures and sub-cultures in a variety of subtle ways, what secularism required is a broadening of the base of religion as humane culture by ridding it of superstition, ritualism and blind conformity to scriptures and tradition and revivifying it as a constructive and liberating social force. On the other hand, he considered it disastrous to try and cast different religions into the mould of single dominant religion, however, eclectic it may claim to be. Great religious men [no doubt realise that they stand on the same broad ground, irrespective of their personal beliefs and religious practices. But the common man is afflicted by the differences that divide and is less impressed by the common elements that unite. Rammohun Roy had realised that unless religious conflicts interwoven into culture conflicts were resolved, the different religious communities would never be able to achieve, either their own welfare or that of the nation as a whole. He, therefore, planned to have the nucleus of a new *elite*, which, by example and precept, will act as a spearhead of a movement for the resolution this conflict on the national level. His Brahma Sabha was designed to be a forum, not for the masses who were to follow a new religious doctrine, but for the select few who would be able to shed the narrowness of religious communities pitted against one another. The great task he asked them to undertake was to remove the obstacle to nation-building by making it possible for men belonging to different religions to respect the tenets of different faiths. This was the essence of secularism which was not mere not-intervention based on equal indifference to all religions. In other words, secularism meant realising the identity as well as the universality of all religions without losing one's commitment to religion as such and to one's own religion, in particular. To Rammohun Roy, secularism did not mean irreligion or materialism or atheism which is understandably an intellectual's response to the irrationality of organised religion as a negative force in society and politics.

Rammohun Roy derived his concept of freedom from the ideal of humanism, humanism being understood in its broad sense. To him, humanism meant the liberation of the human spirit form the bondage of ritualism, dogma, superstition and false other-worldiness. It meant liberation from communal prejudice that stood in the way of real nation-building. But it also meant the recognition of the dignity of the individual. He was too near the French Revolution not be impressed by its ideal of humanism that sought to obliterate the distinctions of birth, wealth, status or privilege—the ideal of glorification of man. When, however, we remember Rammohun Roy's Indian background we can appreciate why neither the abstract man nor man reduced to the lowest common measure could impress him too much. He could not assume that all men can be equal in capacity or performance and therefore the stressed the role of education in developing the cast potentialities of power and achievement lying dormant in human beings. He therefore wanted equality through recognition of inequalities objectively present in society; unity through recognition of human differences and inequalities. But recognition of objective reality did not mean passive acquiescence. Rammohun Roy was therefore principally a reformer and an activist within the constraints of his environment. And his inspiration came from his reasoned faith in the worth and dignity of the individual. The *Upanishadic* philosophy taught him that one who sees all enveloped in supreme consciousness and sees the supreme consciousness in every individual, cannot artificially separate man from man by interposing distinctions of race, language, religion, caste, wealth or privilege. Thus he came to the conclusion that man *qua* man has certain inalienable rights which cannot be taken away, on the pretext of maintaining the stability of a social or religious order or satisfying the pragmatic requirements of an economic or political system. This was broadly in consonance with the spirit underlying the doctrine of 'natural rights' which was sweeping contemporary Europe with the violence of a revolutionary tidal wave. Thus in harmony with the spirit of the age and in consonance with his own understanding of *Upanishadic* idealism, Rammohun Roy fought against all social or administrative arrangements which offended against human dignity and freedom and rested upon domination and exploration of man by man.

Rammohun Roy demanded freedom as part of the process of liberation of the human spirit—true renaissance. In retrospect, it is clear that this process was thwarted, among other things, by the conflict between the Eastern and Western cultures that followed in the wake of our imbibing the heady wine of English education and Western thought. Rammohun Roy did not consider this conflict to be inevitable when he fought relentlessly for the introduction of Western educational as part of Government's educational policy. His famous letter to Lord Amherst, containing a strong and closely reasoned case for English education, was written in 1824. It was in 1833 after a debate lasting for nine years that the 'Anglicists' prevailed against the 'orientalists'. The early products of the new system of education after Rammohun Roy death were swept off their feet by the ideals of liberty, equality and fraternity enshrined by the French Revolution, which had given birth to a romantic movement in Europe. This species of romanticism had not overwhelmed Rammohun Roy and his generation of intellectuals. But what Rammohun Roy had not considered to be inevitable actually happened. The new generation of educated Indians glorified individualism, materialism and rationality. They broke away from all social and religious norms, all restraints and all conventions sanctified by tradition. For some, it was a revolt against religion on the score of its irrationality. For others, it was the revolutionary exercise of the right of private judgment in favour of principled conversion to Christianity. It was a 'cultural revolution', the essence of which was scrupulous regard for truth at all costs. Although there were occasional excesses and lapses, as a contemporary remarked, "indeed the college boy was a synonym for truth." The answer to this new challenge was not the backlash of Hindu orthodoxy which failed, but Rammohun Roy's proposed synthesis which as clearly far in advance of the times. But it was Hume's philosophy of individualism that eventually won the day. It acted as dissolvent in a altogether alien social and political milieu which was none the less responsive to it in the objective circumstances of the time. But the significance of this phenomenon should not be exaggerated. The 'cultural revolution' was confined to the chosen few—the new *elite*. The vast masses of the population remained more or less immune. Indeed, it was an unfinished revolution even so far as the limited class of educated intellectuals was concerned.

It would be instructive to answer a few questions bearing on Rammohun Roy's political thinking, which one may formulate in the frame of reference of certain modern categories of political thought.

Was Rammohun Roy a republican radical? During his sojourn in England towards the end of his life, some of his English friends used to maintain that he was republican. James Sutherland has recalled that, when news reached Calcutta of the famous 'Three Days' (21-29 July, 1830), Rammohun Roy was so full of enthusiasm that "he could think and talk of nothing else". On his way to Europe when he saw a French frigate on the Cape Bay flying the tri-colour he was carried away by emotion and, in spite of fracturd leg which he was nursing as the result of an accident, he insisted on being taken on board the French frigate where he was received most cordially. Later on the made it known that, if the Reform Bills were lost, he would leave the British Empire and become an American citizen. Some have discovered in Rammohun Roy, not without reason, a pronounced radical shift during his last years (particularly after his visit to France of Louis Philippe). There is evidence that he shared the disillusionment of the British working class with the Reform Bill. On the whole however it world be correct to say that he accepted republicanism as an abstract principle, that he felt that it worked well in the United States of America, but that it remained an abstract principle when he saw himself "surrounded by power, more or less arbitrary, from the form of government existing in his own country", as an English friend appraised his concrete position.

This brings us to the questions, what was Rammohun Roy's attitude to the British rule? According to the testimony of Sandford Arnot, his English Secretary (whose moral scruple and veracity have been questioned), Rammohun Roy used to tell his English friends that India would need British rule for another forty of fifty years. The point of this testimony was that Rammohun Roy was moderate in his political views. What was no however equally stressed was his assumption that the British rule would be an agency of India's social, political and economic modernisation. One may say that this was an act of faith, but without this perspective of faith much of Rammohun Roy's reformist activism would not be intelligible. Nevertheless, perhaps he had a logical ground for his belief. In his days, British rule was unsure of itself and uncertain about the further. The Western system of education was an instrument by which an *elite*, allied to the British rulers, could be crated, but there was a danger that the heady wine of Western thought might also produced social revolutionaries of one kind or another, who would end up as political radicals. That explains the initial opposition of the British rulers to Western education particularly because a small but self-conscious intellectual *elite* keenly desired it. After the battle was won, Rammohun Roy probably came to the conclusion, that the British rulers had opted for India's modernisation as a matter of enlightened self-interest. He had no doubt however about the ultimate effects of modernisation in the context of historical forces. One can therefore adduce evidence in favour of the thesis that Rammohun Roy believed, and, indeed, anticipated, that India would sooner or later win her political independence, sooner rather than later than when it actually materialised. Perhaps Rammohun Roy's most explicit observations that my be quoted in this connection are contained in the following extracts from a letter dated 18 August, 1828 addressed to Mr. J. Crawford : "Supporting that some 100 years hence the native character becomes elevated from constant intercourse with European and the acquirements of general and political knowledge as well as modern arts and sciences, is it possible that they will not have the *spirit* and *inclination* to resist *effectually* any unjust and oppressive measures serving to degrade them in the scale of society? It should not be lost sight of that the position of India is very different from that of Ireland, to any quarter of which an English fleet may suddenly covey a body of troops that may force its way to any requisite direction and succeed in suppressing every effort of a refractory spirit.... In could be *an ally of British Empire or troublesome and annoying as a determined enemy".*

Was Rammohun Roy inclined towards Owenite socialism? The recent discovery of his letter to Robert Dale Owen, Robert Owen's son, throws light on a possible answer to this question. This letter, dated 13 April, 1833, was written towards the end of his life. The following extracts from this letter seem to be illuminating : "It is not necessary either in England or in America to oppose Religion in promoting the social, domestic and political welfare of their inhabitants, particularly a system of Religions which inculcates the doctrine of universal love and charity. Did such philanthropists as Locke of Newton oppose Religion? No.... I grieve to observe that by opposing Religion your most benbevolent father has hither to impeded his success.... My desire to see you and your father crowned with success in your benevolent undertakings has imboldened me to make these observations." There was considerable force in the argument that it was unnecessary to divorce religion from Robert Owen's brand of utopian socialism, which Rammohun Roy rightly or wrongly, identified with benevolence of philanthrophy. Nevertheless, I have lighted up on passage in a letter dated 31 July, 1832 to William Rathbone in which Rammohun Roy appears closest to the prevailing socialistic stance in England. In this letter, he speaks of "the complete success of the Reform Bills" In spite of the opposition of the aristocrats, and makes the following comment : "The nation can no longer be a prey of the few who used to fill their purses at the expense, nay, to the ruin of the people, for a period of upwards of fifty years." This was certainly not the context of benevolence or philanthropy, but the context of economic exploitation of the many by the few, which had been sharply accentuated in the wake of the Industrial Revolution England.

Was Rammohun Roy a Benthamite liberal, a 'philosophical radical'? Bentham was fascinated by what he had heard about Rammohun Roy from common friends. Bentham's deep respect and admiration for him is clearly evident form a letter which he wrote to him and the contents of which are briefly analysed below. Suterland has, however, called our attention to remarkable incident narrated in his own words as follows : "Strange to say, long after he had retired to rest (just after Rammohun Roy's arrival in London on his first visit to this city) the venerable Bentham, who had not for many years called on anyone or left his house, I believe except to take his habitual walk in the garden, found his way to the hotel, and left a characteristic note for him." One does not know exactly what the possible points of intellectual contact between the two were. One can however speculate on the basis of available evidence. One is however left in no doubt about the fact that Bentham had found in Rammohun Roy a kindred spirit. The somewhat long letter mentioned above is an important key to our understanding of his phenomenon. While praising his cultivated English style, Bentham refers in this letter to his 'character' he had come to know from common friends. Apparently, Bentham had discovered in him a revolutionary with a kindred spirit who applied rational criteria of thought; exposed the superstition, the fanaticism and the obscurantism of his countrymen as well as foreigners (Christian missionaries and administrators); and had dedicated himself completely to the service of mankind. These were also the characteristics of Bentham's own life-style. The following characterization of Rammohun Roy by Robert Montgomery Martin would be true of Bentham also : "At times with a rough, unsparing, ruthless hand he burst asunder the meshes of sophistry, error and bigotry to which it might be attempted to entangle him."

In his letter, Bentham writes : "Now at the brink of the grave ... among the most delightful of reflections is the hope... of rendering my labours of some considerable use" to the people under the British rule in India. He refers, in this connection, to James Mill as a 'disciple' though whom his ideas of legal reform were bearing fruit. He mentions his work on the Law of Evidence. "A grand object of his ambition," he says, "has been to provide for British India, in the room of the abominable existing system, a good system of judical procedure." He also tells Rammohun Roy that James Mill was aimining at "*giving stability and security of landed property in the hands of the greatest number throughout British India*". This was, indeed, revolutionary application of the Benthamite principle of "the greatest good of the greatest number"—a principle which Rammohun Roy made his own when the dealt with the problems of land reform and inheritance. Bentham's projects (as he explains in his letter) included a judicial inquiry into India custom and its bearing on land laws and inheritance laws. In Rammohun Roy Bentham found a like-minded reformist who also stressed the importance of customary law. But Rammohun Roy's inspiration was singularly Indian in the sense that the stressed *lokaci ıra* as co-ordinate with the sovereign's command and sanction—a theory deeply embedded in the dharmasastras. Thus while Bentham's *Fragment on Government* was directed against Blackstone's 'antipathy to reform' (Bentham), Rammohun Roy's parallel endeavour was to demolish opposition to legal reform not only on grounds of 'equity' and 'natural rights', but also on the ground of returning to the true spirit of the dharmasastras.

Although Bentham was close to Adam Smith version of *laissez faire,* on the principle of "the greatest good of the greatest number", Bentham advocated certain measures of taxation and succession to property, which were in conflict with individualism. Similarly, Rammohun Roy's proposal to tax the rich for the sake of relieving the poverty of the masses of the population and his progressive views on the laws of inheritance (to be discussed in the second part of this essay) seem to bear a Benthamite stamp. If socialism were defined as a system which reconciles the good of the individual with the good of the greatest number, Bentham's principle of "the greatest good of the greatest number", pushed to its logical consequence, leads to socialism. Therefore, the following comment of Brajendranath Seal on Rammohun Roy's social and political philosophy seems to be profoundly perceptive and logical : "In the sphere of social construction, he aimed at reconciling the good of the individual with the good of the greatest number—in other words, at harmonising individualism and socialism"

(*Rammohun Roy, the Universal Man.* Death Anniversary address. Bangalore. September 27, 1924.

What were Rommohun Roy's positive ideas on the construction of a future Indian Polity? Rammohun Roy believed that it was possible to glean from India's past experience the essential elements for the construction of a modern Indian polity. Brajendranath Seal, in the course of his address referred to above, mentions three important elements which Rammohun Roy had identified : (1) an original separation between the legislative and the executive functions; (2) the origin of Indian law in custom and *achara* as co-ordinate with the sovereign's command and sanction; (3) the strategic position of the village community and the Panchayat in the Indian polity and the importance of the ryot's tenurial rights and right of ownership. As Seal has rightly said Rammohun Roy "gave a modern meaning and purpose to these ancient and mediaeval elements of Indian polity".

Rammohun Roy's thinking on contemporary economic problems clustered around strategy of modernisation of the Indian economy in the perspective of the economic distortions and mass poverty which were as much the consequences of socio-economic backwardness as the outcome of the lapses of the administrative system. While fighting for the removal of specific grievances on rational grounds. Rammohun Roy never lost sight of the broader perspective of the requisite conditions of economic progress—a suitable economic infrastructure needed for the development of a modern economy.

Broadly, the strategy implicit in his economic (as well as political) philosophy can be briefly defined as follows : widely disseminated Western education; assimilation of Western Science and technology; growth of an enlightened *bourgeois elite* with a spirit of enterprise and rationality and continuously vigilant about social justice, amelioration of the social and economic conditions of under-privileged masses and vulnerable groups and any threat to human rights that came from alien administrators; partnership, on the basis of enlightened interest, between foreign capital, skill and enterprise and whatever enterprise was left amongst the masses of the population, in order to raise the latter to a higher level of economic efficiency; removal of legal barriers to the development of a free enterprise system, which were either the result of an antiquated social system or the consequences of ill-conceived administrative measures; and lastly, moderating the excesses of a colonial economy. (Rammohun Roy was never tempted by the prospect of 'colonial self-government' which was not based on enlightened partnership).

Rammohun Roy's estimate of Indian economic conditions bears evidence of his keen sociological insight. He refers to the debilitating effects of the Indian climate and dietary habits not very congenial to physical efficiency. Peasants living away from cities, courts and administrative centres were 'innocent, temperate and moral', but Rammohun Roy thought that these were characteristics of 'primitive simplicity'. The new urban class, according to Rommohun Roy, was passing through a phase of "imbibing the habits and opinions" of an alien civilization; its religious convictions had been shaken without "any other principles being implanted in their place". A great many belonging to this class were inferior to the peasants from the point of view of character. The 'while-collar' class, not very numerous, was still worse, because members of this class could not rise by dint of merit. Rammohun Roy felt that, if the rising urban *bourgeoisie* found opportunities in trade (as the result of free trade that he advocated), there could be an improvement in its character. He had noticed men of character in the upper layer of urban society who had distinguished themselves in trade. The upper strata however was dependent upon the generally demoralised lower strata who were the agents of the alien traders. With freedom of trade and enterprise, Rammohun Roy thought, honesty, merit and efficiency would be rewarded rather than fraud, dishonesty and nepotism which flourish in mercantist regime of privilege. Therefore, starting from the base right up to the top, there would be an improvement in the quality of the new urban classes if freedom of trade and enterprise were encouraged.

Rammohun Roy had observed economic disparities between the towns and the countryside in the early period of the modern type of urbanisation. He had noted the Malthusian spectre of the rapid increase of population, and, a *la* Malthus, spoke of 'occasional natural checks to this superabundance' of population. (Rammohun Roy was a contemporary of Malthus.) But he did not stop at Malthusianism. He turned his attention to other dimensions of mass poverty. He had observed certain progressive trends in the Indian economy, but he had also noted that prosperity was not being sufficiently diffused amongst the masses. The selling-value of estates, according to him, had generally increased ten-fold, in some cases twenty-fold, between 1793 and around 1831. Rammohun Roy attributed this enormous increase to (1) extensive cultivation of wasteland and (2) rise of rents payable by the cultivators. He understood the phenomenon of 'unearned increment' of land value when he said : "It is true the common increase of wealth has an irresistible tendency to augment the price, without any improving change in the property." Therefore he was able to explain how there had been no 'common increase of wealth' in the sense that the increase was confined to the favoured few and had not been generally diffused in the countryside. Extensive cultivation of wastelands under the stimulus of Permanent Settlement and a certain degree of freedom of trade that had been permitted, had enriched the few more than the peasants, in general, who were generally steeped in object poverty. Apart from the landlords and dealers in commodities, according to Rammohun Roy's analysis, Government was an important share of the 'increased wealth'. Indeed, he strongly advocated that the Government should share the large revenue coming to its coffers with the poor peasants according to a rational plan of readjustment of agrarian economic relations on an equitable and mutually advantageous basis.

What was his plan of agrarian reform? One can appraise this plan only in the light of his *Critique* of the prevailing systems of land tenure. Within the limits of this essay I can only offer a bare summary of his refreshingly rational position on the agrarian question. The interesting point that he made was that, whatever the system, the peasant came worse off. While some landlords had better security, they paid an irrationally high price for it, but compensated themselves at the cost of tenants who were merely tenants-at-will. Those who faced insecurity of assessment and possession were driven to irresponsibility and equally successfully compensated themselves by rack-renting. This was particularly true of revenue farmers. The important aspect of Rammohun Roy's analysis was that he demonstrated by means of statistics that Government also did not benefit so much by the State landlordism as it imagined it did. As regards tenants who were virtually tenants-at-will the economic evil was not merely the absolutely high incidence of rent, but the economic insecurity due to the uncertainty of the incidence of rent. Payment of rent in kind or in terms of labour service, rendered the incidence of rent unresponsive to the rise of prices, which had occurred as the result of the comparative freedom of internal trade. Even the introduction of cash rents had not made much difference. Rammohun Roy's main objection to the prevailing land system was that it stood in the way of capital accumulation by the actual tillers of the soil. His observations on the relationship between price fluctuations and the size of the possible economic surplus obtained by the peasant show an unusual economic insight : "Very often when grain is abundant and therefore cheap, the cultivators are obliged to sell their whole produce to satisfy the demands of their landholders and to subsist themselves by their own labour. In scarce and dear years they may be able to retain some portion of their crop to form part of their subsistence, but by no means sufficient for the whole."

To Rammohun Roy, the basic question was how to rationalise the agrarian relations so as to achieve "the greatest good of the greatest number", to relieve the economic distress of the common tiller of the soil who should normally be able to feel that he has a sake in the land, at least as an occupying tenant enjoying fixity of rent and tenure, if not as an owner-cultivator. Rammohun Roy, therefore, make a number of rather revolutionary proposals as follows :

(1) Government should "on no consideration allow the present settled and recognised extent of land to be disturbed by 'pretended and measurement' which had become a racket and an engine of oppression".

(2) Government should "absolutely interdict any further increase of rent on any pretence whatsoever". Rammohun Roy thought that Government should be "induced to fix a maximum standard" (based on the average actually paid during a given term of years) and prohibit any increase beyond the standard maximum. For the benefit of those who were sticklers for the *status quo* (Permanent Settlement). Rammohun Roy quoted Regulation I of 1793 (the very basis of the Permanent Settlement), which expressly declared that it was "the duty of the ruling power to protect all classes of people, and more particularly those who, from their situation, are most helpless". As he argued, Regulation VII provided for the permanent right of *Khud-Kasht* Tenant to retain *possession* of land at a fixed rent and protected him against cancellation of his title-deeds except under certain conditions (although the 'exceptions' were abused). Could not these rights be generalized in the spirit of Regulational?

(3) Rammohun Roy understood that freezing the rents at existing levels meant freezing the existing situation which was too bad for the peasant masses. They needed immediate relief through a education of rent charges already pitched at too high a level. It was no realistic to ask the Government of a trading company to sacrifice revenue. Therefore he made out a case for two alternative fiscal measures which could even be combined, but he did not consider it expedient to combine them. By themselves, his suggested remedies were quite radical in the context of his age.

The first alternative was for Government to "raise part of its revenue by taxes on luxuries and such articles of consumption as are not necessaries of life and make a proportionate reduction in the rents of cultivators and in the revenues of the Zamindars to whom their lands belonged". To argue in favour of redistributive indirect taxation with the objection of transferring income from the rich to the poor was socialist radicalism in India of 1830's. But Rammohun Roy was evidently following the Benthamite logic of utilitarianism. He had no doubt that wealth had begun to accumulate in the hands of landlords and dealers in commodities—a new class of *bourgeoisie*—as the result of the Permanent Settlement, extension of cultivation into wastelands and the free flow of trade. While he welcomed free trade and economic enterprise in the interest of the country's economic prosperity, he was anxious to see that the poor masses share part of this prosperity or at least be prevented from being exploited further. Trade in rice, including export trade in rice, had become quite lucrative. Raja Rammohun Roy clearly saw that export of rice was calculated to aggravate the effects of famine in the countryside in years of scarcity. In third issue of *Samvad Kaumudi* he therefore appealed to Government to suspend the rule of free trade in the case of rice exported from Bengal to foreign ports. The economic transition in India made it quite feasible for the Government to tap new sources of indirect taxation like transit duties, export duties and excises. Why could not the luxury consumption of landlords, dealers in commodities and the classes dependent upon them as well as the rich traders-cum-rulers be taxed to compensate for the loss of revenue, which may sustained, as the result of the reduction of rents payable by rackrented tennants? Rammohun Roy did not like the *Rytwari system*, because, relatively speaking, it had an inhibiting effect upon the development of the sources of revenue in general. That the budgetary resources of the Government could increase so much more if the peasant masses were progressively better off, could very well be a legitimate inference from Rammohun Roy's logic of diffusion of prosperity in the vast Indian countryside.

In this connection, Rammohun Roy used another argument supported by broader consideration of political economy. As the result of the Permanent Settlement and the political security it had ensured, the ruling class had created a class of landlords and an upper layer of the middle-class which were "firmly attached to the Government", as he put it. Rammohun Roy argued that, "if the benefit of Permanent Settlement were also extended to the cultivators, the farmers and labourers in every part of the country, they would be equally attached to the Government and ready to rise in defence of if, as a militia or any other-shape that might be required." In this way the Government would not need progressively increased land revenue to support a growing standing army. This logic of Benthamite liberalism was obviously lost on the contemporary ruling class.

Rammohun Roy's second alternative (if the first was not acceptable) was to bridge the budgetary gap by "reducing the revenue establishment". As a experienced former *Dewan* of the East India Company, he was able to make a few concrete suggestion. Covenanted European employees to the Company were employed as superintendents (revenue 'collectors') on a salary of Rs. 1000-1500 per month, "whereas their duties were chiefly performed by native officers" Recruited on a salary of only Rs. 300. per month, they could easily replace European collectors. This would mean substantial economy, while it encouraged local talent, character and initiative. Under the existing system, the Indian employees, the "real managers of the business", were overlooked and neglected, and most of them were "indifferent to anything but their temporary interest". Only six to eight European 'circuit collectors' would be needed to check the records and proceedings of the Indian collectors whose efficiency could easily be ensured by the requirement that no one would be a 'collector', unless he had been in revenue service for at least ten years.

Rammohun Roy pleaded strongly for legal protection of tenancy rights. The existing system of land revenue administration had become an engine of oppression. The peasants were "too poor and too timid to underatake the hazardous and expensive enterprise of seeking redress". He made a number of practical suggestion. As already said he suggested that measurement of land at the instance of the *Zamindar* must not be permitted. European officers could not travel much in a hot climate and "depended chiefly on two or three persons who were around them". Therefore, the simple procedure must be "to take the survey and settlement of the preceding years as the standard and prevent any future measurement and assessment". The advantage would be that "this system would relieve the cultivators from the apprehension of future exaction". The judicial officers must not proceed with the sale of distrained property for the recovery of rent, unless they were satisfied that the Zamindar's demand did not exceed the rate paid in the perevious year. The court should be in session once a week to hear such cases. A penalty should be imposed on a *Zamindar* who was held to be guilty of charging rent in excess of the rent of the previous year. An officer charged with negligence or connivance must be severely punished. The Collector must prepare a register of cultivators containing their names, identification of land ownership and the rent-rate fixed. As early as 1831 Rammohun Roy suggested that "Collectors should not by any means by armed with magisterial power", because "these powers very often proved injurious to those who attempted to maintain their own right against the claims of Government whose agents the collectors were."

Rammohun Roy maintained that the modernisation of the Indian economy needed a proper interpretation of the law of inheritance. He interpreted authoritative scriptures, commentaries and the legal tradition in defence of a 'progressive' economic philosophy of property rights and inheritance. He argued that the judges had interpreted the *Dayabhaga* law of Bengal in such a way that it upset the modern economic arrangements slowly emerging in the country. Mitakshara system (prevailing outside Bengal) recognised a distinction between ancestral and personally acquired property, but *Dayabhaga* recognised no such distinction. Under the changed economic conditions the absence of this distinction had an interesting economic consequence. Rammohun Roy said : "Large sums of money have been laid out in purchase of land without reference to any distinction between acquired and ancestral property." The Calcutta Supreme Court, however, resolved to introduced new maxims into the 'law of inheritance' and declared null and void "every disposition by a father of his ancestral property without the sanction of his sons and grandsons" The 'sudden change', Rammohun Roy contended, meant that "ruin must triumph over the welfare of a proportion of those who have their chief interest in landed property'. He was evidently thinking of the process of capital formation (formation of bourgeois property) and the growth of capitalistic enterprise, as the result of landed property becoming a fluid capital asset. His contention was that, under the established law of the land, this process, had never been frowned upon thwarted. The ruling of the judges was thus bound to bring about a narrowing of the base of 'credit' in mortgage or loan transactions incidental to trade or manufacture. The expansion of the credit system, which had been well under way, would, therefore, be arrested and, as Rammohun Roy put it, a great majority of the rising capitalists would "unavoidably curtail their respective establishments, much more their luxuries, a circumstance which would virtually impede the progress of domestic and foreign commerce".

That Rammohun Roy broadly understood the dynamics of internal capital formation in evidenced by his views on two related controversies : (1) the induction of foreign capital, skill and enterprise into the Indian economy as a whole and particularly into the agricultural sector; and (2) the drain of wealth from India. These two controversies had a common frame of reference, *viz.* the conflict (1) the mercantilist remnants of the regime of economic privilege which the East India Company was unwilling to discard and (2) the new free trade doctrine which had triumphed early in the 19th century.

In India the conflict appeared in Rammohun Roy's generation as one between the forces of progress and the forces of reaction. If social and political freedom absence of privilege, it also meant, in the sphere of economic life, abolition of commercial privilege, freedom of trade, and freedom of not only holding property, but also disposing of it as one liked in his own economic interest, subject, however, to the overriding principle of the 'greatest good of the greatest number'. The controversialists on the two sides were not divided on racial lines. On the side of restrictionism, monopoly and privilege there was a combination of India landlords, members of the 'Establishment' in the East Indian Company (European were a divided house), and the orthodox, obscurantist elements in the Indian society who were opposed to any change that disturbed the status quo. On the side of free trade and progress were ranged modernist Indians, like Rammohun Roy, who were themselves either landlords or merchants : 'liberal' East India hands and European merchants, traders and industrialists who felt inhibited by the Company's monopolistic privilege and the restrictions it had imposed on freedom of enterprise. In the correlation of forces Rammohun Roy and his fellow-workers took a position not of *comprador* elements in a colonial economy, but of enlightened patriots who sought a modernised economy and polity by aligning themselves with 'progressive force' released by the industrial Revolution in England. They thought, perhaps naively, that the ultimate social, economic and political emancipation of India would come about through rapid socioeconomic transformation of the basis of the partnership of foreign capital, skill and enterprise supported by the enlightened self interest a liberal British administration.

The case of the 'progressive' was remarkably stated by Lord William Bentinck in his report to the Board of Directors of the East India Company in 1829 . We catch a glimpse in it of certain 'progressive' trends in the Indian economy in the first two decades of the last century. Bentinck's main contention was that British science and technology would benefit India. Spread of knowledge and technique would be too slow a process unless the Europeans identified themselves with the economic life of India and demonstrated the utility of western knowledge and technique by their actual results. To doubt this possibility was to doubt the possibility of unity on the basis of common language, common urges and common economic interests. To doubt it was to question the effect of the investment of skill, technique, capital and credit in creating a vast potential market in India. India was a poverty-stricken land. In the absence of a sound economic infra-structure, the increase of wealth witnessed in the country seemed merely to aggravate the crisis. Was not Indian agriculture practised with a low breed of draught cattle, bad seeds and a lack of skill and enterprise? Were not the skilled workers in a wretched economic condition? Was not trade a lifeless process and handicapped by ignorance? With the exception of commodities the qualities of which had been improved by the Europeans, there were none the quality of which was not lower than that of comparable goods in other countries? Indian agriculture, manufacture and trade were handicapped by excessive rates of interest on loan capital—a situation which indicated the association of poverty with the difficulty of obtaining credit. The existing sources of revenues were inelastic and barely adequate for meeting the requirements of defence and administration; nobody could think of financing out of revenues the construction of roads and irrigation works, and provision of social services like education. Bentinck argued that the vicious circle could be broken if the European could settle in India and acquire landed property more *freely* (not absolutely freely).

The main thrust of Bentinck's argument was that, if the traditional Indian crafts were destroyed and not replaced by production of new kinds of commodities, East India Company's expert trade would suffer and accumulation of capital in Europe, as the result of a thriving export trade, would be restricted. Bentinck also had in mind the adverse effects on internal prices, foreign exchange and internal revenues. The way out of the crisis was the development of India's productive resources.

He referred, in this connection, to the project of a cotton spinning mill run by steam-driven machinery and the trend towards increasing cultivation of a better quality of cotton and tobacco which could stand American competition. The administrative requirement that foreign machinery could not be imported unless payment was made in advance and the circumstance that European firms had to operate in the outlying areas through agents whom they would not otherwise have cared to employ, were obstacles in the way of rational economic enterprise. In this context, Bentinck maintained that the indigo plantations and the factory industry that they supported were an agency of economic progress in the countryside, although one must admit that there were cases where indigo planters were misbehaving as oppressors.

Bentainck was opposed to importation of merely foreign labour, because foreign labour by itself was more expensive than Indian labour. It was imported that knowledge and skill flowed in, which would raise the level of the Indian worker's skill and efficiency. India wanted European capital and technological skill and offered in exchanges a potentially cast consumers' market.

Rammohun Roy was very close to Lord William Bentinck, I have quoted Bentinck at length in order to explain the background as well as the distinctive features of Rammohun Roy's essay, *Remarks on Settlement in India by Europeans contained in General Appendix to the Report of the Select Committee of the House of commons on the affairs of the East India Company (1832).*

After 1815 there was prolific public controversy in England on the subject of overseas emigration for a number of reasons. The employees of the East India Company had also been drawn into this controversy. Rammohun Roy referred in his essay to the fact that they had stated the pros and cons of settlement of Eropean immigrants in India and that, in the Indian context, this was seen, as Rammohun Roy said, as a 'political measure'. He summed up the *pros and cons* and, on the whole, supported European immigration and settlement without any illusions. It was conditional support on broad utilitarian grounds and in the broader perspective of colonialism. One could think of a colonial economy dominated by temporary migrants—the 'birds of passage'—who had no real stake in the country and depended on a system of remote control exercised by the centre of metropolitan power. This was the pattern that was growing in India. Rammohun Roy was apprehensive of this type of colonialism. He preferred a system based on the assimilation of the right kind of European into Indian society to speed up India's, political and economic modernisation. This implied that Europeans should be *selectively* permitted to hold property and settle down in India. There was no rational case, from the Indian point of view, for unrestricted entry of the British unemployed in order to lessen the burden of poor relief in England.

Rammohun Roy listed the benefits of controlled immigration as follows : (1) European settles would bring better agricultural techniques and raise the quality of agricultural products, such as sugarcane and indigo; (2) they would introduce "improvements in mechanical arts"; (3) by contact with Europeans, Indians will shed their prejudices and superstitions which pre-disposed them against 'useful exertions', *i.e.* economics activity; (4) the presence of settlers would be a curb on the excesses of both landlords and officials; (5) there would be diffusion, throughout the country, of the knowledge of European arts and science; (6) the Europeans would be a channel of 'authentic information' on which the British legislature could rely; (7) in the event of foreign invasion an Indian population enjoying civil and political rights would be a bulwark of strength in conjunction with European settlers with an economic and political stake in the country.

Rammohun Roy did not wish to overstate the case and, therefore, took care to present the dark side of the picture. "The European settlers being a distinct race and belonging to the class of rulers will dominate Indians and try to enjoy exclusive rights and privileges. "On grounds of differences of religion, colour and habits, they will be inclined to hurt the susceptibilities of Indians. Rammohun Roy therefore, wanted, at least to begin with, educated European" of character and capital" as settlers. Without equality of civil rights and a system of trial by juries "composed imparitially of both classes", one, however, could not expect any good results. The existing situation was quite depressing. There was, therefore, a clear possibility of settlers "having readier access to persons in authority" and becoming a privileged class. European civil officers and disciplined soldiers had created an inferiority complex, in Indians. Rammohun Roy thought that when European settlers came as private citizens this complex might be dissipated. But he also anticipated that, in the long run, conflict of interest and a clash of mutual prejudices might eventually lead to a situation where either the Europeans or the Indians would try to dominate and "no government could mediate between them with effect or ensure public tranquility. The only safeguard against such an eventually was to open the door to a class "who, in general might be expected to raise the European character still higher" and also to win the affection of the people by helping them to emancipate themselves from "the bondage of ignorance and superstition". Rammohun Roy believed in the possible rise of 'mixed community'. He was not unmindful of the climatic handicap which did not stand in the way of European settlement in Canada and the United States of America. He suggested that the headquarters of the settlers might be in "cool and healthy sports", forgetting that, apart from the difficulties of remote control, isolated pockets of people, generally cut off from the mainstream of the country's life, could hardly be expected to serve the historic purpose he had in mind on the whole, Rammohun Roy's arguments were mainly directed against a system of colonialism based on absentee ownership, as in Ireland, which meant administration and exploitation by proxy, the evil effects of which he understood fully well in the light of the misfortunes of the Irish people.

[B.N. Ganguli]

5 SATI PRACTICE AND HIS OPPOSITION

I

History records that Mughal Emperor Akbar tried to suppress this practice among the Hindus and it is also said that earlier Jehangir too made a law of death penalty for this offence but could not carry it out in action. From time to time many administrators tried to stop it but even their best efforts proved to be nothing more than nibbling at the problem of its eradication. Evidently the custom was all the time looked down upon as inhuman but since numerous orthodox Hindus considered this as an act of merit which would ultimately bring eternal peace in Heaven, the practice continued among Hindu widows. This conviction added strength to the tradition and the practice continued without caring for warnings. In European countries, instances of cruel punishments to those who held views against the current traditions and against views held by the ruling clergy are numerous—the practice of burning of old women under the pretext of their witch craft abounds the pages of history all over the world in the middle ages but such cold-blooded, destruction of young women on the pretext of their husbands' death was not heard of excepting in India. Though these acts were more than cruel the custom persisted specially in India and the society glossed over this for centuries. Rammohun was the first Hindu who not only severely condemned this practice but also made emphatic public protest challenging its validity by quoting the scriptural texts. In every possible way, he tired his best to show that the practice was not corroborated by the most important law, givers of the ancient times—one or two much lesser men might have given expression of approval probably under special circumstances and for reasons which have no moral sanction or nothing to do with public morality.

Until Rammohun shook the public conscience, the custom was persisting in Bengal severely irrespective of classes and the society leaders were unmoved by it. It is difficult to believe that the learned scholars and educated leaders of the orthodox Hindu society like Raja Radhakant Dev and Dewan Ramkamal Sen did not feel their conscience hurt by such self-immolation—more atrocious it is when we find there is no record that this practice was followed in their own families. Contrary to our expectation and to our utter dismay we notice that these two leaders together with a host of Rajas, Maharajas and Pundits not only approved the custom but opposed Rammohun's movement for its abolition. It is curious that neither in Bengal not in any part of Hindu India any movement or protest ever took place, what is worst is that even in Benares, not a single group of pious or religious men or highly cultured Vedantists organised any public protest, leave aside Calcutta which was specially known for *Tantra-influence* and kali worship. What adds to the tragedy of the situation is that Radhakanta Dev was later given the public honour of a Magistrate and Justice of Peace by the Government and Ramkamal Sen was raised to higher and higher status. We are also at a loss to find absence of condemnation by foreigners in the English newspapers. These were the past incidents on which hardly any serious literature has been built up by the anthropologists.

The clouded mentality of the big and small people of Bengal (where incident of *Suttee* was the largest) who bore silently the inhuman atrocities cannot be explained. It is an undisputed fact that Calcutta had the worst of rigours of this custom. The Calcutta figures are alarming compared with the figures in other regions. Yet nobody can dispute that the soil of Bengal was most propitious for acceptance of Buddhism and Ahimsa and also acceptance of Vaishnavism of Chaitaniya Mahaprabhu with his flood love, sweeping the country throughout its length and breadth. The past records of Bengal as compared with the other regions of India bore clear evidence of these incidents in much larger degree. In the south and in the western regions of India, the incidence of this atrocity has been quite low. To–day suitable explanations for this state of affairs extremely inadequate and the sociologists have to work on them. In explaining the causes why Burdwan and Hooghly regions showed the large incidence, Mr. Oakley (Magistrate of Hooghly) said the following :

> ....In Calcutta there was an excess of profligacy and immorality of conduct and the worshippers of Kali, who indulged in drinking and other immoral practices, considered the burning of *Suttees* as a choice, entertainment rather as a religious act. The worship of Kali was not very popular in other districts and consequently the number of *Suttees* in those places was comparatively small. With regard to the sudden rise, the District Magistrate said that it was possibly due to interference of the Government. The Government regulation was in a way legalising the practice and people found that the Sastras sanctioning the inhuman practice were recognised by the Government. The Governor-General (Lord Hastings) therefore suspended any further action...

If one has to attempt to explain the origin of the practice, he should primarily begin with the law of inheritance to see in what direction and with what emphasis, peoples' minds were working. This may be evident from the fact that in Bengal where Dayabhag obtains (on the death of the husband the entire property would be inherited by the wire) *Suttee* affected roughly one widow out of every thirty whereas in the upper provinces where Mitakshara obtains (on the death of the husband property would be divided amongst all successors including the widow) one widow out of a thousand felt victim to the practice.

The primary explanation might have been the law of inheritance, but there was also a secondary explanation, in respect of which Rammohun's own writings can be quoted :

> Therefore any quotation from other authorities or detached passages attributed to Manu, but not be found in his code,

and inconsistent with it cannot be considered as of any validity. Then, whence, it asked, arose a practice so repugnant to reason, and so contrary to the most ancient and highest legislative authority of the Hindus? Only (1 reply) from the jealousy of their Princes, who were unable to tolerate the idea of their wives proving forgetful of them and associating with other men after their deaths,...while their surviving relations did not fail to encourage the practice for the reasons above explained, to promote their own interest...to support their views, by interpolations, and inventions, under the name of traditions, and quotations, from the Poorans and Tantras, which all acknowledge to have no limit or certain standard..

Leaving the general question taking the particular case of Rammohun's own family, it may be pointed out that even his mother did not become a *Suttee* after her husband's death but, it was in her presence that her daughter-in-law (eldest son Jugmohan's wife) did adopt *Suttee*-practice. It is commonly held that on this self-immolation by Jugmohan's wife in 1811, Rammohun vowed to start a regular campaign relentlessly against this inhuman practice until its eradication. We have already seen that Rammohun made up his mind while in Benares between 1798 and 1803 where he had witnessed horrible scenes of *Suttee* as well as child-sacrifice. In 1818 we find Rammohun raising his voice in Armiya Sabha in condemnation of not only these inhuman practices but also other social evils. He expressed indignation in public meetings and through his writings. It is said that he even visited these funeral scenes whenever possible to plead personally for saving the victims. His campaign started from 1811 and was re-inforced from 1818, when after a serious study of the law he wrote a tract. Rammohun's tract created a strong commotion in the orthodox section of the Hindu society and at last he was able to move the Government to action, particularly when these cases were found to be increasing in number upto 1818.

In February 1822, a Government order was issued under the signature of the Adjutant-General prohibiting the concermation of a pregnant woman or one having a child of tender age or of any girl not yet arrived at full age or one forced against her wish. The Government order ran thus :

> Whereas it has appeared that during the Ceremony denominated *Suttee*, (at which Hindu women burn themselves) certain acts have been occasionally committed, in direct opposition to the rules laid down in the religious institutes of the Hindus, by which that practice is authorized, and forbiden in particular cases : as for instance, at several places pregnant women, and girls not yet arrived at their full age have been burnt alive, and people after having intoxicated women by administering intoxicating substances, have burnt them without their assent whilst insensible; and in as much as this conduct is contrary to the Shastras, and perfectly inconsistent with every principle of humanity...it will be then their duty to exert themselves in restraining them; and at the same time to let them know that it is not the intention of the Government to check or forbid any act authorised by the tenets of the Religion of the inhabitants of their dominions; or even to require any express leave or permission being required previously to the performance of the act of *Suttee*; and the Police Officer are not to interfere and prevent any such act from taking place. And lastly, it will be their duty to transmit immediately for the information of the Magistrates, a full detail of any measures which they may have adopted on this subject, and also on every occasion when within the limits of Thannahs this Ceremony of *Suttee* may take place, the same being lawfully conducted, they will insert it in the Monthly Reports.

The activities and sentiments of the Government were communicated to the Court of Directors and the latter wrote back the Parliament had already been put in possession of the facts of the situation in the country. Buckingham, already in England after deportation from India, added his share of publicity through the *Oriental Herald* describing all that he had been doing while in India with the help of his *Calcutta Journal.*

Lord Hastings was then the Governor General. Though he tried to stop the practice, the fear of a revolt among the Sepoys refrained him from any strong decisive step. The same fear worked also on Lord Amherst, his successor, who recorded his decision in March 1827:

> ... I must frankly confess, though at the risk of being considered insensible to the enormity of the evil, that I am inclined to recommend our trusting to the progress now making in the diffusion of knowledge amongst the natives, for the gradual suppression of this detestable supersition. I cannot believe it possible that the burning or burying alive of widows will long survive the advancement which every year brings with it...I wish that the substance of Mr. Harington's excellent preamble to his proposed regulation could be embodied in some of the books of instruction which are distributed to generally, and in such large numbers, by our School Book Society.....

After Lord Amherst, came Lord Bentinck as Governor-General. Bentinck, before leaving London, was reported to have made up his mind to stop anyhow this inhuman and immoral practice. After reaching India, he however, started consultation with those administrators specially known to have India's good at heart. He was in possession of some facts quite early in his administration, an account of which is given below :

> In the Delhi Territory, Sir Charles Metcalfe never permitted a *Suttee* to be performed.

> In Jessore, one of the districts of the Calcutta Division, in 1824 there were 30 *Suttees*; in 1825, 16; in 1826, 3; in 1828, there were none. To no other cause can this be assigned, than to a power beyond the law, exercised by the Acting Magistrate, against which however, no public remonstrance was made. Mr. Pigou has been since

> appointed to Cuttack, and has pursued the same strong interference as in Jessore, but his course, although most humane, was properly arrested, as being illegal, by the Commissioners. Though the case of Jessore is perhaps one of the strongest example of efficacious and unopposed interposition, I really believe that there are few Districts in which the same arbitrary power is not exercised to prevent the practice. In the last week, in the report of the Acting Commissioner, Mr. Smith, he states that in Ghazipore in the last year 16, and the preceding year 7, *Suttees* had been prevented by the persuasions, or rather it should be said, by the threats of the police...Having made inquiries also how far *Suttees* are permitted in the European Foreign Settlements, I find from Dr Carey that at Chinsurah to such sacrifices had even been permitted by the Dutch Government. That within the limits of Chandernogore itself they were also prevented, but allowed to be performed in the British territories. The Danish Government of Serampore has not forbidden the rite in conformity to the example of the British Government.

When he consulted Mr. Horace Wilson, one of the most sincere friends of India, the reputed orientalist noted in his reply:

> ...My opinions are adverse to only authoritative interference with the practice of infant sacrifice at Sagor and in was not only unauthorised by any part of the Hindu code....It was of rare and restrictive occurrence. This affords no parallel to the performance of an act observed throughout India for many ages, under every form of Government and enjoyed by texts which all orthodox. Hindus regarded as holy.. the practice of female infanticide was of very limited observance. Its suppression was the work of persuasion and personal influence...the practice has never been abolished.. the enjoyment of settled property.. may have contributed to render the murder of female infants comparatively rare but there is no doubt

that both in Gujarat and in the Gangetic provinces female children are still destroyed by Particular tribes...the capital punishment of Brahmins are alluded to in your letter as an instance of safe interference with Hindu prejudices. It is true that no open opposition has been made to the execution of such a sentence—the Mohamedan Government is not likely to have held the persons of Brahmins inviolable and their being condemned to death was therefore no innovation...these considerations therefore appear to me of little weight. The analogies are fallacious and it seems a dangerous evasion of the real difficulties attending the question of abolishing the *Suttee* to adduce them as proof of the impunity with which its abolition may be affected...of a similar character is the attempt to represent it as not essentially a part of the Hindu religion. A widow, it is true, is not commanded[5] to burn in every case and Manu is silent on the subject of concentration. Other authorities of equal sanctity are sufficiently explicit... the *Suttee* cannot be put down without interference with the Hindu religion......

I am confident that his Lordship will do me the justice to believe that I should be one of the warmest advocates for the abolition of so inhuman a rite if I was not strongly impressed with the apprehension that serious evil may attend any measures proposed for its absolute suppression.

Then Bentinck wrote pointing out the following :

H.H. Wilson thinks that the attempt to put down the practice will inspire extensive dissatisfaction. I agree also in this opinion. I must acknowledge that a similar opinion as to the probable excitation of a deep distruct of our future intentions was mentioned was mentioned to me in conversation by that enlighetened native, Rammohun Roy, a warm advocate for the abolition of *Suttee* and of all other superstitions and corruptions engrafted on the Hindu religion.....

Bentinck appreciated the cautious views of H.H. Wilson and the possibility of deeper distrust but they fell short in a matter like this. He then wrote to Lord Hastings in England for his opinion and the latter replied :

> The subject which you wish to discuss is one which must interest one's feelings most deeply, but it is one of most extreme nicety when I mention that in one of the years during my administration of Govt. in India above 800 widows sacrificed themselves within the provinces comprised in the Presidency of Bengal, to which number I very much suspect that very many not notified to the magistrates should be added. I will hope to have credit for being acutely sensible to such an outrage against humanity. At the same time, I was aware how much danger might attend the endevouring to suppress forcibly a practice so rooted in the religious belief of the natives. No men of low caste are admitted into the ranks of the Bengal Army. Therefore the whole of the formidable body must be regarded as blindly partial to a custom which they consider as equally referable to family honour and to points of faith. To attempt the extinction of the horrid superstition without being supported in the procedure by a real concurrence on part of the army would be distinctly perilous. I have no scruple to say that I did believe I could have carried with me the assent of the army towards such an object. That persuasion, however, arose from circumstances which gave me peculiar influence over native troops.

Thus Bentinck had before him the views of several administrators and also of the well-wishers of India. He had also before him several published tracts which Rammohun wrote pointing out the views of the illustrious ancient law-givers. He fully appreciated the impassioned appeals of Rammohun and he now invited him for a consulation of the momentous issue before him. After some discussions Rammohun suggested :

> That any practice might be suppressed quietly and unobservedly by increasing the difficulties and by the indirect agency of the police.

Rammohun apprehended :

> That any public enactment might give rise to general apprehension, that the reasoning would be, while the English were contending for power, they deemed it politic to allow universal toleration and to respect our religion but having obtained the supremacy, their first act is a violation of their profession and the next will probably be, like the Mohamedan conquerors, to force upon us their own religion.

Then Bentinck disclosed his intention of suppressing this evil practice by legal enactment. Rammohun at first felt that in social problems, legal enactment would be very undesirable but in the next moment he not only gave approval but assured him all help that he was capable of rendering.

When the orthodox community led by Raja Radhakanta Dev came to know that Bentinck had finally decided to lean in favour of Rammohun's appeals and to abolish the practice by law, *Samachar Chandrika* wrote :

> Rammohun, no doubt, was born in a Hindu family, but how could be represent all or majority of the Hindus. He cannot claim to represent his own forefathers or the clan, not the speak of the community.

Benthock's consulations ended and he made his decision with extreme boldness (in spite of what had already happened two decades back at Vellore). He finally wrote :

The first and primary object of my heart is the benefit of the Hindus. I know nothing so important to the improvement of their future condition as the establishment of a purer morality, whatever their belief, and more just conception of the will of God. The first step for this better understanding will be dissociation of religious belief and practice from blood and murder. They will then, when no longer under this brutalising excitement view with more calmness acknowledged truths. They will see that there can be no inconsistency in the ways of providence, that to the command received as divine by all races of men. 'No innocent blood shall be split' there can be no exception, and when they shall have been convinced of error of this first and most criminal of their customs, may it not be hoped that others, which stand in the way in the way of their improvement, may likewise pass away, and thus emancipated from those chains and shackles upon their minds and actions, they may not longer continue, as they have done, the slaves of every foreign conqueror, but that they may assume their first places among the great families of mankind? I disown in these remarks, or in this measure, any view whatever to conversion to our own faith. I write and feel as a legislator for the Hindus, and as I believe many enlightened Hindus think and feel.

Descending from these higher considerations, it cannot be a dishonest ambition that the Government of which If form a part should have the credit of an act which is to wash out a foul stain upon British rule, and to stay the sacrifice of humanity and justice to a doubtful expendiency, and finally as a branch of the general administration of the Empire, I may be permitted to feel deeply anxious that our course shall be in accordance with the noble example set to us by the British Government at home, and that the adaptation, when practicable to the circumstances of this vast Indian population, of the same enlightened principles, may promote here as well as there the general prosperity, and may exalt the character of our nation.

It will be seen that Bentinck passed through a great mental struggle between expediency and caution on one side and duty on the other, between what was expected of him as an efficient administrator and what was incumbent on him as a Governor-General with a large vision and fully possessed of a sense of progress to rehabilitate India to a stable position. Bentinck had also a keen sense of social justice consistent with conservation of national traditions. This being the background, the studied opinion of Mrityunjay Vidyalankar (who had already understood Government's learnings to abolition of the practice) and the strong support received from Rammohun's tracts must have given Bentinck a distinct spurt in taking a bold decision, Further a portion of the translations by Sir William Jones must have strengthened Bentinck still more.

Administrator's Way

Bentinck now adopted a courageous stand with a stout heart completed the Minute to abolish the cruel practice by the promulgation of an ordinance. The concluding part of his historic Minute stated :

> ....It is upon this first and highest consideration alone, the good of mankind, that the tolerance of this inhuman and impious rite can in my opinion be justified on the part of the Government of a civilised nation. While the solution of this question is appalling from the unparalleled magnitude of its possible results, the considerations belonging to it are such as to make even the stoutest mind distrust its decision. On the one hand, Religion, Humanity, under the most appalling form as well as Vanity and Ambition—in short, all the powerful influences over the human heart...are arrayed to bias and mislead the judgment. On the other side, the section of countless ages, the example of all the Mussulman conquerors, the unanimous concurrence in the name of policy of our most able rulers together with the universal veneration of the people, seem authoritatively to forbid, both to feeling and to reason, and interference in the exercise of their natural prerogative. In venturing to be the first to deviate from this practice it becomes us to show that nothing has been yielded to feeling, but that reason, and reason alone, has governed the decision...
>
> .....Prudence and self-interest would counsel me to tread in the foot-steps of my predecessors. But in a case of such momentous importance to humanity and civilisation that man must be reckless of all his present to future happiness

> who could listen to the dictates of so wicked and selfish a policy. With the firm undoubting conviction entertained upon this question, I should be guilty of little short of the crime of multiplied murder if I could hesitate in the performance of this soleman obligation. I have been already stung with this feeling. Every day's delay adds a victim to the dreadful list....

Bentinck signed the Minute on November 8, 1829, making the *Suttee* practice illegal and punishable by law. On this basis the Government issued the Regulation on December 4, 1829. Rammohun won his life's most ardent objective but the enforcement of the law took more time than was expected. The enlightened liberal section Hindu Bengal paid congratulatory address to the Governor-General; the Europeans presented a separate address; but the orthodox section of Hindu Bengal led by Raja Radhakanta Dev went to Bentinck on January 14, 1830 with a long representation bearing a thousand signatures including those of many learned Pundits and citizens.

Rammohun's study of the Sastirc provisions for widows had convinced him that concremation was not a part of Hindu religion but only practice, loosely followed, over a long period. The idea of eternal happiness which largely prompted this action had nothing to do with Hinduism. The smaller authorities like Angira, Harita, etc., and endorsed the *Suttee* practice but it was more for a show of purism—some half-hearted and others forced. In fact the greatest and oldest lawgivers Manu and Jajnavalkya who stand supreme as law-givers in India had not recommended the self killing practice for widows. They, on the other hand prescribed a strictly virtuous and austere life for them. Rammohun was guided by these law-givers and brought social plessure for stopping this evil practice. But it was seen that his personal intervention (when he opposed this practice during his stay in Benares) had no effect. He thus came to the conclusion that much more effective and strong measures from Government side were essential for stopping this evil.

In spite of Rammohun's ceaseless efforts, he has not been given, by one group of Indian scholars, his due share of credit, after the abolition of the *Suttee* practice ostensibly on the ground that when Bentinck wanted Rammohun's opinion on his proposed legal measure, the latter did not favour it whole heartedly.

Reformer's Way

Rammohun said the following to Bentinck :

> ....The practice might be suppressed quietly and unobservedly by increasing the difficulties and by indirect agency of the police.

How absurd it is to construe the above, as has been done by a reputed historian, that Rammohun's mind was not fully made up for abolition of the practice. Let in the repeated here that it was Rammohun who having felt deeply oppressed by the barbarity of the practice, wrote tract after tract, exposing the evil effects when the whole country was indifferent and when the orthodox section was distinctly against any interference with the existing practice. In writing out tracts, he carried out deep study of the ancient texts, since he realised that the only means for achieving his objective was to convince the orthodox leaders, for it was they who invariably led or coerced the common people to form their views of what was to be done or not to be done—unfortunately, it was not by the dictates of common people's conscience, since that freedom was denied to them by their conscience-keepers, *i.e.,* the Zamindars.

It would be nothing short of a flagrant travesty of truth, if, despite Rammohun's long record of persuasions by all means, Rammohun is accused of having had no clear objective. Rammohun had his own views on the "means" of abolition of the practice but about "abolition itself", his stand was clear, positive and final. The choice of "means" is what distinguishes the Reformer from the Administrator. Rammohun knew that it was always wise to adopt the means which least disturbs the minds of the common people. A reformer like Rammohun who dedicated his whole life in ridding the society of the evils of caste system, polygamy, child-marriage, child-sacrifice, widow-oppression culminating in *Suttee* practice, would naturally emphasise on the need for spontaneous efforts from below through the people as against legal enactments from above. It would be absurd, if for every reform, legal enactments are resorted to instead of quietly permeating new ideas into the society supplemented by physical impediments.

The reputed historian, R.C. Majumdar, referred to above, has very ungenerously and without the slightest justification interpreted Rammohun as below :

> According to Bentinck's Minute, Roy recommended that the practice might be suppressed quietly and unobservedly by increasing the difficulties and by indirect agency of the Police. It is rather extraordinary that Roy should have made this suggestion... The averaging force of fact remains that when Bentinck was determined to legislate on *Suttee*, Roy lurched and staggered.

But Rammohun did not stagger for nothing; he must have felt that his reformatory objective of getting the evil practice abandoned by the people themselves out of disgust, futility and sheer helplessness, was not being achieved; that on the contrary, a positive violation, however well-internationed and however gloriously conceived, might give a jerk in the Sepoy's mind. Our reputed historian has himself pointed out :

> Roy opposed legislative enactment on the ground that public enactment would not only violate the British profession of religious neutrality on which the (Britishers) had prided themselves but would create mistrust in the minds of the Hindus about the British intentions.

Having pointed out, it does not behove him to cast reflection on Rammohun's so–called faltering by stating :

> ....faltering in resolution in the part he played in the prelude to the abolition of *Suttee*.

It was not faltering in the sense of "hesitating to take action on abolition" but hesitating to adopt" legal enactment," where social impediments and obstructions, strengthened by administrative measures, should have achieved the objective. R.C. Majumdar's emphasis, however, on violation of religious neutrality, has lent a great support to the historian S.N. Sen's analysis of the causes of the Sepoy Mutiny which runs as follow :

> ....An atmosphere of distrust and suspicion had been created by a series of well-intentioned but ill-judged legislative and administrative measures which shook to its very core the sepoy's faith in the bonafides of the Sarkar, and successive Governors-General contributed unconsciously to the steady deterioration of public confidence to their good faith. Lord Dalhousie has generally been held responsible for the outbreak but no single act of his by itself would have caused the revolt. Lord William Bentinck, Lord Amherst, Lord Auckland, and Lord Ellenborough had each by some act of omission or commission either alinated orthodox opinion in the country or interfered with ancient right and privileges dearly cherished by the people.
>
> The alien government was based not on the loyalty of the people but open its armed force. The sepoy felt that his was the strong arm that had sustained it so long, and he could overthrow it whenever he wanted. He had hitherto remained loyal to his salt, but when he thought that his employers aimed at nothing less than his ancestral faith, the very basis of that loyalty was shattered.......The revolt had been long brewing, the greased cartridge only hastened it.

Taking a long view, Rammohun felt in one way which was the Reformer's way and it was to effect a through change in the people's mentality, but in the circumstances in which he was placed, he felt that it was upto the administrator to take recourse to his own line of action, in view of his own administrative responsibilities. He only indicated his preference and left the matter in Bentinck's hands. As the decision came. Rammohun felt relieved but still unhappy at the thought of its possible repercussion on the Sepoys. He must have sensed a faint streak of cloud gathering on the horizon. In course of time, several such lapses (as appeared to the Sepoys) from the original assurance on the part of the British administration deepened the faint streak of cloud until it burst with a thunder, in the uprising of 1857. True, Rammohun staggered as any thinking-man would stagger, so did also Bentinck (as any Reformer would do) which will be more than clear as one reads the final portion of Bentinck's note.

It is inconceivable, though it is a fact, that two learned, well established God-fearing men like Dewan Ramkamal Sen and Raja Radhakanta Dev along with their numerous orthodox Hindu supporters, opposed Bentinck's decision—a progressive measure. The role of these two men in particular and of the followers in general was tantamount to sacrificing countless widows (including very young widows) on the plea of religious injunctions, a kind of mass sacrifice under social pressure, merely on the plea of husband's death. Therefore opposition to the abolition only meant that the orthodox leaders of the Hindu society were slaves of a cruel practice, yet it must be noted that it was not compulsory—Rammohun's mother did not become *Suttee*. If the leaders of the society had a good understanding of the *sastric* provision, they could not support this practice since the essence of Hinduism is that man is a spark of the Divine and therefore self-immolation be a serious crime, and that those who were involved in this killing would be equally punishable.

If Radhakanta Dev and Ramkamal Sen realised the true spirit of *sastric* provision they as leaders of the Hindu society could not have debased themselves in opposing the abolition of the custom, for it was such unfortunate widows who really deserved their sympathy and protection. It is difficult to imagine how these leaders set aside the greatest of law-givers like Manu. The leaders missed the wholesome teachings of *sastras* and degraded their religion by associating it with the *Suttee* custom. The charge that Hinduism put little stress on ethical principle of life and that Buddhism provided that necessary stress as did also Christianity, seems true to a large measure. Rammohun guided by ethical principles opposed all unethical practices, however ancient they might be, by tracts and by persuasion.

Bentinck, as a Christian guided by ethical principles and administrative ideals, felt impelled to rise to his full stature rather than blindly act on "British assurance of religious neutrality" without a fuller assessment in the light of national growth. Evidently Bentinck did not take these practices as part of religion. Bentainck's bold utterances in all their progressive measures will reverberate from age to age, and from one corner to another. It is worth remembering Bentinck's firm words :

> ....when Governor of Madras, I saw, in the Mutiny of Vellore, the dreadful consequences of a supposed violation of religious custom upon the minds of the native population and soldiery. I cannot forget that I was then the innocent victim of that unfortunate catastrophe and I might reasonable dread, when he responsibility would justly attach to me in the event of failure, a recurrence of the same fate. Prudence and self-interest would counsel me to trend in the footsteps of my predecessors. But in a case of such momentous importance to humanity and civilisation, that man must be receive of all his present or future happiness who could listen to the dictates upon this question. I should be guilty of little short of crime of multiplied murder, if I would hesitate in the performance of this solemn obligation.

Bentinck responded fully where his predecessors deemed it wiser and safer to keep quiet. Both Bentinck and Rammohun performed their part in deep conviction, yet if one has to apportion the credit in this matter, it may not be wrong to give the larger share to Rammohun, because Rammohun voluntarily espoused the cause. He worked over thirty long years from 1799 to 1833.

It is interesting to read a letter of an admiring lady, Mrs. Martin, who overwhelmed by the great courage of Rammohun wrote the following in the *Bengal Hurkara* :

> The statesman whose name is associated with the proceedings of this memorable juncture merits the loud applause of those whose interests are more immediately identified with the Government over which he presides, as having exhibited that Government in a point of view at once interesting and novel—in an attitude of independence it had never before assumed...and as being free to co-operate for, and sufficiently powerful to the establishment of measures in, the advocacy of Justice and the public weal.
>
> This, Sir, is the circumstance which will render the rule of Lord Bentinck in India more illustrious than that of any of his predecessors...this confirms his claim to that constitutional liberality of character, without which a great and good man never existed....
>
> But, Sir, in the further investigation of this affair, the full onus of merit will be perceived to rest, not on the Government, but on one of the most eminent Philanthropists that any country has ever produced, and without whose extraordinary and unceasing exertions, it would be supererogatory to instinuate that the act of council, now so generally applauded might never have been passed. Your observation that "Europe will resound with praises on the exertions of the Indian Government on this occasion" should certainly have been modified; the series of grievances to which its imbecility in this respect has given protracted continuance can surely not be cancelled by the mere trady introduction of a measure which a disgraceful apprehension of danger, alone prevented from being earlier adopted.. and which, as I have before observed, would not low, in the utmost probability,

have been brought into effect, (though to diffuse a peculiar radiance even over the present administration) but for the powerful though unacknowledged did of the great Hindu Philosopher, Rammohun Roy....and in....

Frozen indeed must be those emotions, and superficial, vitiated, and contemptible those political theorems, which unconscious to the enthusiasm of philanthropy in the one instance, or trembling at the supposititious embarrassment in the other, renounce alike the honor, the greatness and the immoral glory to which the performance of courageous and generous deeds conducts!

But a dawn is bursting on a new and happier prospect, the triumphs of liberty, whether over object system of polity or national error are necessarily remarkable for an emanation of splendour, which dissipating the surrounding darkness chases the fugitive shadows to the gloom of the eternal past...at least to the countrywomen of the Hindu Patriot may it prove so, ...at least to those prodigies of fortitude the Indian widows may the present era prove a fubilee which enfranchises them for ever,.. and in commemorating the amiable and highly polite administration of Lord Bentinck, may they never cease to remember the glowing sympathy, intelligence, and fearless energy displayed through a course of eighteen years, by their great and at length successful advocate, Rammohun Roy.

To the above letter *Bengal Hurkara* referred in its next issue as follows :

In a preceding page we have inserted a letter from Mrs. Martin on the abolition of the *Suttee*. Our fair correspondent has paid a just tribute to the labours of that learned Brahman and ardent philanthropist, Rammohun Roy. This enlightened Hindu has long laboured to prove to his countrymen that the custom is not only abborrent to every principle of humanity but is actually in contradiction to the Sastras or Sacred writings. It must indeed be a proud and happy reflection to this eminent and worthy native gentlemen that his exertions and his hopes are now about to be consummated by the manliness and good feeling of the present Government. The fervent eulogy of an English lady, thus openly and nobly bestowed upon this excellent Individual, we are quite sure will not be undervalued by him, however accustomed he may be to the voice of praises from almost every quarter of the globe. We cannot, however, help regretting that our fair correspondent should have made rather an invidious distinction between Lord William Bentinck and Rammohun Roy, with reference to their peculiar share to the glory to accrue from the suppression of so ancient and detestable a practice as the *Suttee*. Lord William Bentinck has done all that a Governor should do. If he has not devoted so many years of labour and anxiety to the accomplishment of the same object, he has evinced the same sincerity of purpose, and has seized on the first opportunity of effecting, at one blow, what Rammohun Roy has prepared the way for, by the energy of argument and the grace of eloquence. Let us not therefore offer our exclusive praise and gratitude either to Rammohun Roy or to Lord Bentinck. The former would never have succeeded in his patriotic and enlightened labours without the co-operation of the latter, nor would Lord Bentinck, have ventured on so desirable a measure, if the minds of the natives had not been prepared to abandon the worst of superstitions, by the unwearied labours of their distinguished countrymen.

Once Bentinck adopted his own way of abolishing the practice Rammohun assured him all his support in case of any untoward event. Some correspondence, it is believed, took place between Bentinck and Rammohun when the former got upset by the commotion created by the orthodox adherents of Radhakanta Dev. In a meeting at Bolepur (West Bengal) on September 10, 1977, Prof. Dilip Biswas, the most eminent authority on Rammohun, told us that he had discovered scraps of scribbling of Rammohun giving Bentinck full assurance of all help, if any untoward event took place at all.

REFERENCES

1. Table of Suttee cases :

Year	Calcutta Div.	Dacca	Murshidabad	Patna	Benares	Bareilly*	total
1815	253	31	11	29	48	15	387
1816	289	24	21	29	65	13	441
1817	442	52	42	49	103	19	707
1818	544	58	30	57	137	14	839
1819	421	55	25	40	92	17	650
1820	370	51	21	42	93	20	597
1821	391	52	12	69	104	15	654
1822	528	45	22	70	102	16	583
1823	340	40	13	49	121	12	565
1824	373	40	14	59	76	10	572
1825	398	101	21	47	55	17	639
1826	324	65	8	65	48	8	518
1827	337	49	9	55	49	18	517
1828	308	47	10	55	33	19	463

*Bareilly represents what were the upper provinces of British India.

2. Rammohun in his *Essay On the Rights of Hindus Over Ancestral Property According to the Law of Bengal* (Calcutta, 1830) writes :

"6. From a regard for the usages of the country, the practice of the British courts in Bengal, as far as related to the law of inheritance, has been hitherto consistent with the principles laid down in the Dayabhaga, and judgments have accordingly been given on its authority in many most important cases of frequent occurrence which have been fully discussed, and invariably decided by the judicial tribunals in Bengal, in conformity with the doctrines of Jimutavahana.

"First. If a member of an undivided family dies, leaving no male issue, his widow shall not be entitled to her husband's share according to the Mitakshara : but according to the Dayabhaga, she shall inherit such undividual portion :

"Second. A childless widow, inheriting the property of her deceased husband, is authorised to dispose it, according to the Mitakshara : but according to the Dayabhaga, she is not entitled to sell or give it away.

"Third. If a man dies, leaving one daughter having issue, and another without issue, the latte shall inherit the property left by her father, according to the Mitakshara : while the former shall receive it according to the Dayabhaga.

"Fourth. If a man dies without issue or brothers, leaving a sister's son and a paternal uncle, the latter is entitled to the property, according to the Mitakshara : and the former according to the Dayabhaga.

"Fifth. A man, having a share of undivided real property, is not authorised to make a sale or gift of it without the consent of the rest of his partners, according to the Mitakshara : but according to the Dayabhaga, he can dispose of it at his free will.

"Sixth. A man in possession of ancestral real property, though not under any tenure limiting it to suceessive generations of his family, is not authorised to dispose of it, by sale or gift, without the consent of his sons and grandsons, according to the Mitakshara : while according to the Dayabhaga, he has the power to alienate the property at his free will".

According to Colebrooke's translation of the Dayabhaga (Chapter XI), "the whole wealth of a deceased husband who had no male issue, shall belong to his widow though there be brothers of whole blood, paternal uncles, daughter's sons and other heirs", still too much of stress on "motive of inheritance" only not be correct interpretation, because looking into Parliamentary Papers one will find a number of cases of *Suttee* where family means were extremely meagre and the question of inheritance negligible. It will also be apparent that apart from Brahmins, lower castes also were involved.

3. Apart from being inhuman, the practice was irrational. Rammohun's emphasis on rationality (as against religious convention) was something unique at that time. any serious student of ancient history would know that India produced many great rationalists among whom was Buddha who told his disciples that if at any time they had doubts about the efficacy of his doctrines, they should not hesitate to change them. Brihaspati the law-giver was another.
4. See J.K. Majumdar, *op. cit.*, p. XXVIII.
5. True, some widows destroyed themselves of their own wish but in many cases, they were induced by drugging. In the

concluding paragraphs of his recently discovered fourth tract (published in England) Rammohun took his stand on the code of Manu (pp. 75-76) and not on humanitarian or other considerations. Modern Hindu social reformers cannot be expected to possess his faith in the sacred books where two courses were provided for the widow : ascetic life or *anumarana*. But the earlier codes prescribed quite a different course *niyoga*, appointment, analogous to the Jewish Levirate, a custom by which a dead man's brother or next of kin or even a member of the caste could raise issue on the widow. The widow was first made to lie down by her dead husband on the funeral pyre. She was then made to rise and return home with the receitation of the following stanza which occurs both in the Rigveda (X. 188) and the Aṭharvaveda (XVIII. 3.1) : "Go up, o woman, to the world of the living; thou liest by this one who is deceased; come to him who grasps *thy* hand, *thy* second spouse thou hast now entered into the relation of wife to husband." This shows that in the Vedic period the primitive custom of self-immolation of the widow was forbidden among the progressive elements of the population.

The picture of *Suttee* practice abolition will not be complete without the following information regarding the authorities for the abolition :

(a) Those of persons in favour of an immediate and total suppression of the rite by the authority of Government (25 in number);

(b) Those recommending the immediate suppression of the rite by the authorised interference of the local magistrates (1 in number);

(c) Persons recommending a total and immediate prohibition of the rite by Legislative enactments, as expedient, safe and practicable (8 in number);

(d) Persons recommending a gradual abolition of the Rite by the authorised interference of the Magistrates (10 in number);

(e) Persons who abstained from giving any opinion on the subject at large, but apprehended no danger from a prohibition of the rite, as regards the Native army (3 in number);

(f) Persons adverse to a direct prohibition of the rite by Government (11 in number);

(g) Persons adverse to a total prohibition of the rite as being premature (2 in number);

(h) Persons adverse to every species of official interference with the Rite of *Suttee* (4 in number);

(i) Persons adverse to prohibition of the Rite, as being a departure from the principles of toleration, but who conceived it would be safe though productive of dissatisfaction (2 in number);

(Abstracted from the Appendix to the Statement submitted by the East India Company, to the King's most Honourable Privy Council).

7. "......the translations of the institutes of Manu, by Sir William Jones, which is before the public, and which, to use the language of that immortal work, is a system of duties, religious and civil, promulgated in the beginning of the time of Manu...the first of created beings and to the oldest only, but holiest of legislators, a system so comprehensive and so minutely exact, that it may be considered as the institutes of Hindu Law". (Sir W. Jones Works, Vol. VIII, Preface). This great legislator, in prescribing the duties of widows, thus ordains : "Let her (the widow) continue till death, forgiving all injuries; performing harsh duties, avoiding every sensual pleasure, and cheerfully practising the incomparable rules of virtue, which have been followed by such women, as were devoted to one only husband"; and like those abstemious men, a virtuous wife ascends to heaven though she has no child if after the decrease of her lord, she devote herself to pious austerity (Verse 160)...It cannot be alleged that the Veda may have justified the practice and superseded the authority of Manu; since he Veda itself declares that "Whatever Manu pronounced was a medicine for the soul".—(Sir William Jones *Works,* Vol. VII, p. 83).

8. One January 14, 1830, a representation to Lord Bentinck against the prohibition of *Suttee* was made under the signature of over a thousand citizens including :

Maharaja Girish Chandra Roy Bahadur,	Raja Radhakanta Deb,
Maharaja Shib Kissein Roy Bahadur	Babu Gopi Mohan Deb,

Maharaja Kali Kissein Roy Bahadur,

Babu Ramgopal Mullick,

Maharaja Gour Ballav Roy Bahadur,

Babu Prankissan Biswas,

Babu Radhamadhab Banerjee,

beside more than a hundred Sanskrit Pundits. The signature of one very important man, Dewan Ram Kamal Sen, was not there. On further scrutiny it was found that Ram Kamal Sen, though he did not put signature, supported the representation, for, we find that in the inaugural meeting of he Dharma Sabha, as Chairman, he said :

> "according to the orders of the Governor-General, an appel must be made to His Majesty relative to the regulations forbidding *Suttee*....."

The meeting established the Dharma Sabha on February 6, 1830 and elected the following as committee members :

Maharaja Kali Kissein Bahadur.

Maharaja Ashutosh Dey,

Maharaja Gokulnath Mullik,

Raja Radhakanta Deb,

Ram Kamal Sen,

Ramgopal Mullik,

Gopi Mohan Deb,

Tarini Churn Mitra

We find elsewhere that—According to the orders on 2nd August, 1830, Dharma Sabha met and Ram Kamal Sen said :

> "All the members have equally laboured in the establishment of the society and in the promoting of its chief object, the dispatch of the petition to England...."

The Governor-General forwarded the representation to the Council in London. The appeal was heard by the Privy Council and was rejected on July 11, 1833. This was the final seal on the abolition.

Its authoritative work is "Collect" Raja Rammohun Roy".

6 VIEWS ON REVENUE SYSTEM

Engagements, public and private, recorded and unrecorded were numerous and these discussions and discourses, by and large religious, social and political, related also to economic and legal subject which needed serious, well-thought-out and sympathetic consideration of the Government. An urgent and comprehensive treatment was particularly needed for subjects like the revenue and judicial systems prevailing in India. Land revenue questions concerned vitally the cultivators, landholders and the Government, no less the British Parliament. The judicial problems were equally important and vast. Naturally Rammohun concentrated all his thoughts, on problems and their solutions so that the Government might make the best use of them for the levelling up of the country's administration in the coming revision of the Charter. He wrote five Papers[1] :

1. *Revenue System of India* : 54 questions were put and their replies will go down in history as a stupendous work achieved within a short time. The replies were in the form of a paper appended with a statement (August, 19, 1931).

2. *Judicial System of India* : 78 questions were put and his own answers were in the form of a paper (September 19, 1831).

3. *Additional Queries respecting the Conditions of India* : 13 questions and their replies (September 28, 1831).

4. *General Character and Condition of the Native Inhabitants* (September 28, 1831).

5. *Settlement of Europeans in India* (July 14, 1832).

Revenue System of India

It is known that before Lord Cornwallis, a year-to-year arrangement was the practice which was followed by a decimal settlement. Lord Cornwallis introduced Permanent Settlement.[2] The incidence of rent which came into force was as follows :

> It is considered in theory that the cultivator pays half the produce to the landholder, out of which half, 10-11ths or 9-10ths constitute the revenue paid to Government, and 1-10th or 1-11th the net rent of the landholder. This half of the produce is a very heavy demand upon the cultivator, after he has borne the whole expense of seed and labour, but in the practice, under the permanent settlement since 1793, the landholders have adopted every measure to raise the rents by means of the power put into their hands (Nag and Burman : *English Works of Raja Rammohun Roy*. Part III, p. 40, 7A and p. 57, 13).

All Round Improvements Stated

The amount of assessment fixed on the lands of those provinces at the time of Permanent Settlement (1793), was as high as had ever been assessed and in many instance higher than ever before been realized by the exertions of any government : Mohammedan or British. Therefore the Government sacrified nothing in concluding the settlement. If it had not been formed the landholders (Zamindars) would always have taken care to prevent the revenue from increasing by not bringing the waste lands into cultivation, and by elusive arrangements to elude further demands (Nag and Burman : *English Works of Rammohun Roy*, Part III, p. 47, 37A).

At the time of the Permanent Settlement (1793), the amount of the revenue which had been paid on each estate (Zamindari) in the preceding year was taken as a standard of assessment, subject to certain modification, Estates (Taluka) which had paid a revenue directly to Government for the twelve years previous without fluctuation were to be assessed at the rate, and the principle of that assessment was considered to be nearly one-half of the gross produce. In Behar and other places the gross amount of the rents arising from an estate was fixed up on the rate of Government assessment, allowing, however, a deduction of ten per cent to the landholder (Zamindar), in the name of proprietor's dues (Malikana) and also something for the expense of collecting the rents. (Nag and Burman : *English Works of Raja Rammohun Roy*, Part III, P. 41, 10A).

Improvements in the Condition of the Landholders

Their condition has been much improved : because, being secured by the Permanent Settlement against further demands of revenue, in proportion to the improvement of their estates they have in consequence brought the waste lands into cultivation, and raised the rents of their tenantry, and thus increased their own income, as well as the resources of the country..... I would propose, first, that the collectors should not by any means he armed with magisterial power, secondly, that my charge against the revenue officers should be at once investigated by the judicial courts (Nag and Burman : *English Works of Raja Rammohun Roy*, Part III, p. 47, 36A).

The new system acted upon during the last forty years, having enabled the landholders to ascertain the full measurement of the lands is their own satisfaction, and by successive exactions to raise the rents of the cultivators to the utmost possible extent, the very least I can propose and the least which Government can do for bettering the condition of the peasantry, is absolutely to interdict any further increase of rest on any pretence whatsoever; particularly on no consideration to allow the present settled and recognized extent of the land to be disturbed by pretended re-measurements; and informing the Permanent Settlement. (Nag and Burman : *English Works of Rammohun Roy*, Part III, p. 45. 31A).

On finding any Zamindar guilty of demanding more than the rent of the preceding year, should subject such offender to a severe fine; and on discovering any police officer or native commissioner guilty of connivance or neglect, he should subject them to fine and dismissal from service. (Nag and Burman : *English Works of Rammohun Roy*, Part III, p. 46, 34A).

Some Important Observations Made

When the revenue of an estate falls into arrear, the Government by its own authority sells property. But the proprietor cannot sell the property of a cultivator, except by the means of the judicial authority, which generally expedites the recovery of such balance. (Nag and Burman : *English Works of Rammohun Roy*, Part III, p. 43, 20A).

Important Comments on Perpetual Settlement of Public Revenue[3] (Rammohun's Paper on Revenue System, (Nag and Burman : *English Works of Rammohun Roy*, Part III).

2. ..... To avoid the demand of an increase of revenue on the part of Government, proprietors in general and then wilfully to neglect the cultivation, which very often proved utterly ruinous to themselves, and excessively inconvenient to Government, in managing, farming or selling such estates for the purpose of realizing their revenues. (Nag and Burman : *English Works of Rammohun Roy*, Part III, p. 55).

3. ..... This enormous augmentation of the price of land is principally to be attributed to the extensive cultivation of waste, lands, which has taken place in every part of the country, and to the rise of rents payable by the cultivations, and not to any other cause that I can trace...... (Nag and Burman : *English Works of Rammohun Roy*, Part III, p. 55).

4. It is true the common increase of wealth has an irresistible tendency to augment the price, without any improving change in the property, but when we reflect on the extent of overwhelming poverty throughout the country (towns and their vicinity excepted), we cannot admit that increase of wealth in general has been the cause of actual rise in the value of landed estates. To those who have ever made a tour of the provinces, either on public duty or from motives of curiosity, it is well-known that within a circle of a hundred miles in any part of the country there are to be found very few, if

any (besides proprietor's lands), that have the least pretension to wealth or independence, or even the common comforts of life. (Nag and Burman : *English Works of Rammohun Roy*, Part III, p. 56).

5. It has been asserted, and perhaps the justly, that much of the increased wealth of Bengal in late years is to be ascribed to the opening to trade in 1814, thereby occasioning a greatly increased demand for produce of lands. In as far, however, as this cause may have operated to increase of wealth, it is confined to landholders and dealers in commodities. (Nag and Bruman : *English Works of Rammohun Roy*, Part III, p. 56).

8. None will, I think, hesitate to rejoice in the augmentation of the incomes of proprietors derived from the extension of cultivation, as every man is entitled by law and reason to enjoy the fruits of his honest labour and good management. But as to the policy of vesting in the proprietors themselves, exempted from any increase of tax, the power of augmenting rents due from their Khund-Kasht tenants, I must confess it to be a subject that requires examination. (Nag and Burman : *English Works of Rammohun Roy,* Part III, p. 56).

11. In short, there were three parties, acknowledge to have had a fixed right in the soil : Ist, the Ryots to cultivate the land, and receive one-half of the produce in return for the seed and labour, 2nd, the Government, in return for its general protection, to receive the other half, with the exception of one tenth or eleventh, 3rd, the Zamindars, or landholders, to receive the tenth or eleventh for their local protection, and for their intervention between the Government, and the peasantry. (Nag and Burman : *English Works of Rammohun Roy*, Part III, p. 57).

14. With a view to facilitate the collection of revenue and

to encourage proprietors to improve their estates, Government liberally relieved them in the year 1793 from the distress and difficulties originating in the uncertainty of assessment, by concluding a perpetual settlement with them. But I am at a lost to conceive why this indulgence was not extended to their tenants, by requiring proprietors to follow the example of Government, in fixing a definite rent to be receive from each cultivator, according to the average sum actually collected from him during a given term of years; or why the feeling of compassion excited by the miserable condition of the cultivators do not now induce the government to fix a maximum standard, corresponding with the sum of rent now paid by each cultivator in one year, and positively interdict any further increase. (Nag and Burman : *English Works of Rammohun Roy,* Part, p. 57).

15. Some however, doubt whether government can now assume the power of bettering the condition of they immense portion of its subjects, without violating the long-standing practice of the country (Nag and Burman : *English Works of Rammohun Roy,* Part III, p. 58).

16. With respect to the Regulations, however, there would be no real violation to them, as in Regulation 1 of 1793, which is the basis of the Permanent Settlement, the Government thus expressly declares, that "it being the duty of the ruling power to protect all classes of people, and more particularly those who from their situation are most helpless, the Governor General in council will, whenever he may deem it proper, enact such regulations as he may think necessary, for the protection and welfare of the dependant Talookdars, Ryots, and other cultivators of the soil : and no Zamindar, independent Talookdar, or other actual proprietors of land, shall be entitled on this account to make any objection to the discharge of the fixed assessment which

they have respectively agreed to pay. (Nag and Burman : *English Works of Rammohun Roy*, Part III, p. 58).

22. With respect to the expediency and advantage of appointing native revenue officers to the higher situations in the revenue department, I am strongly supported by the opinions of persons whose sentiments have great weight with the governing party as well as with the party governed. I can safely quote the remarks of many distinguished servants of the Honourable East India Company, such as Sir Thomas Munro, Mr. Robert Rickards, Mr. H. Ellis, and others. (Nag and Burman : *English Works of Rammohun Roy*, Part III, p. 60).

24. "For the present, perhaps, it would be proper to transfer the duty of selling the property of defaulting lanholders to the registrars; and the judge, instead of referring causes to the revenue officers, should submit them to Sudder Ameens or native commissioners already appointed to decide causes under a certain amount. (Nag and Burman : *English Works of Rammohun* Roy, Part III, p. 60).

25. In order to prevent the exercise of any undue influence or bribery in obtaining the situation of native collectors of revenue, it is requisite that all the present Serishtadars or head native officers attached to the different collectorships, should each be confirmed, at once, in the situation of collecting, and in case of his death or removal, the next in rank should succeed him.... (Nag and Burman : *English Works of Rammohun Roy*, Part III, p. 60).

26. The present collectors may be transferred, if found qualified, to the judicial or some other department, or allowed to retire on suitable pensions. Besides the Board of Revenue, who should exercise a constant superintendence over the revenue branch, there should be six or eight European civil servants of the Company,

who stand high in the estimation of the Government, appointed under the denomination of circuit collectors, to examine personally, from time to time, the records kept, and the proceeding held by the native collectors. (Nag and Burman : *English Works of Rammohun Roy*, Part III, p. 61).

27. At all events I must conclude with beseeching any and authority to devise some mode of alleviating the present miseries of the agricultural peasantry of India and thus discharge their duty every their fellow-creatures and fellow subjects. (Nag and Burman : *English Works of Rammohun Roy*, Part III, p. 61).

Warren Hastings

Rammohun was in his teens (about 16/17 years old) when Hastings was ruling. Rammohun was living in his own cell of intellectualism engrossed in thoughts for social regeneration of Bengal and the country.

Hastings was preoccupied with his own problems of administration due to disturbances and hostilities in different parts of India. This led him to make arbitrary exactions and means tactics of economic exploitation. In the administration he could not straighten out many knotty problems and became high-handed in land revenue matters.

He however did some great unique things in Bengal, *viz.*, engaging some bright young civilians of that time to revive the past glories of India's contributions in different branched of knowledge which ultimately led to what came to be known as Bengal Renaissance.

Lord Cornwallis

Cornwallis came and gave his whole attention to administrative affairs without caring much for other improvement in the life of the people. He wanted economic improvement in greater financial solvency for the State. Therefore the first thing to which his attention was directed was the question of raising and stabilising land revenue and along with it the question of improving agriculture. He felt that larger revenues were essential for carrying out also was project. He also felt that the people of Bengal should fully realize the huge possibilities of development in various directions. At home in England, he studied the working of the perpetual settlement of land revenue and the idea obsessed him that such a settlement should be equally beneficial for India. He set himself to this task and in this he was depending upon several friends and also Sir John shore and other British experts.

Cornwallis in Full Appreciation

Cornwallis honesty felt that Providence had placed in charge of a great country with large potentialities but whose economic progress was miserably slow. Along with his other English friends, Cornwallis thought that Permanent Settlement would go a long way to solve the many problems which Bengal was facing. We read the following in a Minute written in 1790 on the economic condition of Bengal :

> Cornwallis wrote that England was fortunate in establishing her domination over one of the most fertile countries on the face of the globe. The population according to his description, was mild and industrious. The real value of the possessions depended upon the ability to furnish a large annual investment to Europe to give considerable assistance to the treasury at Canton, and to supply the wants of other presidencies. At a consequence of the heavy drain of wealth from these causes with the addition of that which was occasioned by the remittance of private fortunes there was great domination of the current specie, and a langour had spread over the cultivation and general commerce of the country. He, therefore, thought that a material alteration in the general principles of management was necessary so that the inhabitants might be roused and their industry increased. His panacea was the Permanent Settlement of that land revenue of Bengal. The diagnosis was not wrong though the remedy prescribed could not effect the cure. (Dr. N.K. Sinha : *Economic History of Bengal,* Vol. I, pp. 238).

Charles Grant

This was in the early nineties of the Eighteenth century. But going back even earlier, by at least 14/15 years, one would see that the dominant figure of Charles Grant was presiding over Bengal's destiny in the hands of East India Company, in many ways. He had his own conservative ideas which were very much against the advancing interest of India. Besides, he was one of those who, strangely enough, thought that India needed Christianity for better life and progress. He further believed that India was as intimately tied up with England and India's economy and progress were so bound up with England that if East India Company's monopoly was withdrawn, at any time, India would cease to continue to grow and would lapse into inefficiency. In other words, Grant firmly believed that India's progress depended on British administration and monopoly. There were however other Englishmen (British traders, manufacturers, shipping interests, etc.), who strongly favoured the abolition of monopoly in the hope that healthy and fair competition would tend to increase the volume of trade between India and England. As the idea of free trade began to gain ground, the influence and stature of Charles Grant began to suffer. Round about this time, Grant left for England and Rammohun's activities began to be more and more intense, thought, to the economic field, his energies were directed much later. However much we may regret, probably it was all for the good of Bengal that his mental propensities naturally directed him first to social, moral and then religious reform.

It will be seen that even after Permanent Settlement came, due to apathy of the East India Company of the one hand and lack of Indian capital on the other, industrial and agriculture development made very slow progress during the twenty years which followed. Without absolving the Indian peasantry of its main responsibility for this backwardness, it can be argued that the Government also should have done much in that direction, since a steady flow of revenue game into the coffers of the Government which met all demands of the state including heavy expenditure on wars etc. No doubt the landlords also benefited enormously[4] and the state being in a healthy condition, money should have flowed under certain stipulations towards improving agriculture. With the renewal of the Charter in 1813, which incorporated good many liberal measures, Bengal's position should have improved much.

During these twenty years, Rammohun spent all his energies in intellectual pursuits with a view to social reforms, creating an atmosphere in India (particularly Bengal) of liberal and useful thinking which, to a certain extent, drew larger attention. While thus engaged, he was dragged into litigations and harassed by his own kith and kin. Another ten years passed in various social activities when his attention was directed to the complaints in respect of coffee and indigo plantations. When he looked into them he also saw the state of both agriculture and industry in the country. By now his mind was disturbed at the backwardness prevailing in both agriculture and industry for was of technical skill, capital and enterprise. He now boldly pleaded for colonisation of Europeans into the interior of the country under certain conditions. All these brought him to summit of controversy and fame.

Now the Rammohun was in England, and the question of revision of the Charter was before the British Parliament, Rammohun was enlightening the public, in English papers, with his views on Revenue and Judicial matter, as indicated by the Select Committees. He laid stress on the following matters.

Inequity to the Ryots in the Legislation of Permanent Settlement

Rammohun pointed out that the peasantry suffered as much under Permanent Settlement as in the Ryotwari Settlement. In the former, one was a victim of the Zamindar's greed and oppression and in the latter, he was a victim, of endless intrigues and coercion. Rammohun suggested that for the protection of these cultivators from extortion, the least that could be done by the Government would be to take away the magisterial powers from the collectors. He however did not fail to see that when Cornwallis made his plan, he had probably not anticipated all these evils. To say this in favour of Cornwallis or any legislator is a special pleading. In an attempt to remove some of these evils, Bentinck passed several Regulations. Rammohun had his own views, brief extracts of which have been given above all to show how keenly Rammohun felt for the Ryots.

Regulation III—Lakheraj (Lands) Regulation

Some time earlier, in 1828, when Bentinck was the Governor General, a regulation known as Regulation III, otherwise known as the Lakheraj Regulation had been passed and Rammohun had an occasion to protest against the form of the Government's land resumption proceeding since he felt that under this Regulation, the promise given by previous Governor-General was being dishonoured. Regulation XIX (1793) had assured the landholders of rest-free lands that these would not be subjected to payment of revenue, unless, their titles were found defective by courts. The Regulation of 1828 withdrew this above assurance, enabling the Government to confiscate a large number of revenue-free lands. Rammohun criticised it as betrayal on the part of the Government and he drew up a petition on behalf of the landholders or Bengal, Bihar an Orissa, but the petition was rejected. Among the many petitions submitted, the most weighty was that of Rammohun in whose praise the Court of Directors felt impelled to write the following few lines to the dispatch dated February 23, 1830 :

> Among the petitions against Regulation III, 1828, which have been noticed in a preceding part of this dispatch, there is one which we have stated to be anonymous; we have now to notice that an exact duplicate of that petition has since been presented to us, with the signatures of above 200 individuals annexed to it, accompanied by a letter addressed to our secretary in this department by four native, name Dwarkanath Tagore, Kalinath Roy, Pursunno Komar Tagore, and Rammohun Roy. The intelligence of the above-name individuals is acknowledged to be much superior to that of the native aristocracy in general. However much, therefore, we may doubt whether any

considerable number of the petitioners are capable of understanding the arguments which it contains we are not the less disposed to give due consideration to the expression of the sentiments of such individuals on a question which so generally affects the interests of the native community as well as those of the state.

Ryotwari Settlement

Ryotwari Settlement developed in regions of Madras; in a fragmentary and crude it had been in existence for a long time. After studying Madras conditions in detail for 7 years, Thomas Munro left exhaustive notes and reports. At last in 1820, the Ryotwari systems was introduced. The following are the observations on the system as seen and described on the lapse of considerable period of time by the innovators and their associates :

1. Thomas Munro declared in 1807 and in 1813 that in essence it was a permanent as the Zamindari Settlement of Bengal except in regard to wastelands; yet from the following, it will be seen that the results were not as anticipated :

> The Ryotwari system was introduced finally in all unsettled tracts in Madras in 1820, but the permanency of the assessments, recognised and admitted by the Madras Government down to 1862, has since been ignored. The uncertainty of the State demand, now altered at each recurring settlement on grounds which are unintelligible to the people, leaves the agricultural population of Madras in state of perpetual uncertainty and chronic poverty. (R.C. Dutt : *Economic History of India*, p. 103).

2. We find that the Board of Revenue of Madras in 1818 observed :

> The Ryotwari settlement, in fact, was made annually, frequently by the Tahsildars and Sheristadars (subordinate low-paid officers), and was not in general concluded until after the crop had been raised; the system then was to make as high a settlement as it was practicable to realise. If the

crop was good, the demand was raised as high within the survey rates as the means of the Ryots would admit.... (R.C Dutt : *Economic History of India*, p. 100).

3. As Governor of Madras, Sir Thomas Munro did all the could to foster the village institutions; he organised Panchayats, and conferred on them judicial powers and he endeavoured to continue the village communities of India as living and organic institutions such as they had been in the past. But all these endeavours failed. When all real power was taken away from old institution, forms of authority could not keep them alive. (R.C. Dutt : *Economic History of India*, p. 103).

4. Dutt further observed that Collectors were encouraged to break up joint-tenure wherever it existed and to enter into engagements with tenants separately. The high rate of assessment, by which the State demand was fixed at 45 per cent or 55 per cent of the field produce, caused endless oppression and was generally reduced under the considerate administration of Sir Thomas Munro.

5. The eminent economist further observed :

"......we see the growing partiality of Thomas Munro for the Ryotwari system in tracts of country where there were no hereditary Zamindars. In places like Bengal and the Northern Circars, where the prevailing system was the possession of lands by great landlords, the Government had continued that system and made settlement with Zamindars. In other places, where the prevailing system was the payment of the revenues by the ryots or cultivators direct to the State, Munro continued that system and made settlements direct with the ryots. It was necessary and essential to give some permanency to the Government demand, in both cases, for the improvement of agriculture and the prosperity of the people. This was done by Lord Cornwallis in Bengal; and this was desired and recommended by Thomas Munro for Madras, but has never been done. Here lies the fatal defect in land settlements of Southern India." (R.C. Dutt : *Economic History of India*, p. 85).

Dutt has been most eloquent when he described the land revenue matters of Bengal as follows :

> Land revenue matter of Bengal is a measure which has done more to secure the prosperity and happiness of British subject in India than any other single measure of British Government. (R.C. Dutt : *Economic History of India*, p. 6).

While concluding, it is worth recapitulating the sequence of introduction of land revenue measures in India. The Permanent Settlement of the land revenues, which was concluded in Bengal in 1793 was extended to Benares in 1795 and to the Northern Circars and other tracts between 1802 and 1805. It stands out as the most notable and the most beneficent act of civil administration within this period.

As Dutt remarked :

> The land revenue administration had been settled wisely or unwisely in Bengal in 1793, in Madras in 1820 and also in reformed Mahalwari settlement in Northern area in 1833 and Ryotwari Settlement in Bombay in 1835. (R.C. Dutt : *Economic History of India,* pp. 10-11).

Questions that agitated Rammohun's mind for further elucidation :

(a) What other terms could be considered for renting of the farm?

(b) How to stop frequent of rent?

(c) What should be the most satisfactory relation between rent and gross produce of the land?

(d) What effective measures can be adopted to prevent sale of land consequent of revenue arrears?

(e) What precaution can be taken for Collectors' conducts in respect of sales in a fair way?

(f) How could the Government ensure quick revenue collection keeping cultivators' interest safe?

(g) What improvements can be suggested on the basis of revenue assessed by Government on each estate?

Public Criticism of Rammohun' Evidence

On the evidence submitted to the Government by the various parties, the Tory organ *John Bull* expressed the opinion (the liberal English Press kept silent) that Rammohun's evidence was by far the most sensible of the lot.

Fulsome praise came from other newspapers. *Samachar Durpan commnted* (March 1832) :

> We learn from the Indian *Gazette* that a series of questions had been addressed to Rammohun Roy in writing, on the Revenue, Judicial, and commercial system of India, to which has now been preparing replies. Those on the Revenue system have been given in and are said to have afforded the highest gratification. His answers to questions on the Judicial system of India were nearly finished in the beginning of September. The whole, when complete, will present a complete view of the Civil, Criminal and Financial system of the country. He is said to have suggested various improvements, such as the Trial by Jury, Native Judicial Assessors, Joint Judges, Regular Public Register, Codes of Civil and Criminal law, the use of the English instead of Persian language, etc.

Bombay Courier remarked in December 1832 :

> Already we are in a condition to appreciate the advantages likely to result from the visit of the intelligent Hindu who is domicilitated with us. In his answers to some serious questions proposed by the India Board, Rammohun Roy has expressed frankly his sentiments respecting a variety of very important points connected with the internal administration of British India. This evidence, probably the most valuable which has been hitherto recorded on India topics, in printed in one of the voluminous appendices to the Report of the Parliamentary Committee, where it is not likely to attract the attention it deserves....

India Gazette said (June 1832) :

> We are happy to perceive the interest with which Raja Rammohun Roy's replies to the Parliamentary queries on the revenue system of India has been received by the native community. We have now before us the queries made to him and his answers regarding the judicial system now prevalent; but as it would occupy too much of our space to give them entire, we propose to form an abridgement of them, and in our paper of next Saturday to insert the opinion he had given upon the existing system, and, in a subsequent paper, the suggestions which he has made for its improvement. The fact of a native of India's appearance before Parliament to give his opinion upon the character of the system of Government in this empire, is so novel, and the opinions he has expressed are so important, that we feel it unnecessary to apologize for devoting the columns of the *Durpan* to the subject.

As against such appreciative remarks there were the unfavourable[5] ones of, for instance, *Bengal Harkaru* (on June 20, 1832) :

> We have re-published from the Asiatic Journal of March, Rammohun Roy's replies to queries on the Revenue System of India, and we think most of our readers will agree with us in saying that it is not what might have been expected from one of his known talents and professed principles. There are, in many parts, marks of a tendency of soften, a sort of "velvet condemnation" or "sarcenet surety" that, had not his name been attached to them, we could never have supposed the replies to be his. There is no want of clear and explicit information on many heads, but on others we are grieved to find him committing himself sadly. But it will be better to adduce instances of what we are advancing and to comment on them as we proceed." The *Harkaru* then look up the question : "In the event of the tenants falling into arrear with their rents, what means do the proprietors adopt for realizing it?" and gave Rammohun's answer : "They distrain their moveable

property, with some exceptions, by the assistance of the police officers, and get it sold by means of the judicial authorities." Referring to this answer the *Harkaru* commented : "This reply is utter trimming, we will not say it was intended to mislead, but in truth we are at a loss to say for what it could be intended, when we find it again referred to in queries 28-29, and the same shuffling misleading answers given."

The second question which the *Harkaru* took up was : "Does the legal authority seize upon both the moveable property and the person of the tenant for his rent?" To this Rammohun's answer was : "On a summary application to the Police, the moveable property of the tenant, with some exceptions, is distrained by the help of the police officers, and by the ordinary judicial process, the immoveable property of the tenant may be attached, and his person arrested for the recovery of the rent". The *Harkaru* reacted severely : "We say this is a shuffling and a misleading[6] answer; it is the answer of an unwilling witness; of one not inclined to say all he knew of "his order", and thus calculated to mislead the committee and indeed almost every man who had not given the subject his special attention; for it utterly glosses over that which Rammohun Roy must know (and no man better knows it) to be the very plague spot of our administration; the curse on the land; the bend by which the unfortunate ryot it held, and bought, and sold, as the thrall and the serf of the farmer of the revenue for the time being; and through the abuse of which the whole of the settlemented provinces are at the moment racked with illegal exactions to an amount utterly incredible to those unacquainted with the details of the subject; How could Rammohun Roy in these replies, forget the Seventh Regulation of 1799?"

Seventh Regulation of 1799

It makes provisions for special powers of restraint on the part of Zamindars. But it was for emergency only. Zamindars were not expected to take this aggressive role except in very special cases. It always created public agitation.

Taking up the comments from both sides, the *Durpan* remarked warily :

> Rommohan Roy obtains little credit for his evidence. The *Hurkaru* rates him for being too favourable to the Zamindars; the *Chundrika* on the other hand is pereptually decrying him for having injured the Zamindars in his evidence. We offer no opinion on the subject. Great goodwill, we have no doubt, flow to the country from Rammohun Roy's visit to England and from the exertions he is making. If we has any doubt on this subject, they would be dispelled by his having succeeded in displeasing both parties in India. The truth lies between them.

In the Appendix to the Report of the Committee of the House of Commons on India Affairs, submitted in 1831-32, there were papers written by Rammohun Roy when he was in England. These were his replies to the queries raised by the Board of Control, covering seventeen folio pages, with interesting and important observations relating to the position of the Government, Cultivators, Zamindars and others. They threw a flood of light on the working of the existing Judicial System and on Government policy in allied matters. Written by a reformer, a nationalist, a thorough and competent expert like Rammohun Roy, the opinions, observations and recommendations deserved the best consideration of the Government and the public. A large amount of them still holds good even to-day though they were written about a century and a half ago.

Bishop Heber's Views about Land Tax in India

Bishop Heber, who was in Calcutta in 1823, recorded in the Diary of his travels during 1824, 1825, 1826 through different provinces of India that he was struck by the appalling poverty of the people. He ascribed to the heavy land-tax in vogue all over the land. His letter on Hon'ble C.W. Wynn in 1826 noted : Neither native nor European agriculturists, I think, can thrive at the present rate of taxation. Half the gross produce of the soil is demanded by Government and this, which is nearly the average rate wherever there is not a Permanent Settlement is sadly too much to leave an adequate provision for the present, even with the usual frugal habits of the Indians, and the very inartificial and cheap manner in which they cultivate the land. Still more it is an effective bar to anything like improvement, it keeps the people, even in favourable years, in a state of abject penury; and when the crop fails in even a slight degree, it involves a necessity on the part of the Government of enormous outlays in the way of remission and distribution, which, after all, do not prevent men, women, and children dying in the streets in droves, and the roads being strewed with carcasses. In Bengal, where, independent of its exuberant fertility, there is a Permanent Assessment, famine is unknown. In Hindustan (Northern India), on the other hand, I found a general feeling among the King's officers, and I myself was led from some circumstances to agree with them, that the peasantry in the Company Provinces are, on the whole, worse off, poorer, and more dispirited, than the subjects of the Native Princes; and here in Madras, where the soil is, generally speaking, poor, the difference is said to be still more marked. The fact is, no Native Prince demands the rent which we do, and making every allowance for the superior regularity of our system, &c., I met with very few men who will not, in confidence, own their belief that the people are overtaxed, and that the country is in a gradual state of impoverishment...... I am convinced that it is only necessary to draw less money from the peasants, and to spend more of what is drawn within the country, to open some door to Indian industry in Europe, and to admit the natives to some greater share in the magistracy of their own people, to make the Empire as durable as it would be happy. (Bishop Heber : *Memoirs and Correspondence*, Edited by his Widow, London, 1830, Vol. II, p. 413).

Permanent Settlement—Its Larger Significance

It has been authoritatively stated that the Dinajpur (Bengal) records show the efficacy of long-term tenure as against year-to-year tenure. Long-term tenure gets a fair chance of making the economy stable and provides better security to the peasants. The other alternative, *viz.*, year-to-year tenure, is adopted when the administration has not got sufficient time to make a clear survey and foresee the future as may arise. One can read in the British Parliamentary debates that Western Hastings, in resorting to annual leases and arbitrary rents, aggravated the land problems in Bengal by making the financial position of the peasants very uncertain and weak. As it happened, political matters all over India were moving fast and this reflected on the main administration, centred in Bengal. Because of war conditions prevailing in many parts of India for which money had to be found, revenue collection acquired an urgency. Cornwallis felt that long-term agreement was the only way to solve the problem. Among the experts entrusted with such a scheme were Richard Becher, John Shore and James Grant in England. They drafted in 1792 the letter by which the Court of Directors formally brought Permanent Settlement into existence. This benefited most of those who were given the special privilege of collecting revenues on behalf of Government, especially in view of the fact that these rent collectors (later called Zamindars), though compelled to enter into an agreement with the Government on a permanent basis, were not obliged to enter into similar agreements with the ryots which could make their position equally secure. It has been stated that such agreements with the ryots would have been very difficult because the works involved in such a scheme was vast equally risky.

It was natural therefore that the Zamindars in such circumstances were not only grateful but also showed utmost loyalty to the Government. The security of tenure gave them opportunity to concentrate on agricultural improvement and also incentive to give attention to industries connected with agriculture. At that early period of the nineties in Bengal, *laissez faire* was very naturally the order of the time. If after the introduction Permanent Settlement, land attracted people's capital more than industry, it was clear that affluent section in the area of Bengal were swayed by the prospect of easy and certain profits. To ascribe low motives now to the promulgators of Permanent Settlement would be unfair. Certainly Cornwallis wanted Permanent Settlement only for the purpose of quick and sure collection of revenues on which the entire Indian administration depended. It also enabled the Government to impose a high assessment on the Zamindars by compensating them in return by leaving the ryots at their mercy so that the Government revenue realisation could be at its highest.

It is said that permanent Settlement created, for the first time, private property in land. This may be only partially true, for, in some form or the other, private property had been in existence since long and it was a fact that a large amount of merchant-capital in the hands of Indians had come to be invested in land. To some extent this had coincided with the decline of the textile industry in Bengal and break-up of the Company's monopoly after 1813, when private merchants found themselves in need of capital for trade with England. This trend was intensified from 1833 with the replacement of the *Agency Houses* by the Managing Agency system (of private businessmen). Initially, it was the British who could invest and hence they made large profits. Indians followed with good success though the bulk of them chose money-leading or *Mahajani business* and also house-property investments like the Roys of Bhagyakul or the Lahas of Calcutta or the Parsees of Bombay and the Chettis of Madras.

There is strong view that Permanent Settlement acted as a great hindrance to quick modernisation of Bengal by reinforcing the inertia of traditional thinking and inclinations. But while it is a fact that a very large part of capital accumulation that arose in Bengal was diverted to land, it is still a debatable point as to how it arose for, it is equally a fact that modernisation first came to Bengal. The critics of Permanent Settlement might advance the plea that it is the Dayabhag Law which helped the accumulation of capital more in Bengal than in other regions where Mitakshara law prevails. The view is sufficiently forceful.

Summing up, Rammohun's papers on Economic and other issues, his evidence before the Select Communittees in England etc., all go to show that he presented a balanced account of the country's economic situation and its future lines of approach. *Bengal Hurkaru* was vehemently opposed to his evidence as favouring the land-holders' interests and the *Samachar Chundrika* was equally strongly against him as inimical to the landholders' interests. The fact, however, remains somewhere in the middle, for, Rammohun was a hard realist who knew full well that in the situation before the country, too much of a demand complicated in nature would be futile. He knew that in an attempt to improve the ryots' interests in the then economic situation of the country, a greater chaos might come in as the landholders had by now become a strong. Force Rammohun was aware that the liberal paper *Bengal Hurkaru's* comments were hardly sincere in favour of the ryots, for its aim was to tarnish his image. Probably it would be more correct to say that at this time of his life he was more interested in minimising the importance of East India Company's powers and its area of activities in trade and commerce, will be seen that in the renewed Charter of 1833, the Company ceased to be a trading body.

REFERENCES

1. See Nag Burman : Rammohun's English Works, Part III, p 11, Questions and Answers on Judicial System; p. 39, for Question and Answers on Revenue System; p. 55, for his paper on Revenue System. The paper written for evidence communicated by Rammohun were printed in Vol. V, pp. 716-741 of the Report.

2. The Permanent Settlement of 1793 was a frank attempt to apply the Whig philosophy of Government on India (see Eric Stokes : *English Utilitarians and India*). It was a British model and well thought out. It will not be correct to say that serious thoughts were not bestowed on the matter. Under the permanent Zamindari Settlement of 1793 in the province of Bengal, the annual land assessment was to be equal to the *jumma* paid by a Zamindari estate in the preceding year (the

when the land assessment was originally fixed). This was the standard of assessment permanently fixed.

3. Nag, and Burman : English Works of Rammohun's, Part III, p. 55,—Paper on Revenue System.

4. An idea has gone around that the Permanent Settlement system, though undeniably beneficial to the Government, proved too advantageous to the landholders; the vast wealth which they were supported to have derived from it excited in the mind of some an anxiety to devise a ground for overturning it. The fact, however, is that even the greatest landholder in the country, such as the Raja of Burdwan, who paid a land tax of between 30 and 40 lakhs of rupees to the Government, did not receive more than six or eight lakhs, about 20% on the amount collected, for his own share as proprietor. For this sum he incurred an immense responsibility since he was punishable for thefts and robberies committed within the estate and subject to loss by inundation and failure of corps. The generality of the Zamindars were by no means favourably situated, a fact clearly proved by the estates which come under the immediate management of the Government in the Court of Wards and by the frequent sales of estates for arrears of revenue. (Nag and Bruman : *English Works of Rammohun,* Part III, App. IV, p. 72).

5. The Rammohun was full of sympathy for the peasants within the frame-work of the law, will be abundantly clear from Rammohun's answers in paragraphs cited earlier, thus :

..... the very least I can propose and the least which Government can do for bettering the condition of the peasantry, is absolutely to interdict any further increase of rent on any pretence whatsoever, particularly, on no consideration to allow the present settled recognized extent of the land to be disturbed by pretended re-measurements; and......

......on finding any Zamindar guilty of demanding more than the rest of the preceding years, should subject such offender to a severe fine; and on discovering any police officer or native commissioner guilty of connivance or neglect, he should subject them to fine and dismissel from the service.

6. Another point need clarification : regarding the view expressed a little earlier by the Bengal Harkaru, it may be observed that when the journal made unfavourable comments on Rammohun for his answer (in its issue of June 20, 1832), it seems to have forgotten that Rammohun had to state the law on the point and not to dwell on excess on either side.

7 CHAMPION OF FREE PRESS

I

The eighteenth century was an era of darkness and desolation for our country. It was perhaps the darkest age in modern Indian history. An old, decadent society and polity was in the process of crumbling down no ray of hope or light was visible anywhere. The country had lost its link with the fundamental truths of its being and gasped under a crippling load of unreason and irrationalism. All the vital links of society lay prostrate and paralysed. Religious and educational institutions, rural and urban life, agriculture, industry, trade, law and administration were in a state of utter chaos. Dead habit and decadent tradition blocked all channels of creativity in the field of art and culture, religion and politics. In this situation of abject slavery to circumstances and dark gloom of degeneration came forth a light of ray and hope in the emergence of Rammohun Roy, the father of the modern age in India. In this land there arose a conflict of three different cultures, three civilizations, the Hindu, the Muslim and the Christian. Rammohun was the first to evolve a concord and convergence between the three and thus ushered in the modern era which is marked with the gradual evolution of a composite nationality and synthetic civilization for India. He went further. On the same lines of convergency and through the experiences of his universal personality he indicated in the clarity of his clear and synthetic vision, the solution to the larger problem of international culture and civilization.

Rammohun was perhaps the only person of his time who realised completely the significance and importance of the modern age. He understood, as nobody else had done before this time, that human progress lay not in separatism of national independence but in the fraternity of inter-dependence of individuals and nations evolved through rational synthesis of cultural and political interaction. He applied this principle of universal humanism in realms of social, religious, literary and political affairs, with his great depth of scholarship and clarity of vision. He never subjected himself to abject slavery of circumstances and end eavoured most strenuously to make his own people realise the innermost truths of their own culture and civilization and at the time recognise the common link with the essential truths of other civilization and cultures. Keeping this objective in view he make amazing contributions in original thinking in matters of such wide variety as social and political reform, women's emancipation, freedom of speech and the press, judicial and administrative reforms, scientific education and freedom from every kind of oppression and exploitation.

In the present article I shall attempt to dissert only one aspect of his multifarious activities—that is, his activities as a journalist and his fight for the freedom of the press.

The vigorous personality and radical thinking of Rammohun needed greater self-expression than mere discourses in learned circles. He discovered that there was hardly and literary prose in existence, and whatever little that existed was entirely limited to text-book writing. There were some poetical works from the preceding centuries but no prose writing worth the name. Rammohun was the first to lay the foundation of Bengali prose with a positive style. He wrote his tracts not in the obscure language of the learned but in the common language of the people. In 1815 he published his first prose work, the 'Vedanta Grantha'. It was not a text-book but an original writing in Bengali prose. In the introduction to this book Rammohun expounded the rules to be followed in the construction of a sentence and even gave instruction on how to read Bengali prose. This introduction is a remarkable testimony of Rammohun's clear thinking and originality. He was the first to write theistic hymns in Bengali on which Pandit Ramgati Nyayaratna, an eminent scholar of Bengali language and literature, observed : "They appear to possess the power of melting even stony hearts and of making the most irreligious devoted to God."

The liberal upsurge that came in the wake of the manifold reforms—social, educational, economic, political and religious—initiated by Rammohun Roy urgently needed the service of a liberal press. The need of the time led to a general development of the press in Bengal and specially in Calcutta.

The first liberal paper to be started in Calcutta in 1816 was the 'Bengal Gazette', a Bengali weekly. Its conductors were enthusiastic members of Rammohun's 'Atmiya Sabha'. It was in existence till 1820.

The Sriampore Christian Mission started the 'Samachar Durpan', a Bengali weekly, in 1817 and also published an English journal, the 'Friend of India'.

The first liberal paper in English, the 'Calcutta Journal', was published by James Silk Buckingham in October1818.

'Sambad Kaumudi', a Bengali weekly, was started in 1821 by Tarachand Dutta and Bhabani Charan Bandyopadhyay. When Bhabani Charan resigned from the editorship of this weekly in December 1821, Rammohun took charge of it.

The 'Sambad Kaumudi' was intended for the common people and Rammohun here wrote in his newly evolved prose style for the ordinary man.

The first number of 'Sambad Kaumudi' under Rammohun's care appeared on December 4, 1821. Though Bhabani Charan Banerjee was nominally in charge his weekly till its thirteenth issue, Rammohun was its promoter and reality its editor. Reverend William Adam, while delivering a lecture on 'The life and labours of Rammohun" at Boston said : "He established and conducted two native papers, one in Persian and the other in Bengali, and made them the medium of conveying much valuable political information to his countrymen.

In a prospectus for the newspaper he intended publishing which was printed in English and Bengali in November 1821, he appealed to his countrymen to lend him " the support and patronage of all who feel the themselves in the moral and intellectual improvement of our countrymen" for the publication of the 'Sambad Kaumudi'.

In the same prospectus, it was further stated that "religious, moral and political matters, domestic occurrences, foreign as well as local intelligence, including original communications on various hitherto unpublished local topics, etc., would be published in the 'Sambad Kaumudi' on every Tuesday morning".

On December 20, 1821, the 'Calcutta Journal' published an editorial commenting on he starting of a "new Bengali newspaper edited by a Learned Hindu" and also printed the prospectus of the Bengali newspaper and also the 'Appeal to the Bengali public' published in the first issue of the 'Sambad Kaumudi' of 4 December, 1821. The appeal ran as follows : "It is our intention here after to give further currency to the Articles inserted in this paper, by translating the most interesting parts in the different languages of the East, particularly Persian and Hindustanee; but all this will entail considerable expense, the accomplishment of it will of course depend upon the encouragement which we may be able to obtain. The foregoing being an outline of what we are desirous of performing, our countrymen will readily conclude that although the paper in question be conducted by us, and may consequently be considered our property, yet virtually it is the 'Paper of the public' since in it they can at all times have inserted, anything that tends to the public good..."

The 'Sambad Kaumudi' under Rammohun's guidance lasted only for six months till May 1822, but what its effect on the public mind was can be understood from the flowing passage of editorial of the 'Calcutta Journal' February 14, 1823 : 'The paper which was considered so fraught with danger and likely to explode over all India like a spark thrown into a barrel of gun powder, has long since fallen to the ground for want of support : chiefly we understand, because it offended the native community by opposing some of their customs, and particularly the burning of Hindu widows, etc."

The 'Sambad Kaumudi' dealt with diverse subjects of public interest; for example an appeal to the Government for the establishment of a seminary for the gratuitous instruction of the children of the poor, and appeal to the government to extend the boon of trial by Jury to the Moffussil, Zillah and Provincial courts of Judicature, and address to the Hindu Community, stressing the need of giving their children instruction in the grammar of their own languages before imposing upon them the study of foreign languages, and article describing the miserable condition of the Hindus suffering from the prejudices of caste, and article requesting the Hindus to become tradesmen rather than mere copyists or Sircars.

In April 1822 Rammohun Roy started publishing a weekly in Persian language—the 'Mirat-ul-Akhbar'—the Mirror of News. It was his desire to communicate his political and social views to the educated elite in a manner and form suited to their needs. It was also the first periodical in Persian to be published in India.

In the Prospectus of the 'Mirat-ul-Akhbar' published in the first issue of the weekly, Rammohun stated among others : "I solemnly protest that it is not my object to make this paper the channel of exaggerated praise to the great, or to my own friends, that I may here by meet with favour and promotion : nor is it my intention in this my Editorial capacity to permit unmerited blame or reproach to be cast upon others. On the contrary I shall have a due regard for truth."

In the second issue of the 'Mirat-ul-Akhbar', Rammohun wrote an article on the English Constitution.

In 1921 one Pratap Narayan Das succumbed to the injuries caused by whipping ordered by one Mr.John Hayes, Judge of Comilla for the breach of internment order passed by the Judge on Pratap Narayan.

Pratap Narayan got twenty stripes and was then thrown in jail where he was found dead.

The trial of Hayes by the Supreme Court took place in April 1822, and Rammohun wrote an editorial on this trial in the 'Mirat-ul-Akhbar'. This editorial was translated into English and published in the 'Calcutta Journal' of May 14, 1822, by Mr Buckingham, the Editor of the journal, who was a great friend of Rammohun and was well-versed in a quite a few oriental languages.

This particular editorial of the 'Mirat-ul-Akhbar' was translated into English and published in the 'Calcutta Journal'. In it we come across the following observations by Rammohun Roy : "It is necessary that the local Magistrate should be vested with more efficient authority for carrying the orders of Government into execution, and likewise for preventing the powerful from tyrannising over the weak. But there is no remedy whatsoever for the abuse, which is noticed in this case, arising from their being invested with such powers, except Government should adopt such measures as might enable it to become acquainted with the proceedings of its executive officers without the intervention of favour or partiality to screen them. It is probable that this superintendence of the Government would be a sufficient check upon the Police Officers and put them upon their guard. Although the mode of establishing courts of Appeal may be considered as in some degree a substitute for their restraints, yet it fails in some instances to produce the desired effect. For example, after one has been punished with the rattan and thrown into jail, and put in irons by order of a local Magistrate, he cannot recover from that disgrace although the sentence passed upon him by that local Magistrate should be reversed at a subsequent period. If the execution of the sentence passed by a local Magistrate for inflicting corporal punishment upon a person... be deferred in case the person condemned appealed against the order of the local Magistrate and paid the regular fees, until the order of the Supreme Court of Appeal be issued, this might be preventive of excesses on the part of the Police Officers and might secure the Subject, from the injurious consequences arising from their passion or error."

Besides politics and theology, subjects of educational value were treated with distinction in these journals. During the years 1821-24 he published in his Persian weekly several articles on scientific subjects such as 'Echo in Acoustics', 'Properties of the Magnet', Behaviour of Fishes', 'Description of a Balloon', etc. Rammohun also wrote text-books in Bengali on Grammar, Geography, Astronomy and Geometry. His persistent advocacy for the introduction of scientific education through his periodicals bore fruit long after his death. There is not a shadow of doubt that it is he who initiated the movement for the introduction of scientific education in India.

The lead given by Rammohun and his group to journalistic venture on liberal lines was soon emulated by others although not always all on the same line of thinking. The organ of the orthodox Hindus, the 'Samachar Chandrika's was started in March 1822, to counter the reformative zeal of the 'Sambad Kaumudi'. It was typical of the contemporary orthodox Bengali press which pampered the passions and prejudices of the orthodox Hindus.

The Persian editorials of 'Mirat-ul-Akhbar' were written by Rammohun and English translations of several of them were published in the 'Calcutta Journal' edited by James Silk Buckingham. These editorials revealed Rammohun's great learning and deep knowledge about current political affairs. An editorial in 'Mirat-ul-Akhbar' in August 1822, by Rammohun contained certain observations on the doctrines of Trinity which were considered by the authorities as ' exceedingly offensive.' This would appear from the minutes recorded on October10, 1822 by Mr W.B. Beyley of the Governor-General's Supreme Council on the tendency of the native press. Following extracts from the minutes will give and idea as to the nature of he charge against Rammohun :

The contents of the other Persian paper, the 'Mirat-ul-Akhbar' have been much in the same style as the above, but the Editor's known disposition for theological controversy had led him to seize an occasion for publishing remarks on the Trinity, which, although convertly and insidiously conveyed, strike me as being exceedingly offensive. The circumstances in which the discussion originated was a notice in the above paper on the subject of the death of Middleton, the late Bishop of Calcutta. After some laudatory remarks on his learning and dignity, the article concludes by stating that the Bishop, having been now relieved from the care and anxieties of this world, had tumbled on the shoulders of the mercy of God the Father, God the Son, and God the Holy Ghost'.

The expression coming from a known impugner of the doctrine of the Trinity could only be considered as ironical, and was noticed in one of the other papers as objectionable and offensive. It might have been sufficient for the editor of the 'Mirat-ul-Akhbar' to have disclaimed all such intention, and thus to let the subject drop. But this course was not suited to the polemical disposition of the Editor. In the paper of the 19th July he enters into a long justification of his obituary notice, and, affectedly misunderstanding the real purport of the objection taken to this introduction of the mention of (the) Trinity, he makes use of observations, which, in my mind, constitute an aggravation of the offence. He says, "in respect of what was said of God, the father, Son and Holy Ghost, since the Preachers of Christian religion, constantly, in every church, throughout the year, read their articles of faith with a loud voice, not regarding the presence of either Hindu or Musalman, and declare their conviction that salvation is to be found only in the belief of the Three whom I have mentioned." And, again, "But since it seems that the mere mention in the Persian language of the essential principles of the Christian religion is an aspersion on the faith professed by the Governor-General and all its followers, I shall, Therefore, avoid this fault in future."

Coming from a member of the Supreme Council, this was a charge serious enough to cause concern and annoyance in Government circles. Undaunted, Rammohun went on writing his tract against instances of oppression and irrationalism.

Again in an article entitled 'Ireland—the causes of its distress and discontent' which appeared in 'Mirat-ul-Akhbar' on October 11, 1822 the causes of Irish discontent against English domination were set out with a clear exposition :

Although all the inhabitants of his island call themselves the followers of the religion of Jesus Christ (upon whom and the rest of the prophets of God be peace and blessing!), yet a great number of them on account of their differing in some particular points of faith from the religion adopted by the King of England, follow their own clergymen and Pope in the performance of religious duties, and refuse adherence to the royal divines of the Established Church of England; and in consequence the stipends of their own divines are not defrayed from the revenue of the land but depend on the contributions of private individuals. Besides this, on account of the stipends of the royal clergymen who are appointed to officiate in Ireland, the Government of Ireland exact taxes every year from those who positively refuse to be led by these clergymen in religious matters.

A further cause adduced ran thus :

The noble and other landed proprietors of Ireland pass their time in England, either with a view to raise themselves at Court, or to have all the luxuries of life at their command. And they spend in England an immense sum of the revenue of their lands, which they collect by means of stewards or farmers; and consequently the trades-people in England benefit by the liberat manner in which they spend their money, instead of the people of Ireland. And their rapacious stewards or farmers, for their own advantage and order to show their zeal for the interest of their masters, unmercifully increase the rent of the land and extort those rents from the peasantry. So that many from their improper behaviour are now deprived of the means of subsistence...

The reasons for the condition of famine in Ireland at that time were sought to be exposed in these articles and certain liberal—minded European and Indian gentlemen had subscribed for the 'love of God' to give succour to the starving in Ireland. Expression of gratitude from the Irish, who are a proud nation, was also not lacking for this generous gesture for the progressive and nationalist of India.

All this criticism of popular Christian faith, the English foreign policy and of the British insolence on public roads towards the native, was too much for the British administration in India to swallow.

Soon the acting Governor-General came down with a heavy hand for the suppression of the liberty of the press and promulgated a new press ordinance drastically curtailing free expression of opinion through the press. Immediately following the enactment of the ordinance Rammohun closed down the 'Mirat-ul-Akhbar' as a mark of protest. In the last number of his paper he declared "his inability to go on publishing under". What he would represent as to him, "degrading conditions" and he laments that he, one of the most humble of men, "should be no longer able to contribute towards the intellectual improvement of his countrymen".

It may be of interest to give an account here of the gradual evolution of press censorship under the British regime of that period. The freedom of the Indian press was first curtailed by Lord Wellesley by creating on May 13, 1799, a censorship which called for production of proof-sheets of all newspapers before their publication to the Chief Secretary of the Government for inspection. Lord Minto, his successor, imposed more stringent rules on the editors. The Marquis of Hastings who followed Lord Minto, removed, through an order, dated August 19, 1818, the obligation on the editors to produce the proof-sheets to the Government before publications and only laid down certain general rules intended to prevent discussion of subject, which might undermine the authority of the Government or injure public interests. The real intention behind this apparent liberalisation of press censorship was however to remove the discrimination in punitive measures against European editors for violating the censorship rules. When these rules were framed in Wellesley's time, only European owned papers were in existence and European editors were punished with deportation to England for violating the rules. But by Hasting' time many European and Indian editors had come into the picture and the punitive action proposed in the rules could not be made applicable to them. This made Lord Hasting decide upon relaxation of the censorship rules. But official attitudes towards the press started hardening up again consequent upon publication in the 'Calcutta Journal' in October 1818, of an article by James Buckingham which was considered of an offensive and mischievous character, and therefore a violation of the rules. On October 10, 1822, Mr Bayley delivered in Council lengthy memorandum severely criticising the native press and making particular reference to Rammohun's article in the 'Mirat-ul-Akhbar.'

Bayley in his report said : "Feeling as I do that the native press may be converted into an engine of the most serious mischief.... I shall confine my remarks to the Persian ones already published in Calcutta. They are called the 'Jam-i-Jahan Numa' and 'Mirat-ul-Akhbar', epithets both implying 'the Mirror of News'. The first is understood to be the property of, and to be principally conducted by the English Mercantile House in Calcutta. The second is the paper of the well-Known Rammohun Roy."

Then Bayley exclusively dealt with Rammohun's articles in 'Mirat-ul-Akhbar' and concludes : "I consider it essential that the government should be vested with legal powers to control the excesses of the native as well of the European Press...."

On the basis of this report, Lord Hasting's government on October 17, 1822, wrote to the authorities in England to give them powers to control and curb the excesses of the press.

When Lord Hastings sailed for England in January 1823, one J. Adam, a member of the Civil Service succeeded him temporarily and his first act on assumption of office was to deport Buckingham to England for the offence of his diserespectful expression in an article criticising the acceptance by a minister of the Scotch Church of a post under the East

India Company. The journal was gagged and Mr Standford Arnot, Mr Buckingham's Assistant Editor, who later became Rammohun's Private Secretary in England, was arrested and forcibly sent to England.

The Acting Governor-General went on to impose further curbs on the press through a rigorous ordinance which was passed on March 14, 1823. Under provision of this ordinance, proprietors and editors of newspapers and journals had to apply for a licence to the Chief Secretary of the Government giving an undertaking not to discuss certain matters prohibited by law. Violations of the undertaking could result in the licence being cancelled by the Government.

Rammohun and his close associates decided to contest the Ordinance in the Court of Law. The acting Judge Sir Francis Macnaughton directed the objectors to submit a memorandum to the Government. Accordingly Rammohun and five other eminent citizens of Calcutta—Chandra Kumar Tagore, Dwarkanath Tagore, Har Chundra Bose, Gowree Churan Banerjee and Prasanna Commar Tagore submitted a remarkable memorandum written by Rammohun praying for the repeal of the ordinance. This document has rightly been described by Miss Collect, the biographer of Rammohun, as the 'Areopagitica of Indian History'. The following extract from the memorandum depict the clear thinking and sound judgment of the Memorialists :

While your Mmemorialists were indulging the hope that the Government, from a conviction of the manifold advantages of being put in possession of full and impartial information regarding what is passing in all parts of the country, would encourage the establishment of newspapers in the cities and districts under the special patronage and protection of Government that they special patronage and protection of Government that they might furnish the supreme authorities in Calcutta with an accurate account of local occurrences and reports of judicial proceedings,—they have the misfortune to observe, that on the contrary, his Excellency the Governor-General in Council has lately promulgated a Rule and

Ordinance imposing severe restraints on the press and prohibiting all periodical publications even at the Presidency and in the native languages, unless sanctioned by a license from Government, which is to be revocable at pleasure whenever it shall appear to Government that a publication has contained anything of an unsuitable character.

After this Rule and Ordinance shall have been carried into execution, your Memorialists are therefore extremely sorry to observe, that a complete stop will be put to the diffusion of knowledge and the consequent mental improvement now going on, either by translation into the popular dialect of this country from the learned languages of the East, or by the circulation of literary intelligence drawn from foreign publications...

Another evil of equal importance in the eyes of a just Ruler, is, that it will also preclude the natives from making the Government readily acquainted with the errors and injustice that may be committed by its executive officers in the various parts of this extensive country.

Every good ruler who is convinced of the imperfection of human nature, and reverence the Eternal Governor of the World, must be conscious of the great liability to error in managing the affairs of a vast empire and therefore he will be anxious to afford to every individual the readiest means of bringing to his notice whatever may require his interference. *To secure this most important, the Unrestrained liberty of publication is the only* effectual means that can be employed. (emphasis is mine)

In dismissing the memorandum Sir Francis made an outrageous statement that he given his blessing to the ordinance even before the same was enacted or its merits argued before Court.

The following remark made by Mr Turton, an eminent member of the Bar, who was engaged in the case, bears eloquent testimony to the boldness and patriotism of Rammohun in dealing with the Press Ordinance :

A very short time after my arrival in this country an Act was passed by Government which met with the general reprobation of those who were governed; but no one came forward with the manliness and boldness that Rammohun did to express his sentiment in the odious measure. A man born and brought up in Britain could not have come forward more completely heart and soul in support of that which was the cause of his country; than what Rammohun Roy did in 1823. I then made his acquaintance in the first instance, and was surprised and delighted to see an inordinate love of liberty in a man reared and bred in the spirit of dependence, if dependence could exist in such a mind.

The outraged and indignant Raja discontinued, as mentioned before, the publication of his Persian weekly as a mark of protest. Giving his reasons for suspending the publication in a memorable editorial in the last issue of the paper he mentions :

....After incurring the disrepute of solicitation and suffering the dishonour of making Affidavit, the constant apprehension of the licence being recalled by Government which would disgrace the person in the eyes of the world, must create such anxiety as entirely to destroy his peace of mind, because a man, by nature liable to err, in telling the real truth cannot help sometimes making use of words and selecting phrases that might be unpleasant to Government. I, however, here prefer silence to speaking out.

The 'Friend of India', a journal of the European missionaries of India, admitted the beneficient contributions of the native press and maintained that the freedom of the press had on no occasion been abused by them. This press ordinance would utterly block a native expression directed at pointing out the errors and omissions of the Government intended to interfere with natural course of justice (which had enough provision to deal with any delinquency of the press) and take the law in their own hands. Subordinate officials being fallible, Government ought to welcome the check imposed on them by the dread of publicity.

Frustrated in his efforts to restore freedom of the press Rammohun appealed to King of England Council against the Ordinance—an appeal which has been acclaimed by many as "one of the noblest pieces of English to which Rammohun put his hand". It was brilliant exposition in sound judgment and logical reasoning.

In this remarkable petition Rammohun referring to the various restrictions imposed by the Ordinance went on to say :

The above restrictions as they are capable of being interpreted, will in fact afford Government all its functionaries from the highest to the lowest, complete immunity from censure or exposure respecting anything done by them in their official capacity, however, desirable it might be for the interest of the country and also that of this Honourable Company, that the public conduct of such public men should not be allowed to pass unnoticed. It can scarcely be doubted that the real object of these Restrictions is, to afford all the Functionaries of Government complete security against their conduct being made the subject of observation, though it is associated with a number of other restraints totally uncalled for, but well calculated to soothe the supreme authorities in England and win their assent to the main object of the Rule—the suppression of public remark on the conduct of the public officers of Government of India.

...If these conclusions drawn from the particular circumstances of this country, be met with such an argument as that a colony of distant dependency can never safely be entrusted with the liberty of the Press, and that therefore natives of Bengal cannot be allowed to exercise the privileges they have so long enjoyed, this would be in other words to tell them, *that they are condemned to perpetual oppression and degradation from which they can have no hope of being raised during the existence* of the British powers. (emphasis is mine).

The British nation has never yet descended to avow a principle so foreign to their character, and if they could for a moment entertain the idea of preserving their power by keeping their colonies in ignorance, the prohibition of periodical publications is not enough, but printing of all kinds, educations, and every other means of diffusing knowledge should be equally discouraged and put down. For it must be the distant consequences of the diffusion of knowledge that are dreaded by those (if there be any such) who are really apprehensive for the stability of Government since it is well-known to all in the least acquainted with this country, that although every effort was made by periodical as well as other publications, a great number of years must elapse before any considerable change can be made in the existing habits and opinions of the natives of India, so firmly are they wedded to established custom. Should apprehensions so unworthy of the English nation prevail, then unlike the ancient Romans who extended their knowledge and civilisation with their conquests, ignorance and degradation must mark the extent of British Power. Yet surely even this affords no hope of perpetual rule, since not withstanding the tyranny and oppression of Gengis Khan and Tamerlane, their empire was not so lasting as that of the Romans, who to the proud title of conquerors, added the more glorious one of Enlighteners of the World.

...If your Majesty's faithful subjects could conceive for a moment, that he British nation, actuated solely by interested policy, considered India merely as a valuable property and regard nothing but the best means of securing its possession and turning it to advantage, even then it would be of importance to ascertain whether this property be well taken of by their sarvants.. Therefore the existence of a free press is equally necessary for the sake of the Governors and the governed.

The tremendous impression created by Rammohun's appeal to the King in Council and be well gauged from the following extract of a letter from Colonel Leicester Stanhope to Rammohun Roy, dated 9 June, 1825 :

Your appeal to the King of England council demonstrating the usefulness and safety of a free press in British India, and praying for its restoration, I forwarded with a letter, to the Secretary of the Board of Control. He honoured me with Courteous reply stating that it had been graciously received by His Majesty.

The appeal, considering it as the production of a foreigner and a Hindu of this age, displays so much sense, knowledge, argument, and even eloquence that the friends of liberty have dwelt upon it with wonder...

But unfortunately all his arguments and eloquence proved of no avail against British dread of native criticism and the appeal was dismissed by the Privy Council after six months of deliberation.

It is to be noted that soon after suspension of the 'Mirat-ul-Akhbar' in 1823, Rammohun got himself involved with several other periodicals and kept up his relentless crusade against irrationalism and suppression of freedom. In May 1829 the English weekly 'Bengal Herald' was started by one Dr. R.M. Martin in collaboration with Rammohun Roy and Dwarkanath Tagore. It was a liberal organ with progressive outlook. It had also a corresponding vernacular paper called the 'Bengadoot' printed in Bengali, Persian and Nagri script and language under the editorship of Nilratan Halder, a close associate of Rammohun. The 'Bengal Herald' later became amalgamated with the 'India Gazette' and 'Bengal Harkaru'—two of the leading liberal English journals of the time in which Dwarkanath Tagore had large interests.

Reginald Heber, Lord Bishop of Calcutta, in a letter of R.J. Wilmot Harton in December 1823 remarks...

In the Bengali newspapers, of which there are two or three, politics are canvassed with a bias, as I am told, inclining to whiggism, and one of their leading men (Rammohun Roy) gave a great dinner, not long since, in honour of the Spanish Revolution.

Martin in his 'History of British Colonies' (page 254) observes on the press in India in 1833.

The general tone of the English Press as also the native journals is liberal, but some of the Bengali newspapers are of a high orthodox nature; their prejudices or bigotry are however ably met by their own countrymen in the 'Sambad Kaumudi' and other Hindu journals. The 'Reformer' is, it is said, under the management of a distinguished, wealthy and highly talented Hindu Prasanna Coomar Tagore. But to no individual is the Indian Press under greater obligation that to the lamented Rammohun Roy and the munificient Dwarkanath Tagore.

This may be said to apply not only to the case of the native press but that of the English press in India as well. It is seen that some of the enlightened and eminent British gentlemen of the time adjoined Rammohun to foster and advance the cause of liberalism and rationalism in this country. One of them, Mr Samuel Smith, them a leading book-seller and publisher in Calcutta, purchased the 'Bengal Harkaru'—one of the oldest and leading English papers in the early 20's of the last century. Under his care and guidance the paper soon grew in popularity and usefulness. In this acquisitions of the paper he was largely helped financially by Dwarkanath Tagore. Dwarkanath Tagore was also one of the chief proprietors of the 'India Gazette'—another old and leading English paper at the time. The contribution of these papers towards development of the progressive ideas of the country was most significant and they acted as ancillary to the native liberal press led by Rammohun. This progressivism in the press however was opposed by the 'Samachar Chandrika'—an orthodox Hindu organ along with the like-minded Tory organ 'John Bull'. In spite of the bickerings and vexatious opposition from the conservative and reactionary press the cause of progressivism and liberalism made steady progress under the leadership of Rammohun Roy and Dwarkanath Tagore, with the ultimated result that the 'John Bull' had to be sold off in 1832 to an enlightened and liberal-minded journalist J.H. Stocqueler again with a substantial aid from Dwarkanath Tagore. A further notable event that took place about this time was the establishment in 1831 of an English weekly called. 'The Reformer' by the legal celebrity Prasanna Coomar Tagore, a cousin of Dwarkanath Tagore and staunch followers of Rammohun Roy. It maintained and greatly added to the cause of liberal and progressive journalism in the country. This was soon followed by two other journals—one, 'The lnquirer' in English, and the other, 'Gyanaweshun' in Bengali and English started by some enlightened youths of the Calcutta Hindu College. All these papers were conducted on the same line of progressivism started by Rammohun.

Although the liberal and rational line adopted by section of the Indian press was not generally interfered with in spite of the regulation of Adam, it was strongly urged before Lord Bentinck to repeal the Ordinance before the left his post and returned to England. Apetition to this effect under the signature of Dwarkanth Tagore, Rev. W. Adam and others was presented to Bentinck on February 6, 1835, and a favourable and sympathetic reply was given by his Lordship. The next Governor-General Sir Charles Metcaffe took up the same liberal line of Bentinck and eventually liberated the Indian press of its fetters by rescinding the regulation by passing his memorable Act Eleven of 1835. Although his action was highly hailed in India, it was strongly criticised and resented by the Directors of the East India Company. It ultimately led Metcaffe to relinquish his post of Governor-General-ship. The next incumbent however did not in his wisdom decide to repeal the Act. It was allowed to remain in force. Since then the press has continued to remain more or less free in this country excepting for a short period during the troublesom time of the Sepoy Mutiny. Thus the glorious movement which was started by Rammohun on be half of his countrymen me with successful fruition not long after his death.

Rammohun's contributions as an indomitable defender of free press in this country was gratefully acknowledged by his contem-poraries after his death. On the occasion of the Free Press Dinner given in honour of Sir Charles Metcaffe on February 9, 1838, at the Town Hall, Calcutta, Prasanna Coomar Tagore who spoke on behalf of the Indian community, paid eloquent tributes to the great contributions made by Rammohun for the freedom of the press.

In that era of darkness and desolation, surrounded by a people lying prostrate under the yoke of ignorance, superstition and hundreds of years of foreign domination, Rammohun stood out, a nobody else did at his time, as a valiant fighter of freedom not only of the body but of the mind—freedom not only of action but also of thought. Love of freedom was perhaps the strongest passion of his soul. It was a conviction, rationally derived from his firm belief that a well-regulated and self-restrained liberty is the only way that can lead to a noble and purposeful life. He did not seek to limit the enjoyment of freedom to any class, colour or race or nation or religion, but encompassed all mankind within his unbounded sympathies. His fight for the freedom of the press in India was but one manifestation of his great passion for this love of freedom.

8 RAMMOHUN ROY AND BENGALI PROSE

Rammohun thrives on controversy. While alive, he excelled as a controversialist. After death, he remains a centre of cotention. Is he the father of Bengali prose? Did he write better Bengali than his predecessors? These are some of the moot questions, often debated with passion and heat. Any attempt at estimating the Raja's contribution to Bengali language and literature must therefore begin by clarifying one's answer to these questions.

To take up the first question.[1] The point is that the question itself is wrong; for it rests on the false assumption that a single individual can beget the prose of a nationality.

Evidently, Bengalees spoke in porse since long before Rammohun's advent. Nor did he produce the first prose-book in Bengali. His first two volumes of prse, *Vedanta-Grantha and Vedanta-Sar*, were published in 1815, before which number of prose-books had already appeared.

To set the perspective, I should at this point briefly review the state of Bengali prose before 1815.[2] Till the beginning of the nineteenth century, the Bengali literary mind expressed itself, almot exclusively, through the vehicle of verse. Even history, biography and philosophical tracts were written in *payar*, the predominant Bengali metre. The earliest specimens of Bengali prose, that are still extant, do not date from beyond the sixteenth century. And they are all in manuscripts; for "no printing press," as Jadunath Sarkar writes in his *Fall of the Mughal Empire*, "not even the cheapest and smallest lithographic stone was installed" by our royalty and ruling classes, who imported only luxury goods from Europe.[3] These manuscripts are an indispensable source material for reconstructing the prehistory and early history of Bengali prose. The use of prose in sixteenth and seventeenth centuries was confined to letters, deeds and documents, and cryptic philosophical notes, known as *dehakadaca,* relating to esoteric Vaisnavite cults. It appears that Bengali literary prose was being formed in the early part of the eighteenth century. In this century several Sanskrit-texts—*nyaya, smrti, jyotisa* and *ayurveda* tracts—were translated. An eighteenth-century translation of *Bhasa-Pariccheda,* a standard work on *nyaya* is quite worthy of note. I will have occasion to quote from this manuscript at the next section of this essay.

Beginning from the middle of the seventeenth century, the Portugues missionaries made some attempts at writing Bengali prose; the earliest one being that of Dom Antonio, son of a Bengali Zamindar, kidnapped by pirates and later converted to Roman Catholicism. Dom Antonio's book is a catechism of the Christian doctrine in the form of a dialogue between a Brahman and a Roman Catholic. The next notable attempt, made by Manoel da-Assumpcam, an Augustunian friar, is *Crepar Xaxtrer Orth, Bhed* (Lisbon, 1743). This is perhaps the earliest printed book in Bengali. The text was transliterated in Roman script—Bengali types were not yet available—in accordance with their phonetic value in Portuguese. Crepar *Xaxtrer Otho, Bhed* thus mirrors the phonology of the Bengali language of the first half of the eighteenth century.

The year 1778 marks a watershed, when Nathaniel Brassey Halhed published at Hooghly his *Grammar of the Bengali Language*. For Halhed's *Grammar* Bengali types were fabricated by Charles Wilkins, the able assistance of Pancanan Karmakar, a talented mechanic. This event heralded a new era, the era of Bengali printing, and opened up vast new possibilities for the development of Bengali prose. Four books of laws and regulations (including the famous Cornwallis Code), in Bengali translation, were published before the close of the eighteenth century.

The year 1800 constitutes another landmark, when two institutions—Serampore Mission and Fort William College—were set up. The first Bengali Bible (1800-01)and prose text-books were printed from the Mission press at Serampore. The

College of Fort William was founded with the professed aim of training the civilians from "Home" in the languages and literatures of India. Reverend William Carey headed its Bengali department. Under his guidance and drive the following textbooks came out between 1801 and 1815.

1801. Ramram Basu, *Raja Pratapaditya-Caritra*. Historical sketch of Raja Pratapaditya of Jessore.

William Carey, *Kathopakathan*. A compilation of "colloquies or dialogues intended to facilitate the acquiring of the Bengalee language."

1802. Goloknath Sarma, *Hitopades*. Translated from Sanskrit. Ramram Basu, *Lipimala*. Formally, a collection of letters; out, really, "a composition in Bengali prose in the epistolary form".[4]

Mrtyunjay Vidyalamkar, *Batris Simhasan*. Translated from Sanskrit.

1803. Tarinicaran Mitra, *Oriental Fabulist*. "Bungla version" in the Roman character of Aesop's and other ancient fables.

1805. Candicaran Munsi, *Tota Itihas*. Literally, tales of a parrot, it is a translation from a Persian original.

Rajivalocan Mukhopadhyaya, *Maharaj Krsnacandra Rayasya Caritram*. Though purported to be a historical sketch of Raja Krsnacandra Ray, "the memoir is more of a tissue of fables and traditionary tales."[5]

1808. Mrtyunjay Vidyalamkar, Rajavali. A "history of kings based more on tradition than on authentic history."[6]

Mrytyunjay Vidyalamkar, *Hitopades*.

Ramkisor Tarka-cudamani, *Hitopades*.

1812. William Carey, *Itihasmala*.

A compilation of stories collected from diverse sources. It is not officially recorded to be a publication of Fort William College.

1815. Haraprasad Ray, *Purusa pariksa.* Translated from Vidyapati's Sanskrit work of the same title.

Among the writers of the Fort William period, Carey and Mrtyunjay are most eminent. Carey was more an efficient promoter of the language than a proficient writer in Bengali. His own prose, as is evident from the last edition (1833) of the Bengali Bible, *Dharmapustak,* issued during his life-time, never quite lost its un-Bengali ring.[7] Mrtyunjay, however, was a talented writer, a self-conscious craftsman, who experimented with different styles.

Historically, therefore, Rammohun cannot be called the "onlie begetter" of Bengali prose. The prose in Bengali is the product of a process in which Rammohun, amongst others, played a major role. This role I will try to describe in this essay.

Now, to take up the second question : Did Rammohun write better prose than his predecessors? Some literary historians hold that some of the earlier writers, Mrtyunjay in particular, had a superior prose-style.[8] I should preface this discussion by pointing out that scope for comparative style-study is limited. In fact, a major trend both in linguistics and in literary criticism inclines to that view that formally different expressions differ in meaning, and, therefore, are not comparable.[9] Whether one accepts this view or not, it serves as a caution against the practice of drawing improper comparisons, much too prevalent among our critics and historians.[10] Any exercise in comparative style-analysis, to be meaningful, should fulfil two conditions. First, two texts, if they are to be compared at all, must have at least an analogous theme. Secondly, they must be comparable date : there is no point in comparing the immature piece of one writer with the maturer piece of another.

Accordingly, I choose Mrtyujnay's *Vedanta-Candrika* (1817) and Rammohun's *Bhattacaryyer Sahit Vicar* (1817) for comparison. These two pamphlets have a common subject-matter, seen from opposite view-points : the former argues for, while the latter against, the Hindu practice of idol-worship. There is, however, one difference : Mrtyunjay's tract belongs to his maturer phase; but that of Rammohun represents his earlier period and style of writing.

I am not comparing Mrtyunjay and Rammohun—I would like to emphasize—in order to make judgments of worse and better; I am making the comparison simply to elucidate their respective characteristics.

I will now cite two passages, one from Vedanta-Candrika and the other from *Bhattacaryyer Sahit Vicar.*

> *Evan ei sutre sarvvapadopadanahetuk Brahmajijnasottar niskam karmanusthane mumuksur mokser hani hay na yehetuk phaladvarai bandhak karmma hay svarupata hay na tathapi alpayuca-palacittadi dosayukta idanintan puruserder phalabhisandhirahit karmmasvarup nirvvaha karane tattvabhyaser ksatisambh avanate Brahmajijnasot tar niskam karmmanusthane varavighataya kanyodvahah ei nyay upasthit hay ataev yathavidhi sannyas arthat karmmer phalata o svarupata parityagrup sadhansampanna haiya Vedantasravan sastracaryyopadistarthermanan arthat yuktite avadharan o avadharitarthe cittapravahikaranarup nidi-dhyasan o asramocita karmmarup dharmmanusthanetei deha-patparyyanta kal yapan sannyasir karttavya. Asupteramrteh kalat nayedvedantacitaya ityadi sastrapramanyaprayukta. Ihate vividisar purvvei partiyakta nisiddhacaraner nisthutavalehavat [sic] prasaktii ki ataev nisiddhacari anek sannyasi svasisyake acaryya svami parityag kariachilen taharder matanusari dasanama name ek prakar lok adyavadhi lokete prasiddha ache e vivi-disasannyas karane asamarther prati bahudak kuticakra name dui prakar sannyas vihita ache tahate niskam karmmacaran yavajjiva karttavya hay. Evam ati durlabh tattvajnan labh Isvarajnaprapta karmmayog o cittaikagratapara maphalak Vedanta-pratipadita kupitakapikapolavarnapadm \ksamurttyadyupasanatei sulabh haiya avidya tatkaryya prapancasakaler unmulan kariya jivabhinna Brahmasaksatkar kare. Ei saksatkar dehapatpary yenta jivanmukti dehapatotar*

nivrvvanamukti hay. Evamvidha tattvajnanir dandavinirmmokottar samskarvasata kulalacakra-bhramivat purvvapurvvacirabhyastatatta ıanusthanabalat sams-karvasata anuvarttaman hay.

(Mrtyyunjay Vidyalamkar, Vedanta- Candrika[11]*).*

Jagate Brahma haite bhinna vastu nai ataev ye kona vastur upasana Brahmoddese karile Brahmer upasana haite pare e yuktikrame ki devata ki manusya ki pasu ki paksi sakaleri upasanar tulyarupe vidhi paoya gela tabe nikatastha sthavar jangam tyag kariya durastha devata-vigraher upasana kastasadhya evam vises prayojanabhav ataev tahate pravarta haoya yuktisiddha nahe. Yadi bala durastha devata-vigraha evam nikatastha sthavar jangamer upasana karile tulyarupei yadyapi ai Sarvvavyapi Paramesvarer aradhana siddha hay tathapi sastre ai sakal devavigrahe puja karibar anumatir adhikya ache ataev sastranusare devavigraher puja kariya thaki tahar uttar yadi sastranusare devavigraher upasana karttavya hay tabe ai sastrei kahiyachen ye yahar vises bodhadhikar evam Brahmajjijnasa nai sei vyakti keval cittasthirer janya kalpanik \ ruper upasana karibek ar buddhiman vyakti atmar sravanmananrup upasana kariben ataev sastra manile sarvvatra manite hay. Evam gunansarena rupani vivdhani ca. kalpitani hitarthaya bhaktanamalpamedhasam Eirup guner anusare nanaprakar rup alpabuddhi bhaktadiger hiter nimitte kalpana kara giyache Isopanisader bhumikay ihar vises paiben ar atmar upasana keval sravanmanansvarup hay ihar vivaran. (Rammohun Ray, Bhattacaryyer Sahit Vicar [12])

The following table shows the proportion of Sanskrit or *tatsama* words and compounds in each passage :[13]

Thus one an see, Mrtyunjay makes a larger use of compounds, particularly of longish compounds, than does Rammohun. Mrtyunjay's *kupitakapikapolavarnapadmak samurttyadyupasanatei* is truly sesquipedalian. Rammohun avoids such compounds. He has a definite tendency of splitting the compound; he writes, for instance, *guner anusare* instead of gunanusare. Also note how he repeatedly disjoins the compound *sthavar-jangam.*

Vocabulary	*Mrtyunjay*	*Rammohun*
Total number of words	153	151
Number of Compounds	59	21
Compounds with 2 components	39	19
Compounds with 3 components	12	2
Compounds with 4 components	6	0
Compounds with 5 or more than 5 components	2	0
Tatsama and Sanskrit loan-words	127	106
Tadbhava words	26	45
Desi words	0	0
Videsi words	0	0

The Mrtyunjay passage bears the marks of his avowed Sanskritism. However, the more important point to note is : not how many, but, what kind of Sanskrit words Mrtyunjay and Rammohun use. For Rammohun, too, makes a liberal use of the *tatsama* element; his dicion is also Sanskrit-based. But there is one big difference. The words that occur in the Rammohun passage are not difficult, one can read the entire passage with-quite possibly even without-the aid of *Calantika*, the standard dictionary of current Bengali; while Mrtyunjay is fond of pedantic words, one cannot, for instance, find the meaning of such words as vividisasanyas or *nisthutavalehavat* or *kuticakra* in *Calantika.*

It will close this analysis by quoting two more extacts from *Vedanta-Candrika* and *Bhattacaryyer Sahit Vicar*, that throw light on their authors' characteristic attitudes to and ideals of Bengali prose.

> Aro yeman rupalamkarvati saddhvi strir hrdayartha-boddha sucatur purusera digambari asati narir sandarsane paranmukh han temani salamkara sastrarthavati sadhubhasar hrdayartha-boddha satpurusera nagna ucchrmkhala laukik bhasa sravan matretei paranmukh han.
>
> (*Vedanta-Candrika*)[14]

(....and as the intelligent who are admitted to converse

with an adorned beautiful and virtuous woman, turns [sic] away disgusted at the very sight of a naked and wanton female, so those who are acquainted with the secrete of the ornamented and beautiful language of the Shasters, turn away in digust at hearing the unembellished and immethodical style of vulgar language.—-*An Apology for the Present System of Hindu Worship, Mrtyunjay-Granthavali, Calcutta*, 1346 B.S., p.28).

.......Samskrta tyag karia bhasate Vedanter mat evam Upanisadadir vivaran karibar tatparyya ei ye sarvvasadharan lok ihar arthabodh darite paren kintu pragadha pragadha Samskrta sabdasakal icchapurvvak diya granthake durgam kara keval lokke tahare artha haite bancana evam tatparyyer anyatha kara hay ataev prarthana ei ye dvitiya Vedanta-Candrikake pratham Vedanta-Candrika haite sugam bhasate yena Bhattacaryya likehn yahate loker anayase bodhagamya hay.

(*Bhattacaryyer Sahit Vicar*)[15]

(The doctrines of the Vedanta and the contents of the Upanisads are put into the vernacular—without having recourse to Sanskrit —with the purpose that the common people may understand their meaning. But if a book is made difficult by a deliberate use of abstruse Sanskrit words, the people are deprived of the meaning and, thereby, the purpose is defeated. I therefore entreat the learned Brahmin to write the second *Vedanta—Candrika* in a language easier than that of the first).

II

The fact remains the Fort William group of authors, for all their worth, were essentially text-book writers. Their books, highly priced and meant for the British civilians, remained beyond the reach of the reading public. In any case, a series of publications, identified too closely with the apparatus of an alien imperialism, was not likely to attract, much less to enthuse, the people. The contents of these text-books were, naturally, trivial. What these authors wrote were primers of history and biography, besides colloquies and anecdotes; they "provided *ersatz* enterainment from Sanskrit, Persian and English fables."[16] Rammohun not only wrote for a wider public but brought a new content. Of this new content, one can get an idea even by going through the chronological catalogue of his prose works in Bengali :[17]

1. *Vedanta Grantha,* 1815. A commentary on the *Vedanta-Sutra,* which, in the words of Rajnarayan Basu, "became a *brah-mastra*" in Rammohun's hands.

2. *Vedanta-sar,* 1815. An abridged and easier version of *Vedanta-Grantha.*

3. *Talabakaropanisat* or *Kenopanisat,* 1816. Bengali translation based on *Samkara-Bhasya.*

4. *Isopanisat,* 1816. Bengali translation based on *Samkara-Bhasya.*

5. *Bhattacaryyer Sahit Vicar,* 1817. Sastric disputation with Bhattacaryya on idol-worship, a rejoinder to Mrtyujnay Vidyalamkar's *Vedanta-Candrika.* The title of the English version : *A Second Defence of the Monotheistical System of the Vedas.*

6. *Kathopanisat,* 1817. Bengali translation based on *Samkara-Bhasya.*

7. *Mandukyopanisat,* 1817. Bengali translation based on *Samkara-Bhasya.*

8. *Gosvamir Sahit Vicar,* 1818. Sastric disputation with Goswami on monmotheism.

9. *sahamaran Visaye Pravartak o Nivartak Samvad,* 1818. "A Conference between an Advocate for, and an Opponent of, the Practice of Burning Widows Alive."

10. *Gayatrir Artha,* 1818. An explanation of the *Gayatri* mantra.

11. *Mundakopanisat,* 1819. Bengali translation based on *Samkara-Bhasya.*

12. *Atmanatmaviveka,* 1819. (?). Samkaracarya's (?) text along with Bengali translation.

13. *Sahamaraner Visay Pravartak O Nivartaker Dvitiya Samvad,* 1819. "A Second Conference between an Advocate for and an Opponent of the Practice of Burning Widows Alive." In this polemical tract Rammohun gives his rejoinder to Kasinath Tarkavagis *Vidhayak Nisedher Samvad,* an apology for *Sati.*

14. *Kavitakarer Sahit Vicar,* 1820. Sastric disputation with Kavitakar.

15. *Subrahmanya Sastri Sahit Vicar,* 1820. *Sastric* disputation with Subrahmanya Sastri. The title of the English version : *An Apology for the Pursuit of Final Beatitude, Independently of Brahmunical Observances.*

16. *Brahman Sevadhi* : *Brahman O Misinari Samvad* (Numbers 1, 2, & 3),1821. The title in English : The *Brahmunical Magazine : The Missionary and the Brahmun. In Brahman Sevadhi* Rammohun refutes the attacks of the Christian Missionaries upon Hinduism.

17. *Cari Prasner Utter,* 1822. Answer to four questions put by an advocate of orthodox Hinduism.

18. *Prarthanapatra,* 1823. The English version was entitled *Humble Suggestions to his countrymen who believe in One True God.*

19. *Padri O Sisya Samvad,* 1823 (?). Written in the form of an imaginary conversation between a Trinitarian Missionary and three Chinese converts, this polemical tract exposes the fallacies of Trinitarianism.

20. *Gurupaduka,* 1823. The text, a rejoinder to a pseudonymous polemic, has not yet been traced. Its preface was reprinted in *Choto-Galpa,* 1, Paus, 1340 B.S. Vol II, No. 24.

21. *Pathyapradan,* 1823. "Medicine for the Sick, Offered by One who Laments His Inability to Perform All

Rigtheousness." In *Pathyapradan,* perhaps his longest polemic, Rammohun pillories a scurrilous pamphlet, *Pasandapidan* ('A Torment to the irreligous"), written by Kasinath Tarkapancanan on behalf of the orthodox opinion.

22. *Brahmanistha Grhasther Laksman*, 1826. This short track analyses the characteristics of a householder faithful to Brahman.
23. *Kayasther Sahit Madyapan Visayak Vicar,* 1826. *Sastric* disputation with a *kayastha* on drinking wine.
24. *Vajrasuci,* 1827. Sanskrit text along with the Bengali translation of *p.athma-nirnaya of Vajrasuci Upanisat* (a Mahayana Buddhist work) which shows that, in the final analysis, *Brahmana* means a believer in *Brahman.*
25. *Gayatrya Paramopasanavidhanam,* 1827. An exposition both in Bengali and in Sanskrit of the mode of divine worship through the chanting of the *Gayatri.*
26. *Brahmopasana,* 1828. Another track on the mode of divine worship.
27. *Anusthan,* 1829. A catechism that expounds Rammohun's doctrine of divine worship.
28. *Sahamaran Visay,* 1829. Rammohun's last polemic on *Sati.*
29. *Gauydiya Vyakaran,* 1833. Bengali grammar.

These books constitute, in part (the Bengali part), what may be called the canon of Rammohun. Among his apocryphal texts, the popular pamphlet *Brahma-Pauttalik Samvad* or *A Dialogue between a Theist and an Idolater,* 1820, merits particular mention.

Rammohun, it is pertinent to remember, also wrote in periodicals, a medium that catered to a wider public. He published, for instance, his first tract on *Sati* (*Sahamaran Visaye Pravartak O Nivartak Samvad,* 1818) in Bengal Gezeti or Bengal

Gazette, one of the earliest Bengali newspapers. The columns of *Samvad Kaumudi,*[18] with which Rammohun was closely associated, covered a considerable area of contemporary life.[19] Thus one can see, Rammohun gave to Bengali prose a nobler and a wider content—from Vedanta to day to day problems of social life he made the subject-matter of his writings.

His methodology, too, enhanced the content of his prose and introduced a note of high seriousness. He turned prose into a vehicle of conceptual analysis and rigrous logic, accepting *Sruti, Vedanta-Sutra,* inference, perception and common sense as *pramana* or essential means of arriving at valid knowledge.[20] The way he proves Manu to be more authoritative than Angira, Harit and other *smrtis,* show that he was adept in the mechanics of higher criticism.[21] In his logic-based discourses, Rammohun, however, does not spin metaphysical cobwebs.[22] He employs his immense machinery of reasoning mainly for some down-to-earth purposes : abolition of *Sati,* for instance. Thus his prose acquires a social content. Tagore perhaps thought of this rich and varied content when he said that Rammohun had put Bengali literature upon a granite structure.[23]

Now, let us look into the form of his prose.

Those who underestimate or reject Rammohun's literary achievements *en bloc,* seem to view his prose as a particular kind of writing with fixed features, that underwent little or no change.[24] Such a view, however, is unhistorical and wrong. As the bibliography, I have just given, shows : all his Bengali works, with one exception, came out between 1815 and 1829; *Gaudiya Vykaran,* appearing, after a gap of four years, in 1833. Rammohun's prose, therefore, developed over a period of years; in other words, it, too, has a history.

In his first book, *Vedanta-Grantha,* one can find the faltering steps of the beginner. Take, for instance, the which he himself adduced as an illustrative example while instructing his readers how to understand prose :

Brahma jahake sakal Vede gan Karen ar jahar sattar

avalamban kariya jagater nirvvaha caliteche sakaler upasya hayen.

(*Vedanta-Grantha, Anusthan,* 1815, p. 13)

Violating the normal Bengali word-order, here, the antecedent, *Brahma,* precedes the relative clause. As a result, *Brahma jahake sakal vede gan Karen,* becomes, by itself, a simple sentence, conveying a sense, quite the contrary of Rammohun's intended meaning. Moreover, *sattar avalamban kariya and nirvvaha caliteche* are unidiomatic collocations. The final copula, hayen, too, violates Bengali usage.

Let us take a longer passage :

Manusya jahar sat asat vivecannar buddhi ache se ki rupe kriyar dosgun vivecana na kariya savarage Karen ei pramane vyavahar evam paramartha karyya nirvvaha karite pare eimat sarvvatra sarvvakale haile par prthak prthak mat e paryyanta haita na visesata apnader madhye dekhitechije ekjan vaisnaver kule janma laiya sakta haiteche dvitiya vyakti saktakule vaisnav hay ar smartta bhattacaryyer pare jahake ek sata vatsar hay na yavatiya para Martha karma snandan vratopavas prabhrti purvvamater bhinna prakare haiteche ar sakale kahen je panca brahman jekale edse aisen tahader payete moja evam jama ityadi ves evam goyan chila tahar pare pare se sakal vyavahar kichui rahila na ar brahmer yavanadir dasatva kara evam yavaner sastra path kara evam yavanke sastra pth karana kon purvva dharmma chila ataev savarge je upasana o vyavahar Karen tahar bhinna upasana kara evam purvva purvva niyamer tyag apnarai sarvvada svikar karitechi tave kena emata vakye visvas kariya paramarther uttam pather cesta na kara yay ||2||.

(*Vedanta-Grantha, Bhumika,* 1815, pp. 5-6)

In this passage, too, some of the deviations which I have already noted, recur. But what I want to point out here is the inordinate length of the sentence : the whole passage is one single sentence comprising 156 words, strung together by conjunctions *evam* and *ar.* This joining devise reminds one of

George Campbell's precept that "Of all the parts speech, the conjunctions are most unfriendly to vivacity."[25] The next, and an important, point to note is the complete absence of all punctuations except a doubt *dadi* or double stop at the end. Now, punctuation is a reflector as well as a controller of structure and rhythm. This lack of punctuation indicates Rammohun's as yet incomplete mastery of Bengali sentence-structure. In fact, punctuation is an important index of the progress of his prose.

The punctuation system of *Vedanta-Grantha* like that of other early Bengali books printed in Bengali characters—the case being quite different with Bengali books printed in Roman script[26]—is closely modelled on the traditional punctuation system of Bengali manuscripts. Thus *Vedanta-Grantha* has only those punctuation marks that one finds in a Bengali manuscript : *dadi* (1), double *dadi* (11), *kasi* (—), a *kasi* after a single *dadi* (i—) or after a double *dadi* (*ii*—) and a circle between two double *dadis* (11 O 11). The *dadi* is the Bengali counterpart of the full stop. Besides, in *Vedanta-Grantha,*it serves (like the double *dadi*) the function of the quotation marks, the colon and the dash as well. Rommohun usually clinches an argument with a double *dadi* and indicates the close of a chapter or section (*padah*)by a 11 o 11 or a 11 o 11—mark. The *bhumika* or introduction to *Vedanta-Grantha* closes with a II—sign. He being the book by writing the *mangalacaran, om tat sat*, between double *dadis,* traditionally regarded in West Bengal as auspicious. *Pancanan Tarkaratna* in an illuminating article in *Haraprasad-samvardhan-Lekhamala* has explained the *tantric* symbolism and *naiyayik* significance ofsuch use of the double dadi.[27]

Subrahmanya Sastrir Sahit Vicar (1820) may be taken as a representative work of the middle period. In this polemical tract, printed at Baptist Mission Press, Calcutta, Rammohun makes an ampler use of the English punctuation system and also shows a greater command over his medium. In an authoritative account of puncuation marks in Bengali printing. Dr Sukumar Sen, our leading literary historian, states that

Rammohun introduced the quotation marks, but he says that he cannot affirm—as he has no evidence at hand—whether Rammohun used the comma and the semicolon also.[28] However, a first edition copy of *Subrahmanya Sastrir sahit Vicar,* available at Carey Library, Serampore, conclusively proves that Rammohun did use, besides the quotation marks and the English full stop, the comma and the semicolon as well.[29]

> *Brahmavidyar prakaser nimitta varnasram karmmer anusthan kartavya bate, ye hetuk ekatha Vedadi sastrer sahit viruddha nahe, sutaram amrao iha svikar kari; kintu iha sarvvatha amanya hay, ye varnasram karmmer anusthan vyatireke Brahmajnaner utpatti hay na, yehetuk Bhagavan Vedavyyas varnasramkarmmahin vyktirdero Brahmavidyate adhikar ache, iha sutre likhiachen, se ei dui sutra.*
>
> (*Subrahmanya Sastrir Sahit Vicar.* 1820, p. 2)

As one can see from this passage, Rammohun's punctuation in *Subrahmanya Sastrir Sahit Vicar* is structural and logical. It is structural in that it both mirrors and controls the structure of the sentence. It is logical in that it indicates the steps of the argument and highlights the relationship and the meaning by ordering and shaping the expression.

Rammohun's prose has become altogether more mature in *Subrahmanya Sastrir Sahit Vicar*. The faltering steps of *Vedanta-Grantha* are no more; perhaps the language still creaks a little—note the archaisms of *yehetuk, vyaktrider* and the awkward copula, *amanya hay*—but the movement is vastly easier than it was in the *Vedanta-Grantha* period.

I cannot possibly trace here the development of his prose from 1821 to 1829 in any great detail. However, on the basis of available data I will put forward two generalisations :

1. From 1821 onwards there is a further progress in his prose : it becomes, generally, more lucid and more effective as a medium of logical discourse. His journalistic writings in *Samvad Kaumudi,* which began to appear from 4 December 1821, and intense polemicizing, help him, I think, to evolve his

language. Rammohun, indeed, forged his prose while fighting battles for social and religious reforms; the social battle-ground, thus, indirectly reflected itself into the form of his language. He therefore well illustrates C.V. Wedgwood's adage : "Nothing sharpens prose like the necessity to do battle with it."[30]

2. As a parallel development, the use of the punctuation-device tends to increase. In Pathyapradan, printed at "Sungscrit Press" in 1823, for example, almost the entire paraphernalia of the English punctuation system—the comma, the semicolon, the full stop, quotation marks, the note of interrogation, the paranthesis and the dash—is conspicuously present. I do not, however, mean to say that Rammohun's punctuation was as systematic or elaborate as that of Vidyasagar. Besides, in the early days of our printings, it seems, a lot depended upon the printers, not all the whom were equally equipped or sophisticated. That is why punctuation as well as printing varied from printer to printer.

As a specimen of his later style, I will cite a passage from *Anusthan* (1829) :

Sisyer prasna. kahake upasana kahen.

Acaryyer pratyuttar. Tustir uddese yatnake upasana kaha yay, kintu Parabrahma visye jnaner abrittike upasana kahi.

(*Anusthan*, 1829, p. 2)

This passage reads almost like clean modern prose. I would, however, like to point out the similarity of method and structure of this passage with that of a manuscript treatise on logic, *Bhasapariccheda*.[31] The manuscript, which seems to be free translation of a Sanskrit work of the same name, is dated 1181 B.S. (1774 A.D.). *Gotam munike sisya sakale jijnasa kerilen amardiger mukti ki prakare hay taha krpa kariya balaha. Tahate Gotam uttar karitechen. Tavat padartha janilei mukti hay. Tahate sisyera sakale jijnasa karilen. Padartha kota. Tahate Gotam kahitechen. Padartha saptaprakar. Dravya gun karmma samanya vises samavay abhav. Tahar madhye dravya nay prakar.*

My point is that Rammohun did not build his logical language out of void; he had his roots in the traditional prose of the *naiyayik*.

III

From what I have said thus far, it follows that the two prominent achievements of Rammohun's prose are rationally and lucidity. These two qualities are, indeed, interdependent. A language of rational discourse must needs be lucid; ambiguity is an enemy of logical thinking.

Rammohun generally communicates concepts, reasons and facts. He has, therefore, seldom recourse to the affective aspects of language. But at one or two places, this rational prose becomes charged with emotion. One such passage, an eloquent vindication of Indian womanhood, occurs in *Sahamaraner Visay Pravartak o Nivartaker Dvitiya Samvad* (November, 1819). The passage, first quoted fully by Rajnarayan Basu in his survey of Bengali literature (1878), has since become justly famous.[32]

I will cite another passage—a very extra-ordinary one, in the entire corpus of his writings. It is from *Anusthan*, written, as we know, ten years later, in 1829 :

> *Ananta prakar vastu o vyakti samvalita acintaniya racanavisista ye ei jagat, o ghatikayantra apeksakrta atisay ascaryanvita rasi cakre vege dhavaman candra suryya graha naksatradi yukta ye ei jagat, o nanavidha sthavar jangam sarir yahar kona ek anga nisprayojan nahe sei sakal sarir of saririte paripurna ye ei jagat, jhar karan o nirvvahakartta yini tini upasya han.*
>
> (*Anusthan*, 1829, p.2)

In the terminology of modern stylistics the totality of linguistic phenomenon is known as a "sign". The sign is made of two constituents : the signified and the signifier. In this one-sentence passage, the signifier transmits not a concept, but an emotional and intellectual complex. The fact that Rammohun composed a hymn[33] on the same theme and in very similar diction, confirms that these words gushed forth from the entirely of his psyche.

The syntax is unusual; certain wordings (*acintaniya racanavisista, apeksakrta atisay ascaryanvita*) are quaint; the inevitable copula *han* at the end, jars on the ear. Yet the structure, as an instrument of articulation, is strangely effective. Rammohun has to give the sentence a complex and uncommon shape not only because he wishes to articulate the relationships in it precisely, elaborately; but also because he builds up, compulsively, a sustained rhythmical unit : the whole sentence becomes chantable in one breath, as it were. And thus a catechism becomes a hymn.

The phrase *ei jagat* (this word) followed by a conspicuous comma, is repeated three times. This repetition, besides putting the characteristic accent upon this-worldliness, serves to unify, control and reflect the structure. Furthermore, the ordonnance operates by a tension between two concomitant but contrary strands of 'felt' thought; the sentence becomes a balance of opposites : the mystical intuition of the Supreme Being on the one hand, and the rationalist apprehension of the universe as a well-regulated machine on the other. It is interesting to note how the mechanistic image of the universe as a clock—and the implied image of God as the ideal clock-maker—are mingled with such Vedantic epithets as *ananta* (endless) and *acintaniya* (beyond thought). The exultation of the clock-image perhaps indirectly reflects. Rammohun's striving, urges for seeing a rule of law established in the temporal sphere.[34]

IV

It is, however, not my contention that Rammohun has left behind a model prose. The archaisms and lapses in word-order that I have already noted, were perhaps, to some extent, unavoidable in the formative period of our literary prose. But a certain negative feature of his prose-style, which cannot be thus explained away, is that his prose is sundered from the current of common speech. The written language is never quite the same as the spoken language, nor is it perhaps easy to expound *sastric* arguments in the daily language of the people; but one of the elements that determines the quality of a style is its remoteness from or proximity to colloquial speech, the life-sustaining blood-stream of prose literature. From this point of view, there is a marked difference between Rammohun and Luther, with whom he is customarily compared. Collet, for example, writes : "As by ... Luther in Germany, so also by Rammohun in Bengal, the despised dialect of the common people was dame the vehicle of the highest ideas and became thereby permanently elevated."[35] Interestingly enough, even Dr Ramesh Chandra Majumdar, who is now out to explode the "Rammohun-myth," declared in 1960 : "The standard of revolt he [Rammohun] thus raised against the medieval tyranny of dogma unleashed forces which created what may be called Modern India and makes him worthy to rank by the side of Bacon and Luther."[36]

Luther is a maker of German literary prose; his translation of the Bible is the most important work, "not only in the history of the Reformation, but also in the history of language."[37] Luther came of a peasant stock. And though during the peasant uprising, he instigated the nobles to "stab, knock, strangle them [the peasants] at will", he deliberately based his prose upon the language of the people.[38]

He [Luther] drew his inspiration from popular idiom, from metaphors,....phrases and aphorisms current among artisans and peasants, popular proverbs, aphorisms and saying which he loved, sought for an collected. He had some of them written on the walls of his room and in the margins of his psalter so that he could read and re-read one or other every day. He made a collection of popular proverbs which was printed in 1900. And he was delighted when he found he could use any of them in his translation of the Scriptures when he came across a thought or sentiment which his beloved Germans had expressed in popular language.... Even for theological expressions he avoided Latin, turning to his beloved fifteenth-century Rhenish mystics, and, if necessary having recourse to metaphor.[39]

But Rammohun took to an altogether different course. He made the language of the *bhadralok* or elite the foundation of his prose : even though in his Sanskrit-based diction, he generally avoids the elephantine compounds and the pedantic elements, his prose is, none the less, moulded upon *sadhu-bhasa, i.e.*, the so-called elegant Bengali. In the preface to *Vedanta-Grantha*, he expressly acknowledges that his prose is not the easy language of common speech (*samanya alaper bhasa*) and states that people with some knowledge of Sanskrit and *sadhu-bhasa* will be able to pick it up with a little effort.[40] Now, what is this *sadhu-bhasa*? Suniti Kumar Chatterji in his *Origin and Development of the Bengali-Language* aptly describes it as "doubly artificial" and adds, hitting the nail on the head, "with its forms belonging to Middle Bengali, and its vocabulary highly Sanskritized, it [*sadhu-bhasa*] could only be compared to a 'Modern English' with a Chaucerian grammer and a super-Johnsonian vocabulary, if such a thing could be conceived."[41]

Unlike Luther, Rammohun is not known to have a passion for popular idioms and proverbs; nor does he use them much in his own writings. Seldom has he recourse to the concrete, sensuous vocabulary and metaphors of popular language. He tends to become abstract, rather than concrete; and uses similes rather than metaphors. It is significant to note how often in his translations he changes a metaphor into a simile. Take for example, this famous passage from Isopanisat :

Hiranmayen patrena satyasyapihitam mukham. Tattvam pusannapabrnu satyadharmaya drstaye.[42]

(The face of truth if covered with a plate of gold. Remove it, thou sustainer of the universe, and reveal the truth to the seeker.)[43]

Rammohun renders it thus :

He suryya svarnamay patrer nyay ye tomar jyotirmay mandal sei mandaler dvara tomar antaryami ye Paramatma tahar dvarke ruddha kariya rakhiacha tumi sei dvarke tomar upasak ye ami amar prati atmajnan praptir nimitte kholo.[44]

His rendering is more an explication than a translation; he himself significantly calls his translations *bhasa-vivaran*. *Hiranmayena patrena*' (with a plate of gold) becomes *svarnamay patrer nyav ye tomar jyotirmay mandal* (thy spendour, which is like a plate of gold).

"It do not know," Heinrich Heine says, "how Luther's language came into being, but I know that through his Bible the Lutheran language has spread throughout Germany. It is still supreme there ....and this old book is a source of constant rejuvenation for our language. All the expressions, all the phrases found in Luther's Bible are German; writers can make use of them, and since this book is in the hands of the poorest of the people there is no need for them to be given technical instruction in order to express themselves in a literary form."[45] Luther's Bible, it may be added, ran into 377 editions before his death.[46] Rammohun's works never enjoyed a comparable popularity; nor did they reach the masses of the people.

Being sundered from living speech, Rammohun's language becomes estranged from its run and rhythm as well. And as a con-comitant of this estrangement, his prose lacks flow. He builds his prose in a succession of self-sufficient sentences; there is no flowing over of the rhythm from one sentence to another. One might say, borrowing Coleridge's words, the sentences in a page of a Rammohun have the same connection with each other that marbles have with a bag; they touch without adhering.[47] Not that his sentences have no movement. They have; but these movements do not merge with and dissolve into the more sustained—and symphonic, contrapuntal—movement of the paragraph.[48] In this connection one cannot fail to note that in his prose-books, particularly in the earlier ones, the paragraph indentations are few and far between. And even when a paragraph occurs, in indicates either a phase of logic or an additional breathing space, more often the former than the latter, but never a rhythmic unit. Any page of *Pathyapradan*, marked by a greater use of the paragraph as a punctuation-mechanism, will illustrate this point.

A solid accumulation of independent sentences—often each of them representing a logical step—without the all-embracing sweep of a wider movement, tends to become monotonous. And this seems to be the real reason why Rammohun's prose weary the reader's attention. I, therefore, find it difficult to agree with Pramatha Chaudhuri's observation that Rammohun's style has not been accepted in Bengali literature because he proceeds, like the ancient *bhasyakaras*, by stating the opponent's argument at every step.[49] Vidyasagar, and even Tagore also, take to the same procedure in their polemical pieces; but their prose nowhere tires our patience. What animates and shapes their writings, is this rhythm, this *gest*—to borrow Brecht's terminology—that articulates itself into plastic paragraphs.[50]

The points that I have been trying to make, may be corroborated by a study of his *Bengalie Grammar in the English Language* (1826) and *Gaudiya Vyakaran* (1833). The latter, in Bengali, is based on the former.

Space does not permit me to make a detailed analysis of his two grammars, which they deserve. I will concentrate only on those features that have a bearing upon my main argument.

I should briefly note some matters of fact before I give my estimate of Rammohun's grammatical writings. Before Rammohun, a number of European authors wrote treatises on Bengali grammar. Among his European predecessors, Monoel da-Assumpcam (1743), Halhed (1778), Lebedeff (1801) and particularly Carey (1801) deserve mention. It seems, in the days of Rammohun there was an avid demand for Bengali grammar. Thus, a curious request appears in the *Calcutta Gazette*, April 23, 1789, beseeching "any gentlemen" to undertake for public benefit the composition of a Bengali grammar (Seton-Karr, *Selections from Calcutta Gazette*, ii, 497).[51] In a similar vein, the *Vangadut* of 20 February 1830 exhorts its "learned readers" to find ways and means for producing a Bengali grammar for the benefit of *apamar sadharan* or general public.[52]

Till recently, scholars were haling Rammohun "as the first

Bengali to write a grammar of the mother tongue."[53] But he seems to have been dislodged from his position of pre-eminence in 1970, when Shri Tarapada Mukhopadhyaya published a manuscript grammar supposedly written 1807 and 1811.[54] The manuscript was found among the papers of John Leyden (1775-1811), the brilliant orientalist. Shri Mukhopadhyaya has given it the title *Bangala Bhasar Vyakaran* and ascribed its authorship to Mrtyunjay Vidyalamkar on some external and internal evidences. Carey's Grammar, it may be added, bears an amazing resemblance with *Bangala Bhasar Vyakaran* both in matter in the treatment.

There is also an apparent similarly between Rammohun's *Grammar* and that of Carey's. Rammohun perhaps used Carey's *Grammar* of the *Bengali Language* as his working model. I will give here just one example to substantiate my point. Carey describes the pronunciation of the Bengali consonant ta thus : "The sound of the first of these letters [ta] is expressed in the provincial pronunciation of *butter* in Yorkshire."[55] Rammohun's description is almost identical : "The provincial sound of *t* in the word butter expresses *ta* exactly."[56]

However, though Rammohun owes much to Carey, his is the superior work. His Grammar is partly prescriptive and partly descriptive; in fact, the latter element preponderates over the former. It means : Rammohun is not so much out to legislate, to promulgate a set of more or less arbitrary rules. On the contrary, his attitude to the linguistic phenomenon is permeated with self-consciousness : he stands, it will be truer to say, he tries to stand, "objectively outside the language he is studying."[57] The "rules" are therefore not what he had to obey blindly; but what he observed when he examined how his contemporary Bengalees actually used their mother tongue. One reason why Rammohun could take up and sustain this attitude is that he wrote his *Bengali Grammar in the English Language for foreigners*—for "European philanthropists." To use his won words. It is a paradox : you come to know your won language, when you teach it to a foreigner. Whatever the reason, this attitude led him largely to a discovery of his own language : Bengali is to him, not a mere replica not an aberration of Sanskrit, but a distinctive language with a genius of its own. This linguistic sense and sensibility mark him out not only from Carey or Mrtyunjay, but from most of the later grammarians also. Indeed, this sensibility, this awareness, pervades his grammatical conscience and has left its stamp upon his technique as well as up his collection of language material.

In evaluating a grammar the basic criterion is the language material. If the material collected by a grammarian is not sufficiently representative, his description of the language will necessarily be inadequate. And precisely in this respect. Rammohun is—I repeat—far ahead of all his predecessors and most of his successors in the field of grammar-writing. There is a refreshing rationality in the way he, most of the time, puts the emphasis fixedly upon the native Bengali element as distinct from the Sanskrit element, and upon the living speech as distinct from the fossilized and "imitation-antique" forms of *sadhu-bhasa*. Naturally, this makes his language material representative and his grammatical description more adequate.

I find the logic of this same approach in operation in his treatment of cases, compounds and genders. Carey—or Mrtyunjay for that matter—accepts the Sanskrit model and states "There are seven cases [in Bengali] : the Nominative, Accusative, Instrumental, Dative, Ablative, Possessive, and Locative, which answering to the Sungskrita cases, are placed in the same order as in that language."[58]

Rammohun, in the other hand, can clearly see that Bengali, unlike Sanskrit, has only four cases : "In Bengalee, cases may be reduced to four; the nominative, accusative, locative and genitive."[59] Accordingly, the paradigm of the noun that he gives, has only four inflected cases :[60]

Singular

Nom.	goru	a Cow
Acc.	goruke	a Cow or to a Cow
Loc.	gorute	in a Cow
Gen.	gorur	of a Cow or a Cow's

Plural

Nom.	gorusakal	Cows
Acc.	gorusakalke	
	or	in Cows
	gorusakalete	
Gen.	gorusakaler	of Cows

While Carey and Mrtyunjay make a six-fold classifacation of *samasas* or compounds, Rammohun writes : "those [*compounds*] may be reduced to four classes."[61] What is more important, the examples (*hatbhanga gachpaka* etc.) given by him represent the purely Bengali element; but those of Mrtyunjay are mostly Sanskritic. One such example, common to both Mrtyunjay and Carey, is a little long : *pallava-phala-puspa-stavaka-manjari*, and, characteristically, it occurs in Mrtyunjay's *Batris-Simhasan*. In his *Gaudiya Vyakaran* Rammohun has plainly stated that compound words cannot be much used in Bengali.[62] For he knew full well that long-draw-out compounds do not quite suit its genius.

On adjectives or *visesana*, Carey maintains : "A *visheshuna* must be of the same gender with its vishishya."[63] Here too Carey misunderstands the structure of Bengali in his attempt to make it conform to the model of Sanskrit. Rammohun, on the other hand, very sensibly writes : "When nouns are expressed, the adjectives that join them admit no variation of case, number of gender; as *bada manusyera* superior men; *bada kanyake* to the elder daughter; except those Sungskrit adjectives that are used in Bengalee, which frequently admit of the variation of gender; as *jyestha kanyake* to the-eldest daughter; *jyestha putrake* to the eldest son."[64] Again, on page 59, he states categorically : "Bengalee adjectives have not distinction of gender."

Not everywhere, however, is Rammohun's discription of the facts of Bengali language correct or consistent : to err is natural for one, who breaks new ground. There is therefore no point in making a list of his blunders; I will discuss only those that throw interesting sidelights or show an insufficient comprehension of the living speech.

"Prepositions," Rammohun writes, "may be defined to be

such words, as, when correctly placed before or after a word, express the relation of another attribute or noun to that word; as, *Se nagar haite gela* he went from the Town, expressing relation between the act of going out and the Town, the motion having had its beginning in the Town."[65] This definition, however, is self-contradictory. How can a *pre*position be placed *after* a word? The indeclinable *haite* is, not a preposition, but a post-position; the notion of the preposition is irrelevant in Bengali. Rammohun makes this mistake because the imports a category of English grammar into the grammar of Bengali. Nothing really is so little useful "as reasoning by the analogy from Europe to India."[66]

An instance of Rammohun's inadequate comprehension or incomplete acceptance of the living speech is his insistence upon retaining the copula. A sentence, he insists, must have a verb.[67] The Bengali—as well as the Sanskrit—usage, however, is to leave the 'be' verb generally understood. Thus; Ram *bhalo chele* (Ram good boy=Ram is a good boy) is good Bengali; while, *Ram bhalo chele hay* (Ram good boy is) is unidiomatic. Rammohun persistenty wrote the latter kind of sentences.

Nothing reveals Rammohun's insufficient appreciation of the rhythm of Bengali more than the chapter on prosody, where he affirms, "the natives of Bengal have neither music nor a language well adapted for poetry."[68] This statement betrays his ignorance not only of his native folk-poetry and folk-songs but also of Vaisnava lyrics.[69] (This, again, shows his difference with Luther whose knowledge of and passion for German musical tradition is well-known "Please collect for me all the German metaphors, rhymes and songs, as well as all the poems of the *Meistersingers* [German lyric poets and musicians of 14th-16th centuries, organized in guilds] which have been described, put into verse, composed and printed by you poets and draughtsmen in Nuremberg," he wrote in 1535, to his friend link, who happened to be in that town.[70]) Naturally, Roy could describe only three metrical patterns : *payar, tripadi* and *totak*. He obviously did not make a systematic classification of the Bengali metre; he did not attempt it, either. Even then, his analysis of the *payar* is far from complete. The *payar*, he says, has fourteen *aksars* of letters and not less than seven of more than fourteen syllables.[71] However, the Bengali rhythm, whether in verse of prose, is not a matter of letters, not even of syllables as such; but of a configuration of open and closed syllables. The *payar*, which approximates the speech-rhythm, is a pattern of such syllables. And the peculiarity of the pattern lies in that *payar* line has two feet : the first having eight and the second six *matras* or moras.

VI

I have tried to describe the important role that Rammohun played in evolving the discursive prose in Bengali. Further I have shown that his contributions in this field were not without certain deeply contradictory aspects. In the first place, his prose, being moulded on the *sadhu-bhasa*, is divorced from the living speech. Secondly, though in this *Grammar* he goes very far in accepting the living speech, he hardly resorts to its natural and indestructible resources in his own writings. There is thus a contradiction between Rammohun's theory of prose as a grammarian and his practice as a prose writer. Thirdly, while he largely succeeds in making his prose an efficient vehicle of reason, he fails, in general, to enliven it with the all-pervasive sweep of a wider rhythm. In a way the history of modern prose of the Bengali languages differs fundamentally from that of some other language—of English, for example. Historians of the English language say that the English sentence took the modern form during the end of the seventeenth century. In the seventeenth century, the century of English revolution, the English prose moved towards the common speech. The Puritan and Protestant tradition, the political pamphleteers and journalism, the scientists, and even the Royal Society "preferring the language of artisans, countrymen and merchants"[72] to that of wits and scholars, added their influences to this massive movement towards the common speech. Modern Bengali prose, on the other hand, in its formative period, based itself upon the ossified forms of the *sadhu-bhasa*, and moved toward an opposite direction.

Historically, this disjunction between the living speech and the *sadhu-bhasu* constitutes the basic contradiction, that has determined the development of Bengali prose in modern times. The question inevitably arises : why, at all, did this cleavage take place in the days of Rammohun? Why did out "modern" prose become estranged from the common speech? I cannot possibly embark upon a full-scale analysis of the causes here. But I believe, the cleavage cannot be emplaned in literary terms alone; to find anything like a complete answer, one must go beyond the frontiers of literature. For prose like language, is social product. And, therefore, the contradictions of our ninteenth-century prose reflect the dialecties of our nineteenth-century society : the estrangement of our prose from "the language of artisans, countrymen" mirrors the alienation and identity crisis of the newly emergent urban *bhadralok*.

REFERENCES

1. On this issue the literary historians are divided. One group ascribes the parentage of Bengali prose to Rammohun. R.C. Dutt (AR CY DAE), for instance wrote in his Literature of Bengal in 1877 that Rammohun "formed the Prose Literature of Bengal," Next year Rajnarayan Basu hailed Rammohun as the "father of Bengali prose." See *Basu, Bangala Bhasa O Sahitya Visayak Baktrta* (Calcutta, 1878), p. 22. The other group holds that this ascription is illegitimate. Brajendranath Bandyopadhyaya, for example, would like to bestow the title upon Mrtyunjay Vidyalamkar; Sushil Kumar De seems to take the view that both Carey and Mrytunjay have better claims to this title. See Bandyopadhyaya, Rammohun Roy (in Bengali), *Sahitya-Sadhak-Caritmala,* no. 16, 3rd edition (Calcutta 1350 B.S.), p. 70 and De, Bengali Literature in the *Nineteenth Century,* 2nd edition (Calcutta, 1962), pp. 140-43 and 543-45. Sukumar Sen, however, sensibly enough, does not at all seek a father-figure of Bengali prose. See Sen, Bangala Sahitye Gadya, 3rd edition (Calcutta, 1356 B.S.).
2. I have heavily drawn upon the researches of Sukumar Sen, Sushil Kumar De, Brajendranath Bandyopadyaya and Sajanikanta Das in giving this rapid survey of early Bengali prose.
3. Judunath Sarkar, *Fall of the Mughal Empire,* Vol. IV. (Orient

Longmans's Ist edition, Calcutta, 1972), p. 345. "It was left to the Purtuguese .... To be pioneers in the field of printed book production as well. Information available to us indicated that early in the 16th century two printing presses were imported into Goa and set up there." See M. Siddique Khan, "William Carey and the Serampore Books (1800-1834)," Libri, Vol. 11, No. 3 (1961), p. 197.

4. Buchanan's description cited by De, *op. cit.*, p. 156.
5. De. *op cit.*, p. 178.
6. *Ibid.*, p. 192.
7. Sen, p. 19. As an example of the kind of sentences that Carey wrote, I cite this from the chapter on syntax in his *Grammar* (4th edition, 1818, p. 93) : *Amar Kichu taka nay* = I have no money.
8. See, for example. De *op. cit.*, p. 544.
9. Graham Hough, *Style and Stylistics* (London, 1969), p, 4.
10. See, for instance Ramesh Chandra Majumdar, On Rammohun Roy, (Calcutta, Asiatic Society, 1972), pp. 44-45, 53-55.
11. Mrtyunjay Vidyalamkar, *Vedanta-Candrika, Rammohun-Granthavali,* edited by Bandhyopadhyaya and Das, vol. I, Vangiya Sahitya Parisat, Calcutta, n.d. (reffered to henceforward as *Granthavali*), p. 133.
12. Rammohun Roy, *Bhattacharyyer Sahit Vicar Grathavali,* Vol. I, pp. 177-78.
13. See S. K. Das, *Early Bengali Prose* (Calcutta, 1966) for similar tables I have found his analysis generally useful. He is, however, mistaken in listing *Utsavananda Vidhyavagiser Sahit Vicar* as one of Rammohun's Bengali books (p. 134). Utsavananda in Sanskrit work, which Rammohun never translated into Bengali.
14. Vidyalamkar, *op.cit.*, 152.
15. Roy, *op. cit.*, p. 155.
16. Amales Tripathi, "Bengali Literature in the 19th Century," *The History of Bengal* (1757-1905), edited by N. K. Sinha (University of Calcutta, 1967), p. 483.
17. I owe much to the bibliographies prepared by the editors of Collets's *Rammohun* and Brajendranath Bandyopadhyaya. See S.D. Collet, *The Life and Letters of Raja Rammohun Roy,*

edited by D.K. Biswas and P.C. Ganguli, 3rd edition (Calcutta, 1962), pp. 526-32; Bandyopadhyaya, *op. cit.*, pp. 82-93. See also *Granthavali*, Vol. 7, *Praisista*, pp. 69-72.

18. "Rammohun Roy was not only the principal promoter but the *de facto* editor of this periodical [*Samvad Kaumudi*], and articles from his own pen often appeared in it." Brajendranath Benerji, "Rammohun Roy as a Journalist," *Modern Review*, April 1931, p. 409.

19. For a translation of the contents of the *Samvad Kaumudi* see J.K. Majumdar, Raja Rammohun Roy and *Progressive Movements in India* (Calcutta, 1941), pp. 285-94. The files of the *Samvad Kaumudi* are not available now.

20. For a discussion of Rammohun's system of *pramana* see Dilipkumar Biswas, "Rammohun Roy O Vedanta," *Visva-Bharati Patrika* (Kartik-Paus, 1379 B.S.),. pp. 137-78.

21. *Sahamaraner Visay Pravartak O Nivartaker Dvitya Samvad*, 1819.

22. Jacquenmout writes : "Logic is also a weapon of which he [Rammohun] makes frequent use and he does not like to put it away.... but Ram Mohan Roy is a practical man. He is not passionate idealist who attempts to realize impossible theories; all that he wants to do is to bring about the possible good; and however limited the measure of the possibility for the good may be, he is resigned to concentrate his efforts within the channel in which it will be useful." See Victor Jacquemont. "A Portrait of Rajah Rammohun Roy" (translated from the French by N. C. Chaudhari), *Modern Review* (June 1926), pp. 689-692.

23. Rabindranath Thakur, "Bankimcandra," *Rabindra-Racanavali*, Vol. XIII, W. B. Govt., centenary edition (Calcutta, 1368 B.S.), p. 892.

24. See, for example, De, *op. cit.*, p. 545, where he says : "Rammohun was the father, not of Bengali prose, but of the particular kind of stilted prose which he created and which now remains isolated as a mere curiosity."

25. George Campbell, *The Philosophy of Rhetoric*, Vol. II (London, 1801), p. 287.

26. We are getting Roman punctuation marks in Bengali books printed in Roman characters from as far back as 1743.

27. For the undercurrent of the *tantric* element along with its characteristic emphasis upon this-worldiness in Rammohun's thought-process, see Dilipkumar Biswas. "Rammohun Rayer Dharma-Mat O Tantra Sastra," *Visva-Bharati Patrika* (Baisakh-Asadh, 1882 Saka), pp. 225-48.
28. Sukumar Sen, "Chapa Bamla Racanay Yaticihna, "Visva-Bharati Patirka (Magh-Caitra, 1885-86 Saka), pp. 284-96.
29. A copy of the original edition of *Sahamaraner Visay Pravartak O Nivartaker Dvitiya Samvad* in the keeping of Sahitya Parisat Library, shows that the comma, the semicolon and the full-stop appeared in 1819. However, in the next book Kavitakarer Sahit Vicar (1820) there are no English punctuation signs, except the quotation marks. A possible explanation is that Haracandra Ray, from whose press *Kavitakar* came out, was perhaps not much equipped as a printer.
30. C.V. Wedgwood, *Seventeenth-Century English Literature*, second edition (Oxford, 1970), p. 71.
31. Sahitya-Parisat-Patrika, Vol. 4, (1304 B.S.), p. 325.
32. Basu, *op. cit.*, pp. 22-24.
33. See *Brahma-Samgit, Granthavali*, Vol. IV, p. 61. Notes the last four stanzas.
34. "India requires" Rammohun says, "many more years of English domination so that she might not have many things to lose while she is reclaiming her political independence." See Jacquemont, *op. cit.*, p. 691. In this connection see also, The *English Works of Raja Rammohun Roy*, edited by Nag and Barman, part I, p. 1, footnote, where he writes : "At present the whole empire (with the exception of a few provinces) has been placed under the British power, and some advantages have already been derived from the prudent management of its rulers, from whose general character a hope of future quiet and happiness is justly entertained."
35. Collect, *op. cit.*, p. 193.
36. Ramesh Chandra Majumdar *Glimpses of Bengal in Nineteenth Century* (Calcutta, 1960), p. 53.
37. G.R. Elton, *Reformation Europe* (London, 1963), p. 289.
38. Cited in Engels, *The Peasant War in Germany (German Revolutions)*, edited by Leonard Krieger (Chicago, 1967), p. 42.

39. Frantz Funck, Brentano, Luther, translated by E. F. Buckley (London, 1936), p. 291.
40. Rammohun Roy, *Vedanta-Grantha, Anusthan* (Calcutta, 1815), p. 12.
41. Suniti Kumar Chatterji, *The Origin & Development of the Bengali Language*, Vol. I, (London, 1970), p. 134.
42. Rammohun Roy, *Isopanisat, Granthavali*, Vol. I, p. 210.
43. T.N. Sen's translation. See Sen, "Western Influence on the Poetry of Tagore," *Rabindranath Tagore : A Century Volume*, (New Delhi, Sahitya Akademi, 1961). P. 253.
44. Ray, *Isopanisat, Granthavali*, p. 210.
45. Cited in Funck-Brentano, *op. cit.*, p. 292.
46. Elton, *op, cit.*, p. 289.
47. S.T. Coleridge, *Specimens of the Table Talk of the Late Samuel Taylor Coleridge* (London, 1835), p. 209.
48. Here my analysis is based on Herbert Read's observations on the paragraph in *English Prose Style*, first Indian edition (Ludhiana, 1968), pp. 52-65.
49. Pramatha Chauduri, "Abhibhasan," *Prabandha Samgraha*, Vol. I, (Calcutta, 1959), p. 52.
50. Bertolt Brecht, *Brecht on Theatre*, edited and translated by John Willet (New York, 1966. 104).
51. De, *op. cit.*, p. 72n.
52. Brajendranath Bandyopadhyaya, Samva Patre Sekaler Katha, Vol. I., second edition (Calcutta, 1344 B.S.), p. 63.
53. Suniti Kumar Chatterji, "Rammohun Roy as a Grammarian," *English Works of Raja Rammohun Roy (Social & & Educational)* (Calcutta, 1934), Note IV, pp. 25-30. Dr Chatterji, however, no longer holds this view. For his recent views see his essay in Bengali, "Vyakarankar Rammohun," *Manisi Smarane* (Calcutta, 1972).
54. Tarapada Mukhopadhyaya (ed.) *Bangala Bhasar Vyakaran* (authorship ascribed to Mrtyunjay Vidyalamkar), (Calcutta, 1377 B.S.).
55. W. Carey, *A Grammar of the Bengali Language*, fourth edition (Serampore, 1818), p. 4.
56. Rammohun Roy, Bengali Grammar in the English Language (Calcutta, 1826), p. 7.

57. Otto Jespersen, "Grammer," *Encyclopaedia Britannica*, Vol. X (London, 1963), p. 615.
58. Carey, *op. cit.,* pp. 11-12.
59. Roy, *op. cit.,* p. 20.
60. *Ibid.,* p. 28.
61. *Ibid.,* p. 38.
62. Ray, *Gaudiya Vyakaran, Granthavali,* Vol. 7, p. 21.
63. Carey, *op. cit.,* p. 89.
64. Roy, *op. cit.,* pp. 54-55.
65. *Ibid.,* p. 118.
66. Canning to the Court of Directors, quoted in Bishnu Dey, *Michael Rabindranath O Anyanya Jijnasa* (Calcutta, 1967), p. 1.
67. "Javat Kriya na paiben tavat paryyanta vakyer ses angikar kariya artha karibar cesta na paiben," (*Vedanta-Granth, Anusthan,* 1815, p. 13).
68. Roy. *op. cit.,* p. 138.
69. See Chatterji, "Rammohun as a Grammarian," p. 29. and Bipin Chandra Pal, *Beginning of Freedom Movement in India* (Calcutta, 1954), p. 53.
70. Funch-Brentano, *op. cit.,* p. 291.
71. *Gaudiya Vyakaran,* p. 66.
72. Sprat, *The History of the Royal Society of London,* (1667), p. 113, quoted in Hill, *Intellectual Origins of the English Revolution,* (London, 1972), p. 129.

9 SELECT COMMITTEES AND THE REFORM BILL

Committees for Renewal of Character

In August 1832, the Special Committees of the House of Commons in charge of renewal of the Charter concluded their sittings and presented the Report to Parliament. The Report went to the Court of Directors in April 1833 and, when the Court agreed with the recommendations, in June 1833 the Bill was drafted and placed before the House of Commons. Rammohun gave several suggestions for inclusion in the Charter after careful study and serious thinking. Some of his suggestions were accepted but many were not, yet on the whole the Charter was satisfactory.

Rammohun knew that renewal of the Charter the East India Company, with the most essential modifications and favourable concessions, would require the unstinted support of the lberal members of the British Parliament and Government. The progressive measures could not be incorporated into the Charter without the strong backing of Parliament which was then preoccupied with its own Reforms Bill. Rammohun felt that the Reform Bill's liberal provisions were essential for India's good and Rammohun used his social popularity in England to win his objective and his attention was, therefore, naturally directed wholly on the passing of the Reform Bill of England.

Reform Bill and Rammohun

The Reform Bill of England was introduced in the House of Commons by Lord Russell in March 1831 but it was defeated in April. The Second Bill was introduced in the House of Commons and was carried at the end of September. When it was placed before the House of Lords, it was rejected in the beginning of October, 1831. At this time, England was passing through a turmoil, almost a civil war. In 1832, the Reform Bill was introduced for the third time in the House of Commons and was carried in March but it had yet to go to the House of Lords for adoption. The decision of the Upper House was awaited with great agony by many because of this long suspense. In a letter from Bedford Square to Miss Kiddell, Rammohun wrote :

> I had lately the pleasure of seeing the Rev. Dr. Carpenter, and hearing from that truly venerable minister that Miss Castle and yourself were perfectly well and deeply interested in the cause of Reform, on the success of which the welfare of England, nay of the world, depends. I should have long before this visited Bristol and done myself the honour of paying you may long promised visit, but I have been impatiently waiting in London to know the result of the Bill. I feel very much obliged by your kind offers of attention to my comforts while I am in that part of the country, of which I hope to be able to avail myself as soon as my mind is relieved on this.

The Upper House was in possession of the Bill and in spite of contrary influences, the second reading of the Bill was carried through by a very small margin by the middle of April 1832. This was a sufficiently exciting even for Rammohun as was reflected in his letter to Mrs. Woodford on 27th April :

> ....It must have afforded Mr. Woodford and yourself much gratification to learn by the first conveyance the division on the second reading of the Reform Bill. The struggles are not merely between the reformers and anti-reformers, but between liberty and oppression throughout the world; between justice and injustice, and between right and wrong, but from a reflection on the past vents of history, we clearly perceive that liberal principles in politics and religion have been gradually but steadily gaining ground not with standing the opposition and obstinacy of despots and bigots. I am still unable to determine the period of my

London and my visit to you in the country, I may perhaps do myself that pleasure...

The reactionary attitude of the peers was persisting even in the third reading of the Bill, yet it was finally passed in June 1832. It may be noted that subsequently the same House of Lord passed similar measures for Ireland and Scotland too. It was at this time, on July 31, 1832, that Rammohun wrote the following to his first host in Liverpool, William Rathbone :

> I am now happy to find myself fully justified in congratulating you and my other friends at Liverpool in the complete success of the Reform Bill, not with standing the violent opposition and want of political principles on the part of the aristocrats. The nation can no longer be prey of the few who used to fill their purses at the expense, nay to the ruin, of the people, for a period of upwards of fifty years. The ministers have honestly and firmly discharged their rights. I hope and pray that the mighty people of England may, now in like manner, do theirs, cherishing public spirit and liberal principles, at the same time banishing bribery, corruption, and selfish interests from public proceedings.
>
> As I publicly avowed that in the event of the Reform Bill being defeated, I would renounce my connection with this country. I refrained from writing to you or any other friend in Liverpool until I knew the result. Thank Heaven, I can now feel proud of being one of your fellow subjects, and heartily rejoice that I have the infinite happiness of witnessing the salvation of the nation, nay of the whole world.
>
> Pray remember me kindly to Mr. Cropper and Mr. Benson and present my best respects to Mrs. Rathbone and my love to the children.
>
> R.M.
>
> P.S. If the German philosopher is still at Liverpool, be good enough to remember me kindly to him, and inform him

that we have succeeded in the Reform question without having recourse to the principles of phrenology.

R.M.

Rammohun's Moral Stature

The above is quite interesting because Rammohun, in the midst of a hard struggle against adverse forces of the administration, kept a soft heart for all. At the same time, he made up his mind to give up all connections with England, if reactionary forces prevented the Reform Bill from being passed into law in the House of Commons or in the House of Lords. One may exclaim : how childish it is for an outsider like Rammohun to say that he would have nothing to do with the British connection. Does his connection matter at all? True it does not, and yet how untrue and short-sighted it would be to little the genuine appreciation and ardent co-operation of the most influential and towering personality of India. The fact of the matter is that Rammohun was conscious of the position he came to occupy in the English social and front-rank political circles as were actively engaged in furthering the forward movement of India. In his heart of hearts, Rammohun must have felt that Britian had honoured him in many possible ways and also given him the status of India's ambassador and his denunciation of Britian in such circumstances, however ineffective, still would only elevate his moral stature as the warmest supporter of world-wide liberalism. The fact was that Rammohun made genuine friendship with some important men of position in England, some belonging to the House of Commons and some to the House of Lords from whom his cause got the fullest support. Surely this gain was incalculable.

The Select Committees of the British Parliament, having got all the papers from various experts and evidence from men connected with administration in India and in England, from East India Company's representatives and from Rammohun, bestowed their serious consideration to many matters some of which were extremely difficult and delicate. Their decisions were far-reaching. Rammohun gave his own views candidly and there is no room to think that at this advanced age of his and with the reputation acquired in England, he would do any injustice to truth and to the wellbeing of India. Yet his well-known critic the *Samachar Chandrika* observed as follows :

> ...For a multitude of reasons of this sort, the Zamindars are too poor to make good the Government revenue and their lands are sold off. The Roy-jee without giving those compassionate gentlemen the slightest information on these subjects, has made this strange reply, that they were reduced to poverty by nuptial entertainments, funeral rites and other religious ceremonies. From this we obtain one conclusion, that it is wish that Hindu religious ceremonies should come to an end or the Sahebs may be pleased with him or such language...

This kind of replies and counter-replies covered the pages of the daily papers. The Select Committees transacting their business in London must have got some indications of landholders' opposition to Rammohun. The Committees were guided by the Memoranda and the Evidences. Letters also appeared in defence of Rammohun as follows :

> Respecting the Rajah's assertion that the Zamindars had profited from the cultivation of the waste lands, and the increased rents of their tenants, when the *Chandrika* accuses him of falsehood and speaks of his opinions being despised in England...Let me now ask the Editor, whether there has been no increase above the revenue from which Maleekana was deducted, according to the accounts of each village at the time of the perpetual settlement? Would the Zamindars depend upon that Maleekana?...

Perhaps these petty bickerings reached England too late or even if they did so in time, the Select Committees did not give much attention, for after all, local differences of opinion and estimates of situations were bound to occur every now and then.

During Rammohun's stay in London from 1831 to 1833, he wrote several papers, *e.g.*, on Revenue questions, Judicial questions, and various other connected matters, and he also brought out a scheme for European colonisation in the interior of India with elaborate arguments for and against. There is no doubt that the formulation of this scheme made a very large demand on Rammohun's imagination, on his experiences and his knowledge of human character. The Select Committees of Parliament must have been much impressed by the forceful arguments of Rammohun whose zeal for leading India to become a respectable partner of British Empire within as short a time as can be imagined, was unbounded.

These efforts to representations must have deeply impressed the Select Committees and England and India were agitated by these proposals, some quarters adversely but among progressive and thoughtful persons quite favourably. There is no denying the fact that the common Britishers did not accept the proposals with any happy feeling due to colour complex etc. and they saw more harm than good for their own race. While heated controversies were going on in both the countries. Rammohun was nearing his end. The Select Committees were finishing their labours as the year 1832 was drawing to a close and in 1833 the renewal of the Charter came with some notable changes[1] and some liberal measures including grant of per mission to European to settle in the interior of the country.[2]

REFERENCES

1. The East India Company ceased to be trading body and it became administrative and political in complexion.
2. "The new Charter Act of 1833 made a provision to the effect that Europeans were free to go to, and settle in, any part of the territories in the possession of the Company before 1800 without licence, but they were excluded from going to, and settling in, the territories obtained by the Company since that period, where they could go and reside only upon licence from the local governments. However, these provisions opened the way and provided the means for the amelioration of the conditions of the people though the agricultural, industrial and commercial development of the country, to which the contribution of Rammohun and his liberal followers..."

10 IMPLICATIONS OF THE CHARTER OF 1833

(a) Its History and Renewal

The eventful years are seen when the whole question of the Company came under enquiry when its Charter was renewed.

The result of the enquiry which lasted from 1808 to 1812, was published in the well-known Fifty Report and it led to the Charter Act of 1813.

There was a great improvement in the East India Company management though its financial position was strong one.

> "It exercised monopoly and control over those who might wish for more freedom from various motives, notably missionary zeal and the two points upon which most attention was directed. Section 33 says of 1813 Act, it begins, whereas, it is the duty of this country of promote the interest and happiness of the native inhabitants of the British dominion of India and such measured subject to be adopted as might tend to the introduction among them of useful knowledge, and of religious and moral improvement."

The Renewal of Charter had often before suggested the idea of political combat, but on no previous occasion were the critics of the East India Company more energetic and more jubilant than on the eve of the long Parliamentary discussion which was to finally strip of its little remaining commercial character.

The Select Committee lasted up to 1833, when the Bill renewing the Charter was passed.

The Charter Bill of 1833 was introduced in the House of Commons by Charles Grant in June 1833.

The Bill was passed finally, clause by clause, without adequate discussion.

The Bill was finally passed into an Act by the British Parliament, on Monday, August 19, 1833, and received the Royal assent on August 28, 1833. This is ranked in the Statute Book as 3 and 4. William IV, C. 85.

The Act was to come in force from April 22, 1834, and to expire on April 30, 1854.

It changed many things, personal, its policies and subsidiary Government.

The Age of Conquest had come to an end. The Age of Reconstruction had begun.

It had nobility of purpose and a keen sense of realisation. This Act was framed with high sense of duty.

It marks a most important stage in the Indian History. It is lengthy and prepared by Ilbert. Lord William Bentinck had reformed the subordinate administration. He brought efficiency in the work. He had understood Indian problems.

New system of Government was established by the Act of 1833.

It was the Age of Reform in England. The Whig systems and principles were adopted. Bentham's Principles were overshadowing the minds of the Law-Reformers. Macaulay was the main spring of the age. James Mill was working as Utilitarian for India.

The outlook was changed. Love for India was increased. Better and new principles were adopted.

The Charter Act of 1833 brought important changes in the system of India Administration. Lord Macaulay described the Act of 1833, as the most important Indian Act passed by the Parliament till 1909.

In 1833 says Cowell,

"the attention of the Parliament was directed to the three leading vices in the process of Indian Government :

(a) The nature of the Laws and Regulations.

(b) It defined authority and power from which those various Laws and Regulations enacted.

(c) The third was the confliating judicatures by which the Laws were administered.

Before the Act was passed, many enquiries in the House of Lords and Commons were conducted.

The same may be seen in the Question Nos. 2815 to 2820, written by Mr. Rickards.

The debates both in the House of Commons and the House of Lords seem reasonable. The tone of debates appears to be in noble form.

The Act was passed and it inaugurated a New Era.

It was to bring a New Heaven and New Earth for India. The relations of England and India to be shaped into New.

History of Renewal of Charters

The Renewals of the Charter took place several times :

*(a)*1600 A.D.

*(b)*1698 A.D.

(c) 1733 and 1766 A.D.

*(d)*1793 A.D.

(e) 1813 with many changes.

The study of the representation of the East India interests in Parliament between 1784 and 1834 reveals the important fact, the strength, influence and Independence of the Court of Directors, as against the Board of Control and the Cabinet.

It always varied in proportion to its strength. "By the Act of 1833, the Director", said Tecker, "will only become a screen interposed between the Government and the British people".

As Wilson said in his history about the importance of the Charter and its Renewal,

> "The question however important to the commerce of the Empire was not confined to commercial business on interests, it involved the whole character of the Government of India, the mode in which it might be best administered for the prosperity and happiness of the people, the reputation of the Legislatures and dignity and rights of the Crown."

Two Speeches were of importance at the passing of the Bill—one by Wynn and the other by Macaulay".

He spoke with the fine language about the Bill,

> "The Company is an anomaly, but it is a part of system where everything is anomaly. I will not, therefore, in a case in which I have neither principle and precedent to guide me, pull down the existing system which is sanctioned by experience".

Parliament was ignorant of all facts, as the Board had acquired the ascendancy over the Court.

By the Act of 1833, the Company was again given lease of life of twenty years.

The Company lost its commercial privileges.

Lord Macaulay said,

> "Paternal feeling towards the people was committed".

He said,

> "I see that toleration is maintained, yet I see that bloody and degrading superstitions gradually losing their power. I see the public mind of India, that public mind which we found debased and contracted by the worst forms of political and religious tyranny expanding itself to the noble and just views of the ends of Government and the social duties of man".

He wrote, "on the part of the Bill, on which, what has

recently passed, I must say to the last day of my life, I shall be proud of having been one of those who assisted in framing the Bill which contains the clause...

"It would be, on the most selfish view of the case, far better for us that the people of India were well governed and independent of us than ill-governed and subject to us. That they were ruled by their own Kings, but wearing our broad cloth and working with our cutlery, that they were performing their salams to English Collectors and English manufactures. To trade with civilized men is indefinitely more profitable than to govern savages. That would, indeed, be a doting wisdom, which order that Indian might remain a dependency, would make it a useless and costly dependency which would keep a hundred millions of men from being our customers in order that they might continue to be our slaves.

"The destinies of our Indian Empire are covered with thick darkness. It may be that the public mind of India may expand under our system till it has outgrown that system; that by good Government, we may educate our subjects into a capacity for better Government : that, having become instructed in European knowledge, they may, in some future age demand European institutions. Whether such a day will ever come, I know not. But, never will I attempt to avert or to retard it. Whenever it comes, it will be the proudest day in English History. To have found a great people sunk in the lowest depths of slavery and superstition, to have so rules them as to have made them desirous and capable of all the privileges of citizens would indeed be a title to glory all our own".

"The sceptre may pass away from us.... Victory may be inconstant to our arms. But there are triumphs which are followed by no reverses. There is an Empire exempt from all natural causes of decay. Those triumphs are the pacific triumphs of reason over barbarism; that Empire is the imperishable Empire of our arts and our morals, our literature and our Laws."

In the field of Administration, for the reform of Government two important debates, were held during the time of Lord William Bentinck.

The Committee submitted the report and desired that the defects might be removed to bring efficiency in the Government. The most important work was done, it was the creation of the superior Government diversed of local charge and disjoined from the Government of a separate presidency.

It had brought inefficiency and inconveniences.

Lord William Bentinck desired that the Supreme Government should act as effective apparatus of control over subordinate Presidencies. No Regulation should be issued without the authority of the Governor-General

Lord William Bentinck the Governor-General in a Minute September 14, 1831, expressed the opinion that local detail pressed so much upon him and his Council that the Supreme Court precluded from the performance of its higher and its most important function and duties of the greater responsibilities, in order to improve the efficiency of the Government.

He put further two important suggestions in order to improve the efficiency of the Government. First, that the Supreme Government be diverted of the different local duties of it, functions be confined to purely its work of supervision. Second, that the seat of Government of India be shifted from the Lower Provinces to the Upper Provinces.

He also suggested that in order to look after the Administration of the Lower Province, there should be vice-President in Council, living at Calcutta and superintending the revenue and Judicial Administration

In the course of his Minute, Bentinck made the following Recommendations for the effective control over the subordinate Presidencies :

1. The interference of the Supreme Government should be rather of check, of a preventing and restraining, than [illegible]tive and meddling character.

2. The Supreme Government should aid the home authorities by countering the defect and weakness arising from distance, from delay in issue of orders and from the imperfect knowledge they must possess of circumstances and the true bearing of local questions.

3. The Supreme Government should prevent all innovations and new expenditures and prohibit changes in the details of Military establishment.

4. The General Superintendence of the Troops as all Presidencies should be vested in the Supreme Government.

5. The Subordinate Government should be required to make all the Reports of their Proceedings direct and in the first instance to the Supreme Government, copies being sent for the information to the Court of Directors.

6. The Supreme Council should include a Councillor from each of the Presidencies.

7. Political and Diplomatic relations to be entirely in the hands of the Supreme Government.

8. There should be one Army and one Commander-in-Chief.

9. Civil Servants might be transferred from the Presidency to another.

10. There should be one Legislative Council for all India.

The Charter Act of 1833 made important changes in the Administration.

The Company lost its importance. It lost its commercial privileges, and Government of India was reconstituted on a New Model. The changes introduced by the Act were as follows :

1. The Presidency of Fort William was to be divided into two Presidencies. But division remained suspended up to 1835.

2. Instead of continuing to invest the Governor General in Council with powers of General control over subordinate

presidencies, the superintendence, direction and control of the whole Civil and Military Government of all the said territories and revenues of India were vested in a Governor-General of India in Council. The Governor-General of Bengal became the Governor-General of India.

3. The Supreme Government of India became divested of any local charge for a separate presidency. In keeping with Bentinck's views, however the home authorities agreed that the Governor-General in India should act as a Governor of the Presidency of Bengal.

4. The Supreme Council of India was to consist in its Executive capacity of three Members of the Indian Service excluding the Commander-in-chief who might be appointed as hereto-afore the extraordinary Members.

5. No Governor was now to create new officers or grant money without the previous Sanction of the Supreme Government, vested with the full powers of command the administration.

6. The Governor-General in Council might, from time to time, pass a Law, authorising the Governor-General to exercise, in course of his tour, to any part of India, all the powers vested in the Council collectively, excepting those of making Laws and regulations. In such a case he was required to nominate a President from among his Councillors to officiate during his absence.

7. The executive Government of each of the subordinate Presidency was vested in a Governor and not more than 3 Councellors. The Court of Directors obtained authority to suspend the appointment of Counsellors or reduce their strength within the limit of 3.

8. The Act provided, for distinct Legislative Council consisting of Governor-General, his Counsellors and Legislative Members who was not of Company's service.

The intention was to offer the seat to an English Lawyer to assist the Government in the work of Legislation, but not to take part in its Executive business.

9. The Act also provided for the appointment of the Indian Law Commission to establish a uniform system of Judiciary, Police and Law in the Country.

10. No disability for holding the office, place or employment under the company was observed in respect of religion place of birth, descent or colour

The Act of Parliament of 1833, by which the Charter was renewed, contained so emphatic declaration in favour of the employment of Indians in their own land, irrespective of caste, colour or creed, as to be found in the clause which runs :

> "That no native of the said territories, nor any natural born subject shall by reason only of his religion, place of birth, descent, colour or any of these be disqualified, from holding any place, of his or employment, under the said Company".

These words are most noble and most worthy, ever legislatively recorded by a conquering power.

The Charter Act of 1833

The Articles 3, 4, 41, 51, 53, 81, 87, 103 and 105 also mentioned.

Anderson, had also taken pains to collect the Charter A.C. Banerjee has collected the Act as a whole as.

Charter Act of 1833

An Act of effecting an arrangement with the East India Company and for the better Government of His Majesty's Indian territories, till the 30th day of April, 1854.

3. Provided always, and be it enacted, that from and after the said 22nd day of April, 1834, the exclusive right of trading with the Dominions of the Emperor of China and of trading in tea, continued to the said Company by the said Act of 53rd year of King George the Third shall cease.

4. And be it enacted, that the said Company shall, with all convenient speed after the said 22nd day of April, 134, retain their commercial business.

19. And be it enacted, that it shall and may be lawful for his Majesty by any Letters Patent or by any Commission or Commissions to be issued under the Great Seal of Great Britain from time to time, to nominate, constitute, and appoint, during pleasure, such persons as His Majesty shall think fit to be and who shall accordingly be and styled Commissioners for the affairs of India; and every Enactment, Provision, Matter and thing relating to the Commissioners for the affairs of India in any other Act or Acts contained, so far as the same are in force and not repealed by or repugnant to this Act, shall be deemed ad taken to be applicable to the Commissioners to be nominated as aforesaid.

20. And be it enacted, that the Lord President of Council, the Lord Privy Seal, the First Lord of Treasury, the Principal Secretaries of State, the Chancellor of the Exchequer for the time-being shall, by virtue of their respective officers, be and they are hereby declared to be Commissioners for the affairs of India, in connection with the persons to be nominated in any such Commission aforesaid, and they shall have the same powers respectively, as if they had been expressly nominated in such Commission in the order in which they are herein mentioned, next after the Commissioner first named therein.

21. And be it enacted, that any two or more of the said Commissioners shall and may form a Board of executing the several powers which, by this Act, or by any other Act are or shall be given to or vested in the Commissioners for the affairs of India; and that the Commissioner first named in any such letters patent or Commission, for the time-being shall be the President of the said Board; and that when any Board shall be formed in the absence of the President, the Commissioner next in order of nomination in this Act or in the said Commission, of those who shall be present, shall for that turn preside the said Board.

22. And be it enacted, that if the Commissioners present at any Board shall be equally divided in opinion with respect to any matter by them discussed, then and no every such occasion the President, or in his absence the Commissioner acting as such shall have to voices or the casting vote.

25. And be it enacted, that the said Board shall have and be invested with full power and authority to superintend, direct, and control all Acts, Operations, and concerns of the said Company which in any wise relate to or concern the Government or Revenue of the said territories, or the property hereby vested in the said Company in Trust as aforesaid, and all grant of salaries, gratuities and allowances, and all other payment and charge whatever out of or upon the said revenues and property respectively, except as here in after is mentioned.

35. And be it enacted, that the said Court of Directors shall from time to time, appoint a Secret Committee, to consist of any number not exceeding three of the said Directors, for the particular purposes in this Act specified; which said Directors so appointed shall, before they or any of them shall act in the Execution of the power and.....hereby respond in them, take oath of the tenure following (that is to say),

> "I (A.B.) do swear, that I will, according to the best of my skill and Judgment faithfully execute the several trusts and powers resposed in me as a Member of Secret Committee appointed by the Court of Directors of the India Company; I will not disclose or make known any of the Secret Orders, Instructions, Dispatches, Official letters or Communications which shall be sent or given to me by the Commissioners for the affairs of India, save only to the other Members of the said Secret Committee, or to the person or person who shall be duly nominated and employed in transcribing or preparing the same respectively, unless I shall be authorised by the said Commissioners to disclose and make known the same. So help me GOD."

36. Provided also, and be it enacted, that if the said Board shall be of opinion that the subject-matter of any of their Deliberations concerning the levying war of making Peace, or treating or negotiating with any of the Native Princes or States, in India, or with any other Princes of States, of touching the Policy to be observed with respect to such Princes or States, intended to be communicated in Orders, Dispatches, Official

letters or Communications, to any of the Governments or Presidencies in India, or to any officers or servants of the said Company, shall be of a nature to require Secrecy, it shall and may be lawful for the said Board to send their orders, dispatches, Official letters or communications, to the secret Committee of the said Court of Directors to be appointed as is by this Act directed who shall thereupon, without disclosing the same, transmit the same according to the Tenor thereof, or pursuant to the Directions of the said Board, to the respective Governments and Presidencies' officers and servants; and that the said Government and Presidencies, officers and servants shall be bound to pay a faithful obedience thereto, in like manner as if such order, dispatches, Official letters or Communications had been sent to them by the said Court of Directors.

38. And be it enatced, that the Territories now subject to the Government of the Presidency of Fort William in Bengal shall be divided into two distinct Presidencies—one of such presidencies, in which shall be included Fort William aforesaid, to be styled the Presidency for Fort William in Bengal, and the other of such Presidencies to be styled as the Presidency of Agra; and that it shall be lawful for the said Court of Directors, under the control by this Act provided, and they are hereby required, to declare and appoint what part or parts of any of the territories under the Government of the said Company shall from time to time be subject to the Government of each of the several Presidencies now subsisting or to be established as aforesaid, and from time to time, as occasion may require, to revoke and alter, in the whole or in part, such appointment, and such new distribution of the same as shall be deemed expedient.

39. And be it enacted, that the Superintendence, Direction and Control of the whole Civil and Military Governments of all the said territories and Revenues in India shall be and is hereby vested in a Governor-General and Counsellors, to be styled "The Governor-general of India in Council.

40. And be it enacted, that there shall be four ordinary Members of the said Council, three of whom shall from time to

time, be appointed by said Court of Directors from amongst such persons as shall be or shall have been servants of the said Company; and each of the said three ordinary Members of Council shall at the time of his appointment have been in the service of the said Company for at least ten years; and if he shall be in the Military service of the said Company, he shall not during his continuance in office as a Member of Council hold any Military Command, or be employed in actual Military Duties, and that the Fourth Ordinary Member of Council shall from time to time be appointed from amongst persons who shall not be servants of the said Company by the said Court of (Agral). The arrangement proposed where was postponed by and Act of 1835, which provided for the appointment of a Lieutenant-Governor of the North-West Province.

Directors, subject to the approbation of His Majesty, to be signified in writing by His Royal Sign Manual, counter-signed by the President of the said Board; provided that such last mentioned Member of Council shall not be entitled to sit or vote in the said Council except at Meetings thereof for making Laws and Regulations; and it shall be lawful for the said Court of Directors to appoint the Commander-in-Chief of the Company's Forces in India, and if there shall be no such Commander-in-Chief, or the Offices of such Commander-in-Chief and of Governor-General of India shall be vested in the same person, then the Commander-in-Chief of the Forces on the Bengal Establishment to be an Extraordinary Member of the said Council, and such extraordinary Member of Council shall have rank and precedence at the Council Board next after the Governor-General.

41. And be it enacted, that the person who shall be Governor-General of the Presidency of Fort William in Bengal on the twenty-second day of April, one thousand eight hundred and thirty-four shall be the First Governor-General of India under this Act, and such persons as shall be Members of Council of the same Presidency on that day shall be respectively Members of the Council constituted by this Act.

42. And be it enacted, that all vacancies happening in the office of Governor-General of India shall from time to time be filled up by the said Court of Directors, subject to the approbation of His Majesty, to be signified in Writing by His Royal Sign Manual, countersigned by the President of the said Board.

43. And be it enacted, that the said Governor-General in Council shall have power to make Laws of Regulations for repealing, or altering any Laws or Regulations whatever, now in force or hereafter to be in force in the said territories or any part thereof, and to make Laws and Regulations for all persons, whether British or Native, Foreigners or others, and for all Courts of Justice, whether established by His Majesty's Charters or otherwise, and the jurisdictions thereof and for all places and things, whatsoever within and throughout the whole and every part of the said territories, and for all servants of the said Company within the dominions of Princes and states in alliance with the said Company; save and except that the said Governor-General in Council shall not have the power of making any Laws or Regulations which shall in any way repeal, vary, suspend, or affect any of the provisions of this Act, or any of the provisions of the Acts for punishing Mutiny and Desertion of officers and soldiers, whether in the service of His Majesty or the said Company, or any provisions of any act hereafter to be passed in any wise affecting the said Company or the said territories or the inhabitants thereof, or any Laws or Regulations which shall in any way affect any Prerogative of the Crown, or the authority of Parliament or the Constitutions or Rights of the said Company, or any part of the Unwritten Laws or Constitution of the United Kingdom of Great Britain and Ireland whereon may depend in any degree of allegiance of any person to the Crown of the United Kingdom, or the Sovereignty or Dominion of the Said Crown over any part of the said territories.

44. Provided always, and be it enacted, that in case the said Court of Directors, under such Control as by this Act is provided, shall signify to the said Governor-General in Council their disallowance of any laws or Regulations by the said

Governor-General in Council made, then and in every such case, upon receipt by the said Governor General in Council of notice of such disallowance, the said Governor-General in Council shall forthwith repeal all Laws and Regulations so disallowed.

45. Provided also, and be it enacted, that all Laws and Regulations made as aforesaid, so long as they shall remain unrepealted, shall be of the same force and effect within and throughout the said territories as any Act of Parliament would or ought the said territories as any Act of Parliament would or ought to be within the same territories, and shall be taken notice of by all Courts of Justice whatsoever within the same territories, in the same manner as any Public Act of Parliament would and ought to be taken notice of; and it shall not be necessary to register or publish in any Court of Justice, any Laws or Regulations made by the said Governor-General in Council.

46. Provided also, and be it enacted, that it shall not be lawful for the said Governor-General in Council, without the previous sanction of the said Court of Directors, to make any Law or Regulations whereby power shall be given to any Courts of Justice, other than the Court of Justice established His Majesty's Charters, to sentence to the punishment of death any of His Majesty's natural-born subjects born in Europe, or the children of such subjects, or which shall abolish any of the Court of Justice established by His Majesty's Charters.

47. And be it enacted, that the said Court of Directors shall forthwith submit for the approbation of the said Board, such Rules as they shall deem expedient for the Procedure of the Governor-General in Council in the discharge and exercise of all powers, functions and duties imposed on or vested in him any other Act or Acts; which Rules shall prescribe the Modes of Promulgation of any Laws or Regulations to be made by the said Governor-General in Council, and of the authentication of all Acts and Proceedings whatsoever of the said Governor-General in Council; and such Rules, when approved by the said Board of Commissioners, shall be of the same Force as if they had been inserted in this Act; provided always that such Rules shall be laid before both Houses of Parliament in—the Session next after the approval thereof.

48. Provided always, and be it enacted, that all Laws and Regulations shall be made at some Meeting of the Council at which the said Governor-General and at least three of the ordinary Members of Council shall be assembled, and that all other functions of the said Governor-General in Council may be exercised by the said Governor-General and one or more ordinary members of Council and that in every case of difference of opinion at Meetings of the said Council where there shall be an equality of voices the said Governor-General shall have two votes or the casting vote.

49. Provided always, and be it enacted, that when and so often as any measure shall be proposed before the said Governor-General in Council, whereby the safety, tranquillity or interests of the British possessions in India, or any part thereof, are or may be, in the Judgment of the said Governor-General, essentially affected and the said Governor-General shall be of opinion either that the measure so proposed ought to be adopted or carried into execution, or that the same ought to be suspended or wholly rejected, and the majority in Council then present, shall differ in and dissent from such opinion, the said Governor-General and Members of Council are hereby directed forthwith mutually to exchange with and communicate to each other in writing under their respective hands, to be recorded at large on their secret consultations, the grounds and reasons of their respective opinions, and if after considering the same the said Governor-General and the majority in Council shall still differ in opinion, it shall be lawful for the said Governor-General, of his own authority and on his own responsibility, to suspend or reject the measure so proposed in part or in whole, or to adopt and carry any measure so proposed into execution as the said Governor General shall think fit and expedient.

50. And be it enacted, that the said Council shall from time to time assemble at such place or place as shall be appointed by the said Governor-General in Council within the said territories, and that as often as the said Council shall assemble within any of the Presidencies of Fort St. George, Bombay, or

Agra, the Governor of such a Presidency shall act as an extraordinary Member of Council.

51. Provided always, and be it enacted, that nothing herein contained shall extend to affect in any way the Right of Parliament to make Laws for the said territories and for all the inhabitants thereof; and it is expressly declared that a full, complete, and constantly, existing right and power is intended to be reserved to Parliament to control, supersede, or prevent all proceedings, and Acts whatsoever of the said Governor-General in Council and to repeal and after at any time any Law or Regulations whatsoever made by the said Governor-General in Council and in all respects to legislate for the said territories and all the inhabitants thereof in as full and ample a manner as if this Act has not been passed; and the better to enable Parliament to exercise at all time such right and power, and Laws and Regulations made by the said Governor in Council shall be transmitted to England, and laid before both the Houses of Parliament, in the same manner as is now by Law provided concerning the Rules and Regulations made by the several Governments in India.

52. And be it enacted, that all Enactments, Provisions, matters, and things relating to the Governor-General of Fort William in Bengal in Council and the Governor-General of Fort William in Bengal alone, respectively, in any other Act or Acts contained, so far as the same are now in force, and not repealed by or repugnant to the provisions of this Act, shall continue and be in force and the applicable to the Governor-General of India in Council, and to the Governor-General of India alone, respectively.

56. And be it enacted, that the Executive Government of each of the several Presidencies of Fort William in Bengal, for St. George, Bombay and Agra shall be administered by a Governor and three Councillors, to be styled "The Governor in Council of the said Presidencies of Fort William in Bengal, Fort St. George, Bombay and Agra respectively and the said Governor and Councillors respectively of each such Presidency shall have the same rights and voices in their assemblies, and

shall observe the same order and course in their proceedings, as the Governors in Council of the Presidencies of Fort St. George and Bombay now have and observe, and that the Governor-General of India for the time-being shall be Governor of the Presidency of Fort William in Bengal.

57. Provided always, and be it enacted, that it shall and may be lawful for the said Court of Directors, under such control as is by this Act provided, to revoke and suspend, so often and for such periods as the said Court shall on their behalf direct, the appointment of Councils in all or any of the said Presidencies, or to reduce the number of Councillors in all or any of the said Councils and during such time as a council shall not be appointed in any such Presidency the Executive Government thereof shall be administered by a Governor alone.

58. And be it enacted, that several persons who on the said twenty-second day of April, one thousand eight hundred and thirty-four shall be Governors of the respective Presidencies of Fort St. George and Bombay, shall be the first Governor of the said Presidencies respectively under this Act and that the office of the Governor of the said Presidency of Agra, and all vacancies happening in the Offices of the Governors of the said Presidencies respectively, shall be filled up by the said Court of Directors, subject to ht approbation of His majesty, to be signified under His Royal Sign Manual, countersigned by the said President of the said Board of Commissioners.

For Fort Saint George, and Bombay, shall be the First Governors of the said Presidencies respectively, under this Act; and that the Office of Governor of the said Presidency of Agra, and all vacancies happening in the offices of the Governors of the said Presidencies respectively, shall be filled up by the said Court of Directors, subject to the approbation of His Majesty, to be signified under His Royal Sign Manual, countersigned by the said President of the said Board of Commissioners.

59. And be it enacted, that in the Presidencies, in which the appointment of a Council shall be suspended under the provision herein before contained, and during such time as

Councils shall not be appointed therein respectively, the Governors appointed under this Act, and in the Presidencies in which Councils shall from time to time be appointed, the said Governor, in their respective Councils, shall have all the rights, powers, duties, functions, and immunities whatsoever, not in any wise repugnant to this Act, which the Governors of Fort Saint George and Bombay, in their respective Councils now have within their respective Presidencies; and that the Governors and Members of Council of Presidencies appointed by or under this Act shall severally have all the rights, powers and immunities respectively, not in any wise repugnant to this Act, which the Governors and Members of Council of the Presidencies of Fort Saint George and Bombay respectively now have in their respective Presidencies; provided that no Governor or Governor-in-Council shall have the power of making or suspending any Regulations or Laws in any case whatever, unless in cases of urgent necessity (the burden of the proof whereof shall be on such Governor or Governor-in-Council), and then only until the decision of the Governor-General of India in Council shall be signified thereon; and provided also, that no Governor or Governor in Council shall have the power of creating any new office, or granting any salary, gratuity, or allowance, without the previous sanction of the Governor-General of India in Council.

60. Provided always, and be it enacted, that when and so often as the said Court of Directors shall neglect for the space of two calendar months, to be computed from the day whereon the Notification of the vacancy of any office or employment, in India in the appointment of the said Court shall have been received by the said Court, to supply such vacancy, then, and in every such case, it shall be lawful for His Majesty to appoint by writing under his Sign Manual, such person as His Majesty shall think proper to supply such vacancy; and that every person so appointed shall have the same powers, privileges, and authorities as if he or they had been appointed by the said Court, and shall not be subject to removal or dismissal without the approbation and consent of His majesty.

61. And be it enacted, that it shall be lawful for the said Court of Directors to appoint any person or persons provisionally to succeed to any of the offices aforesaid, for supplying any vacancy or vacancies therein, when the same shall happen by the death or resignation of the person or persons holding the same office or offices respectively, or on his or their departure from India with intent to return to Europe or on any event or contingency expressed in any such provisional appointment or appointments to the same respectively, and such appointments again to revoke, provided that every provisional appointment to the several offices of Governor-General of India, Governor of a Presidency, and the Member of Council of India, by this Act directed to be appointed from amongst persons who shall not be servants of the said company, shall be subject to he approbation of His Majesty, to be signified as aforesaid, but that no person so appointed to succeed provisionally to any of the said offices shall be entitled to any authority, salary or emolument appertaining thereto until he shall be in the actual possession of such office.

62. And be it enacted, that if any vacancy shall happen in the office of Governor-General of India when no provisional or other successor shall be upon the spot to supply such vacancy, then and in every such case the ordinary Member of Council next in rank to the said Governor-General shall hold and execute the said office of Governor-General of India and Governor of the Presidency of Fort William in Bengal until a successor shall arrive, or until some other person on the spot shall be duly appointed thereto; and that every such acting Governor-General shall, during the time of his continuing to act as such, have and exercise all the rights and powers of Governor-General of India, and shall be entitled to receive the emoluments and advantages appertaining to the office by him supplied, such acting Governor-General foregoing his salary and allowance of a Member of Council for the same Period.

63. And be it enacted, that if any vacancy shall happen in the office of Governor of Fort Saint George, Bombay, or Agra, when no provisional or other successor shall be upon the spot

to supply such vacancy, then and in every such case, if there shall be a Council in the Presidency in which such vacancy shall happen, the Member of such Council, who shall be next in rank to the Governor, other than the Commander-in-Chief of Officer Commanding the Forces of such Presidency, and if there shall be no Council, then the Secretary of Government of the said Presidency who shall be senior in the said office of Secretary, shall hold and execute the said office of Governor until a successor shall arrive, or until some other person on the spot shall be duly appointed thereto; and that every such acting Governor shall, during the time of his continuing to act as such, receive and be entitled to the emoluments and advantages appertaining to the office by him supplied, such acting Governor foregoing all salaries and allowances by him held and enjoyed at the time of his being called to supply such office.

64. And be it enacted, that if any vacancy shall happen in the office of an ordinary Member of Council of India when no person provisionally or otherwise appointed to succeed thereto shall be then present on the spot, then and on every such occasion such vacancy shall be supplied by the appointment of the Governor-General-in-Council, and if any vacancy shall happen in the office of a Member of Council of any Presidency when no person provisionally or otherwise appointed to succeed thereto shall be then present on the spot, then and on every such occasion such vacancy shall be supplied by the appointment of the Governor-in-Council of the Presidency in which such vacancy shall happen, and until a successor shall arrive the person so nominated shall execute the office by him supplied, and shall have all the powers thereof, and shall have and be entitled to the salary and other emoluments and advantages appertaining of the said office during his continuance therein, every such temporary Member of Council foregoing all salaries and allowances by him held and enjoyed at the time of his being appointed to such office : provided always, that no person shall be appointed a temporary Member of Council who might not have been appointed by the said Court of Directors to fill the vacancy supplied by such temporary appointment.

65. And be it further enacted, that the said Governor-General in Council shall have and be invested by virtue of this Act with full power and authority to superintend and control the Governors and Governors-in-Council of Fort William in Bengal, Fort Saint George, Bombay and Agra, in all points relating to the Civil or Military Administration of the said Presidencies respectively, and the said Governors and Governor-in-Council shall be bound to obey such orders and instructions of the said Governor-General-in-Council in all cases whatsoever.

66. And be it enacted, that is shall and may be lawful for the Governors or Governors-in-Council of Fort William in Bengal, Fort Saint George, Bombay, and Agra respectively, to propose to the said Governor-General-in-Council, Drafts or projects of any Laws or Regulations which the said Governors or Governors-in-Council respectively, may think expedient, together with their reasons for proposing the same; and the said Governor-General-in-Council is hereby required to take the same and such reasons into consideration, and to communicate the Resolutions of the said Governor-General-in-Council thereon, the Governor or Governor-in-Council by whom the same shall have been proposed.

67. And be it enacted, that when the said Governor General shall visit any of the Presidencies of Fort Saint George, Bombay or Agra, the powers of the Governors of those Presidencies respectively, shall not by reason of such visit be suspended.

68. And be it enacted, that the said Governors and Governors-in-Council of the said Presidencies of Fort William in Bengal, Fort Saint George, Bombay, and Agra respectively shall and they are hereby respectively required regularly to transmit to the said Governor General-in-Council true and exact copies of all such Orders and Acts of their respective Governments, and also advice and intelligence of all transactions and matters which shall have come to their knowledge, and which they shall deem material to be communicated to the said Governor-General-in-Council as aforesaid, or as the said Governor-General-in-Council shall from time to time require.

69. And be it enacted, that it shall be lawful for the said Governor-General-in-Council, as often as the exigencies of the Public Service may appear to him to require, to appoint such one of the ordinary members of the said Council of India as he may think fit to be Deputy Governor of the said Presidency of Fort William in Bengal, and such Deputy Govenor shall be invested with all the powers and perform all the duties of the said Governor of the Presidency of Fort William in Bengal, but shall receive to additional salary by reason of such appointment.

70. And be it enacted, that whenever the said Governor-General-in-Council shall declare that it is expendient that the said Governor General shoud visit any part of India unaccompanied by any member or members of the Council of India, it shall be lawful for the said Governor-General-in-Council, previously to the departure of the said Governor-General, to nominate some member of the Council of India to be President of the Council, in whom during the absence of the said Governor-General from the said Presidency of Fort William in Bengal, the powers of the said Governor-General in Assemblies of the said Council shall be reposed; and it shall be lawful in every such case for the said Govenror-General-in-Council, by a Law or Regulation for that purpose to be made, to authorise the Governor-General alone to exercise all or any of the powers which might be exercised by the said Governor-General-in-Council except the power of making Laws or Regulations : provided always, that during the absence of the Governor-General no Law or Regulation shall be made by the said President and Council without the assent in writing of the said Governor General.

74. And be it enacted, that it shal be lawful for His Majesty, by any writing under His Sign Manual, counter-signed by the President of the said Board of Commissioners, to remove or dismiss any person holding any office, ekmployment or Commission, Civil or Military, under the said Company in India, and to vacate any appointment or Commission of any person to any such office or employment : provided that a copy of every such writing, attested by the said President, shall within

eight days after the same shall be signed by His Majesty be transmitted or delivered to the Chairman or Deputy Chairman of the said Company.

75. Provided always, and be it enacted, that nothing in this Act contained shall take away the power of the said Court of Directors to remove or dismiss any of the officers or servants of the said Company, but that the said Court shall and may at all times have full liberty to remove or dismiss any of such officers or servants at their will and pleasure; provided that any servant of the said Company appointed by His Majesty through the default of appointment by the said Court of Directors shall not be dismissed or removed without His Majesty's approbation, as here in before is mentioned.

76. And be it enacted, that there shall be paid to the several officers here in after named the several salaries set against the names of such officers, subject to such reduction of the said several salaries respectively as the said Court of Directors, with the Sanction of the said Board, may at any time think fit : (that is to say).

To the Governor General of India,
two hundred and forty thousand sicca rupees :
To each ordinary Member of the Council of India,
ninety-six thousand sicca rupees.
To each Governor of the Presidencies of Fort Saint George, Bombay, and Agra,
one hundred and twenty thousand sicca rupees.
To each member of any Council to be appointed in any Presidency,

sixty thousand sicca rupees :

And the salaries of the said officers respectively shall commence from their respectively taking upon them the execution of their respective offices, and the said salaries shall be the while profit or advantage which the said officers shall enjoy during their continuance in such offices respectively and it shall be and it is hereby declared to be a misdemeanour for any such officers to accept for his own user, in the discharge of his office, any present, gift, donation, gratuity or reward, pecuniary or otherwise whatsoever, or to trade or traffic for his own benefit or for the benefit of any other person or persons whatsoever; and the said Court of Directors are hereby required to pay to all and singular the officers and persons here in after named who shall be residents in the United Kingdom at the time of their respective appointments, for the purpose of defraying the expenses of their equipment and voyage, such sums of money as are set against the names of such officers and persons respectively; (that is to say),

To the Governor General,
five thousand pounds,
To each Member of the Council of India,
one thousand two hundred pounds

To each Governor of the Presidencies of Fort Saint George, Bombay and Agra, two thousand five hundred pounds.

Provided also, that any Governor-Genéral, Governor or Member of Council appointed by or by virtue of this Act, who shall at the time of passsign this Act hold the office of Governor-General, Governor, or Member of Council respectively shall receive the same salary and allowances that he would have received the same salary and allowances that he would have received if this Act had not been passed.

77. Provided always, and be it enacted, that if any Governor-General, Governor, or ordinary Member of the Council of India, or any Member of the Council of any Presidency, shall hold or enjoy any pension, salary, or any place, office, or employment or profit under the Crown or any public office of the said Company, or any annuity payable out of the Civil or Military Fund of the said Company, the salary of his office of the Governor-General of India, Governor or Member of Council, shall be reduced by the amount of the pension, salary, annuity, or profits or office so respectively held or enjoyed by him.

78. And be it enacted, that the said Court of Directors, with the approbation of the said Board of Commissioners, shall and

may from time to time make Regulations for the division and distribution of the patronage and power of nomination of and to the offices, commands and employments in the said territories, and in all or any of the Presidencies thereof, among the said Governor-General-in-Council, Governor-General, Governors-in-Council, Governors, Commander-in-Chief and other Commanding Officers respectively appointed or to be appointed under this Act.

79. And be it enacted, that the return to Europe or the departure from India with intent to return to Europe of any Governor-General of India, Governor, Member of Council or of Commander-in-Chief, shall be deemed in Law, a Resignation and avoidance of his office or employment, and that no Act or Declaration of any Governor-General, or Governor, or member of Council, other than as aforesaid, excepting a Declaration in writing under Hand and Seal, delivered to the Secretary for the Public Department of the presidency wherein he shall be, in order to its being recorded, shall be deemed or held as a resignation or surrender of his said Office; and that the salary and other allowances of any such Governor-General or other officer respectively shall cease from the day of such of his departure, resignation, or surrender; and that if any such Governor-General or Member of Council of India shall leave the said territories, or if any Governor or other officer whatever in the service of the said Company shall leave the Presidency to which he shall belong, other than in the known actual service of the said Company, the salary and allowances, appertaining to his office shall not be paid or payable during his absence to any agent or other person for his use; and in the event of his not returning, or of his coming to Europe, his salary and allowances shall be deemed to have ceased on the day of his leaving the said territories, or the Presidency to which he may have belonged; provided that in shall be lawful for the said Company to make such payment as is now by law permitted to be made to the Representatives of their officers or servants who, having left their stations intending to return thereto, shall die during their absence.

80. And be it enacted, that every wilful disobeying and every wilful omitting, forbearing, or neglecting to execute the Orders or Instructions of the said Court of Directors by any Governor-General of India, Governor, Member of Council, or Commander-in-Chief, or by any other of the officers or servants of the said Company, unless in cases of necessity (the burden of the proof of which necessity shall be on the person so disobeying or omitting, forbearing or neglecting, to execute such orders or instructions as aforesaid); any every wilful breach of the trust and duty of any office or employment by any such Governor-General, Governor, Member or Council, or Commander-in-Chief, or any of the officers of servants of the said Company shall be deemed and taken to be a misdemeanour at Law, and shall or may be proceeded against and punished as such by virtue of this Act.

87. And be it enacted, that no native of the said territories, nor any natural-born subject of His majesty resident therein, shall, by reason only of his religion, place or birth, descent, colour, or any of the, be disabled from holding any place, office, or employment under the said Company.

109. And be it enacted, that every power, authority, and function by this or any other Act or Acts given to and vested in the said Court of Directors shall be deemed and taken to be subject to such control of the said Board of Commissioners as in this Act is mentioned, unless there shall be something in the enactments conferring such powers, authorities, or functions inconsistent with such construction, and except as to any patronage or right of appointing to office vested in or reserved to the said Court.

110. Provided always, and be it enacted, that nothing here in contained shall be construed to enable the said Board of Commissioners to give or cause to be given directions ordering or authorizing the payment of any extraordinary, allowance or gratuity, or increase of any established salary, allowance, or emolument, unless in the cases and subject to the provisions in and subject to which such directions may now be given by the said Board, or to increase the sum now payable by the said

Company on account of the said Board, except only by such salaries or allowances as shall be payable to the officers to be appointed as here in before is mentioned to attend upon the said Board during the winding up of the commercial business of the said Company.

115. And be it enacted, that it shall be lawful for any Court of Justice established by His Majesty's Charters in the said territories to approve, admit and enroll persons as Barristers, advocates and attorneys in such Court without any license from the said Company, anything in any such Charter contained the contrary not with standing : Provided always, that the being entitled to practices as an advocate in the principal courts of Scotland is and shall be deemed and taken to be a qualification for admission as an advocate in any Court in India equal to that of having been called to the Bar in England or Ireland.

116. And be it further enacted, that the Court of Directors of the said Company shall, within the first fourteen sitting days next after the first day of May in every year, lay before both Houses of Parliament an account made up according to the latest advices which shall have been received, of the annual produce of the revenues of the said territories in India, distinguishing the same and the respective heads thereof at each or their several Presidencies or settlements, of all their annual receipts and disbursements at home.

Thus ends the Charter of 1833, in the time of Lord William Bentinck.

(b) The New Outlooking and the Policy towards the Indian People—

Board tendencies of thought can be distinguished in the discussions of the Indian policy during the years 1831 to 1833 A.D.

Had these Acts been acted upon the condition of the great Country would have been quite different.

The English remained responsible for these accounts, especially for the welfare of the vast multitude of its inhabitants, for which they had kept no account and there was no one to call upon the account, but it is better to record here that India could derive great advantage from the men of talent and science and art or the affairs to settle in India by this act of 1833.

Mr. Rickards said,

> "But the presences of such men, is not enough. A people in a state of confirmed and degraded poverty cannot, I apprehend, be roused to energetic habits by mere stimulus of foreign example, on this account, I think that our first attention, should as well as in common justice, as in policy, be directed to the improvement of the State and conditions of the natives of that country".

These are the Tories or Conservatives' view, as they recommended the extreme caution but they were impressed by the value and strength of the Indian institutions. They desired to work for the welfare of the Indians but with great care. H.H. Wilson, who wrote the History of British India, was the great exponent of this view.

The second school which desired to change the atmosphere in the Indian outlook was of liberal Tory.

Metcalf, Munro, Malcolm, Elphistone belonged to this school. They all worked with various degrees and with various shades of opinion. They also accepted the improvements in Western ideas and Western outlook. It is seen in the lines of Sir Malcolm :

> "Let us proceed on the course of gradual improvement and when our rule ceases, as it cease must, though probably a remote period, as the natural consequences, of our success in diffusion of knowledge, we shall as a nation have the proud boast that we have performed the civilization to the continued subject of India, when our power is gone, our name will be recovered for we shall leave a moral movement more noble and imperishable than the hand of men ever constructed".

The third school of thought may be called the Radicals with Nationalist and religious wings.

Bentham and James Mill were most influential nationalists and with Macaulay and William Bentinck as followers.

The light of reason was raised and transferred to India during these years.

Blessed with far more than ordinary measure of political liberty and intellectual light, we are to a race, debased by three thousand of despotism, and priestcraft. We are free we are civilized to little purpose, if we grudge to any portion of the human race, equal measure of freedom, and civilization."

Are we to keep the people ignorant in order that we may keep them submissive, or do we think that we can give them knowledge without awakening ambition, or do we mean to awaken ambition and to provide it with no legitimate event?

Yet one of them must be answered with affirmative by everyone who maintains that to exclude the natives from high office.

These all Schools influenced the opinion at large in the Parliament, and in the Court of Directors.

These groups in thought and in speech in planned manner helped the outlook in India.

They realised that any change which takes place in India, and in the Indian society, must be taken on the Westernised direction, because India's march of culture was static.

The Western system was a great help of India. Macaulay said,

> "We shall never consent to administer the pausta to the whole community to stupefy and paralyse a great people whom God has committed to our charge for the wretched purpose of rendering them more amenable to control. What is power worth, if it is founded on vice, on ignorance, on misery, if we hold it only by violating the most sacred

duties, which as Governors we owe to the governed, and which as people..."

The New Awakening in Indians was followed by the Western Education and Liberty of Press.

The systematic employment of the Indians in Administrative, Judicial, and other high offices was rendered necessary which drew the Indians closer to the European though and to the civilization of modern times.

The important principle did not lose the right even in the view of the Lord William Bentinck, that the Indians should be governed for the benefit of Indians.

REFERENCES

1. W.A.R. Archibold—Outlines of Constitutional History of India, (1926), p. 97.
2. Parliamentary Papers, House of Commons, Public Bills, Vol. II, The East India Company. C.H. Philips, pp. 287-94.
3. A.C. Banerjee—Indian Constitutional Documents, pp. 175-96. Hansard 3rd Series, XIX, 1833, p. 163.
4. Grover—Studies in Modern History, p. 344.
5. Anderson and Subedar—The Development of an Indian Policy, (1921), 1818-58, pp. 25-28.
6. Hansard Series—Parliamentary Debates, Vol. XVIII, 1833.
7. C.H. Philip—The East India Company, 1784-1834, p. 297.
8. *Ibid.*, p. 277.
9. *Ibid.*, p. 278.
10. Hansard Parliamentary History—3rd Series, XVII, 1833. p. 741.
11. Hansard Parliamentary History—3rd Series, Vol. XIX, pp. 504, 506, 513, 516.
12. A.C. Banerjee—Indian Constitutional Document, Vol. I, p. 200.
13. William Digby—Prosperous British India, pp. 62-63.
14. B.B. Mishra—The Central Administration of the East India Company, 1773-1834, p. 55.

11 AS A MAN

A full evaluation of Rammohun as a man[1] will remain incomplete even on taking into account his mental, physical and emotional qualities, for he had a personality which played a very important part in all matters. Undoubtedly one would be much impressed by recounting the events and happenings in his life which brought to focus his kindness and nobility, catholicity, decency and decorum, sense of prestige, sympathy for the distressed, conviction, simplicity and fearlessness.

Rammohun showed his noble heart when he excused his nephew Govindaprasad (Jugmohun's son) who dragged him into litigations. Govindaprasad was instigated by Rammohun's mother who wanted to punish her son for his apostasy. Govindprasad was also supported, apart from his desire for financial gains, by other parties : by some people who felt cornered by being put at a disadvantage by Rammohun's position in the courts and elsewhere, by others including Europeans who took the view that in their religious beliefs Rammohun was an intruder by what he wrote about Christianity. Rammohun's kindness to Govindaprasad went further for he got him appointed in the offices of the East India Company. And Rajaram (reared by Rammohun from childhood to youth) was another instance of Rammohun's kind heart. Rajaram was an orphan boy handed over to Rammohun by one Mr. Dick (East India Company's civilian) from bringing him up. His kindness became more intense as the boy fully responded and also followed Rammohun's mode of living.

Rammohun's catholicity of heart is evident for, in spite of his own strong views he allowed his son Radhaprasad to grow in his own ways and never put any pressure to change them; Rammohun did not interfere even when Radhaprasad showed indifference or opposition to his father's convictions. The available record, however, indicate that as Radhaprasad grew in years he began to realise his father's high ideals, catholic and progressive views. Rammohun also showed more and more attachment for Radhaprasad, as will be evident from the serious attention he gave to bring his son out of the litigations into which he was dragged wrongly, according to Rammohun. He passed through an unusual mental depression caused by these forced involvements as he was convinced that these[2] were clear cases of conspiracy between some corrupt men working in the courts and some fairly-high officers both European and Indian.

An instance of Rammohun's decency and decorum as recorded below by a young lady of London society may be narrated here since it took place in her own house :

> At a small evening party at my house in Grenville Street, principally to met the Rajah, he referred to the doctrine of original sin, in a way that started a lady of low church, a very charming and amiable woman, who had brought her daughter, 'But surely Sir', she exclaimed, 'you do believe in original sin? He looked at her, and she blushed deeply. After a minute, he seemed to comprehended the whole, and very gently inclining, he said, 'I believe it is a doctrine, which, in many well-regulated minds has tended to promote humility, the first of Christian virtues : for my own part I have never been able to see the evidence of it.' The next morning my sweet friend called to apologise for what she had said, and added that she had never seen or heard anything so beautiful as this in society.

Another such instance of decency and courtesy deserves notice for it extended to even his family members. From what Hemalata Devi (the great grand-daughter of Rammohun who married into the Jorasanko Tagore family) had heard, she wrote the following :

> Three chairs used to be placed, two for the wives and one for himself. Rajah would not sit until and wives were

seated. In that again, it was a curious sight, the attendants and other domestic inmates used to peep through windows and used to whisper pointing at them and saying "Look, look, the Karta-Dewanji is standing and would not sit until the ladies took their seats.

Rammohun was a straight-forward and fearless man and he did not hesitate to assert his rights as a citizen where necessary. The Bhagalpur (Bihar) incident of 1809 is a clear instance of this. He was then hardly known outside Bengal and yet had the courage not to let go unchallenged the insolence of high official of the ruling class, a senior civilian who happened to be the District Magistrate of Bhagalpur.

Rammohun's sense of prestige was evident from what has come down to us as his tacit understanding with Digby and Woodford that he would not be treated as an ordinary subordinate and that he would not be kept standing, specially before officials. This understanding was well observed, as there grew a deep mutual respect between them which developed into intimate friendship. As Rammohun worked with Digby for a much longer period, Digby became more intimate with him and after Digby's death, his relations with Woodford family deepened.

Another remarkable story about Rammohun's sense of prestige and self-respect which is still current is that when Lord Bentinck was going to take the final decision about stopping the *Suttee* practice, he sent his secretary to Rammohun for the latter to see him. As the story goes, when the secretary told Rammohun, "His Excellency the Governor-General Lord Bentick has desired you to meet him in the Government House", Rammohun reacted sharply and said gingerly : "I have now given up all worldly avocations and am engaged in religious and cultural work and thought. Kindly express my humble respects to the Governor-General and inform him that I have no inclination to appear before his august presence and therefore I hope that he will kindly pardon me." When the secretary reported this to Lord Bentinck, the latter asked : "What exactly did you say to Rammohun?" On hearing what had happened Bentinck understood and told the secretary : " Please go again and tell him that Mr. William Bentinck would be glad to see him." On hearing this, Rammohun relented and got ready to go. This may be an apocryphical version but brings out the sense of dignity of the man and also Bentinck's greatness.

That Rammohun was true to his conviction would be evident from what took place at his last meetings with his mother just prior to her departure for Srikhetra (Puri). Both of them stood on their respective grounds. His mother asked for financial endowment for the maintenance of the family-deity but Rammohun declined to support this practice, though he offered her monetary donation for the service of the poor and the distressed. His mother was not interested in this and she rejected the offer sternly. One other occasion which again showed his strength of conviction was his dissociation from the solemnisation of the marriage of his grand-daughter (Radhaprasad's daughter Chandrajyoti) because the ceremony was done according to strict Hindu rites with *Salgram-sila* a stone representing the deity. Rammohun who was excommunicated in his village abstained from witnessing the marriage in such a form but he did not choose to interfere either with Radhaprasad's or his wife's inner conviction. Radhaprasad's daughter Chandrajyoti later described[3] her marriage in writings.

In a case of public importance, his boldness was shown in his public protest against the suppression of Press liberty. How deep was the impression that was created in England by his famous representation to the King of England has been recorded as below in Turton's speech on the first anniversary of death of Rammohun Roy :

> A very short time after my arrival in this country, an Act was passed by the Govt, which met with the general reprobation of those who were governed; but no one came forward with the manliness and boldness that Rammohun did to express his sentiments on the odious measures. A man born and bred in Britain could not have come forward more completely heart and soul in support of that which

> was the cause of his country, than Rammohun did in 1823. I than made his acquaintance in the first instance and was surprised, delighted to see an inordinate love of liberty in a man reared and bred in the spirit of dependence, if dependence could exist in such a mind;—I should deem this the happiest and proudest moment of my life.

In this connection, Rammohun asked Prince Dwarkanath Tagore to obtain signatures for the above protest, but the latter having failed, stated :

> ....But none of the natives could I prevail upon to join me and I believe it was though, I should be hanged the next day for my boldness.

Rammohun's dignified bearing and power of restraint, even under the worst provocation, were shown in the case of Baptist Missionaries' attack on Hindu scriptures on the polemical discussions on *Precepts of Jesus*. Rammohun controlled himself and kept his temper cool when he was called a "heathen". This restraint was praiseworthy. In a combat of arguments in Sanskrit between Rammohun and Subrahmanya Sastri, the former showed, all along his arguments, the utmost courtesy and civility as he showed in replying to the provocative and vituperative language of, particularly, Mrityunjoy Vidyalankar who, although a learned Pandit and a highly respected man in the conservative section of the Bengali Hindu community, allowed himself to become the mouthpiece of the arrogant and misinformed missionaries who were then trying to belittle Vedanta and Upanishads. Men like Gourisankar Bhattacharya, Bhabanicharan Bandopadhaya and others used course language, offensively slang terms, and spread the most filthy calumny against Rammohun. Still, Rammohun was cool in his replies.

Rammohun's philanthropy and large-heartedness were well-known. He made free distribution of books including the most valuable translations of Vedanta and Upanishads. He wanted to place before every Indian the current picture of Hindu religion as depicted in Vedanta. His financial donations extended to the Unitarian Association, Unitarian Chapel and the Unitarian Press also. His donations to the construction of Brohmo Mandir and the wide range of his humanitarian work were well known.

An outstanding example of his simplicity was the incident recorded in Fanny Kimble's[4] Diary on December 22, 1832 :

> In the evening the play was 'Isabella', the house very full; I played very well. The Rajah Rammohun Roy was in the Duke of Devonshire's box, and went into fits of crying, poor man.

"Isabella", above quoted, could not have been a play. It is very likely that Isabella was the character of Shakespeare's *Measure for Measure* who was put in very pitiable situations with two sentries on her either side. Witnessing that helpless situation, Rammohun sobbed like a child.

Rammohun's sympathy for the womenfolk[5] of his own society is worth a special mention. The worst case was that of women who were denied education and were yet subjected to slights for lack of it. This impelled him to agitate actively to secure for them proper education so that they could acquire the capacity to manage their husbands' property after their death. Also widows' legitimate shares of their husbands' property were ably discussed by Rammohun in separate tracts.[6]

Rammohun's Intellectual Acquisitions

Rammohun's extensive knowledge of history, literature, philosophy, science, explorations, commerce of different nations and Christian scriptures in particular, was acquired by being in constant touch with Digby's collection of books which contained the Works of Gibbon, Hume, & Voltaire, Bruce's *Annals*, Anderson's *History of Commerce* (in McPherson's Annals), Sir Thomas Roe's *Journal and Letters,* Raynal's *East and West Indies, Orem's Historical Fragments,* Dow's *History,* Malcolm's *Sketch of the Political History of India and Central India, Mill's History of British India, etc.* Rammohun's wide range of studies has been stressed by Nag and Burman in their Preface to *The Precepts of Jesus* :

Rammohun startled his contemporaries by his voluminous writings on Christian theology and by showing his capacity to handle effectively not only the English Bible but the Latin Vulgate or the New Testament as translated by St. Jerome (331-420 A.D.) who left Rome and completed the Latin translation of the New Testament in Bethleham, the native village of Jesus. Trinitarian Christianity was politely reminded by Rammohun of the vast Unitarian Hebrew scripture, the Old Testament, which was translated from Hebrew into Greek and emerged as the Septuagint in the Court of Ptolemy Philadelphys to whom our Emperor Asoka sent his missionaries near about 250 B.C. Why and how did Rammohun drift away from English and Latin Bibles to tackle the Greek and the Hebrew Bibles as well is a problem of capital importance which some future holder of a Rammohun-chair of Comparative Religion should solve.

Rammohun's Study of Three Religions—Hinduism, Christianity and Islam—and Laying the Foundation of Study of Comparative Religion

Rammohun studied the Vedas, Brohmo-sutras, Vedanta, Upanishads, Bhagwatgita, Smriti, Puranas and all systems of Hindu philosophy in order to have a full comprehension of Hindu thought in its long procession from the earliest times. He did not give much importance to the Brahmanas, Samhitas and the Puranas, but stressed the Upanishads of which the five important Vedic Upanishads (Upanishads whose origin is traceable to the Vedas) he himself translated.

Rammohun learnt Persian and Arabic assiduously and with their help studied Koran, Hadis and Shariat. He was well acquainted with the thoughts of the rationalists, Mutazilites, Suffis and, it is said, with the polemic literatures of all the sixty-three schools of Muslim theology.

Rammohun studied the Bible very thoroughly. Deeply impressed by the precepts of Jesus, he commended them to his readers while rejecting miracles and the concept of the divinity of Christ. This led to controversies, with missionaries in particular. He went deeper into these with the help of Hebrew, Greek and Syriac languages, mastering a wide range of subjects including the Old Testament, New Testament, Talmud, Tarjuma and Syriac versions of the scriptures. He was acquainted also with Volney, Tom Paine among others and with the scientific strain in European thought from Bacon to Newton.

Having gone deep into the study of these major religious and having compared them, he became the first man to lay the foundation of the science of Comparative Religion. To strengthen his theological concepts, he went into the origin and development not only of the Christian dogma with special reference to the Arian, the Sebeilian and Pelagian controversies but also the movement of liberal thought and ethical rationalism in the Rabbinical writings of the first century before Christ, especially with reference to the Tarjuma of Jonathan and Hilel. The highest and the best in Semitic culture in both Hebraic and Arabic traditions went to enrich Rammohun's mind. The study of these religions, at that time, was a stupendous achievement and established, beyond doubt, Rammohun's intellectual range stamina and sympathy as well as his understanding and constructive approach, all of which have contributed to make him the builder of Modern India.

Rammohun's Efforts to Improve Administration

He made extensive studies of whatever materials were available in the records and, with his experiences in different fields, wrote on the following :

1. Introduction of Indian Judicial Assessors;
2. Introduction of the System of Joint Judges;
3. Maintenance of Regular Public Registers;
4. Introduction of Trial by Jury;
5. Codification of Civil Law;
6. Codification of Criminal Law;
7. Reform in the Tenure of land;

8. Reform in the Rate of Rent;
9. Reform in the Title to land;
10. Reform in the Revenue System;
11. Improvements of the Condition of people and peasants.

Rammohun's Efforts in Finer Arts (Music)

Rammohun's poems breathe the atmosphere of devotion and they are the ontological expression of his devotional conviction and inner feelings. They do not, however, bear much literary value. His contribution was to Brohmo-Sangeet, in Bengali, probably the earliest. As a matter of fact, it will be more appropriate to take these poems as vehicles for classical music in Bengali, if these were set to classical tunes. It is not widely known that Rammohun was a lover of classical music and that he was also well acquainted with Nidhu Gupta around 1795-97 at Calcutta or Burdwan. Nidhu Gupta (1771-1828) who lived in Bihar for eighteen years was exponent of classical music particularly 'Tappa'. Rammohun took interest in knowing the musicians personally and knew the great kali Mirza (of Guptipara) who travelled all over northern India, learning classical music and giving demonstrations of his own. Rammohun is said to have come in contact with Kali Mirza when the latter was old. In Bengal there were, at that time, two other important masters of classical music : (1) Raghunath Roy of Burdwan who, as the court musician, having the opportunity to meet masters from other parts of India, became a leading exponent in Khayal; (2) Ramsankar Bhattacharjee[7] of Bishnupur. According to some Rammohun, during his many visits to Burdwan, met Raghunath Roy.

Rammohun's Legal Proficiency

Rammohun's acquaintance with English and Scottish laws in certain matters shows his legal acumen. In his essay on the *Rights of Hindus over Ancestral property according to the Law of Bengal* (written in 1830), he tried to bring out the differences between the Laws of legitimacy in England and Scotland and with the peculiarities of the Gavelkind tenure of Kent, showing his extensive interest. In this tract he argued with extraordinary ability against a Supreme Court decision denying to the Dayahbhag father the right of free disposition of ancestral immovables. This paper was presumed to have been written by Rammohun as a comment on the judgment of Sir Hyde East to limit the power of the Hindus in respect of alienation of ancestral property. In this connection Rammohun suggested a legal maxim that what is considered immoral should be made invalid.

For any ticklish point of law, he would go into the principles behind the law to seek clarification[8]. One feels fully justified in holding his as a jurist. His power of understanding, his quick grasp, his varied experiences and his extensive study, all contributed to his eminence in law. Whenever he was required to formulate a proposal or interpret an ambiguity, he invariably did so in a progressive and liberal spirit. He could be said to have been guided by the Benthamite principle—greatest good for the greatest number. Rammohun was a worthy successor to India's ancient law-givers like Jimutabahana (author of *Dayabhaga*), Vijnaneswara (author of *Mitakshara*), Raghunandan (author of *Smriti-tattwa*) and the commentators Srikrishna Tarkalankar and Jagannath.

Rammohun's Financial Stability

In 1845, long after Rammohun's death, Kissorichand Mitra wrote in the *Calcutta Gazette* an article in which he cast doubt on his rectitude by raising the question as to how he could manage to purchase big Calcutta houses and bear other expenses. This thought of illegal gratification is most unfortunate, for to quote Lenonard's *History of Brahmo Samaj*, "it is no great achievement to amass by frugality and thrift, a lakh of rupees after ten year's service, the value of a depended Taluk of Rs. 10,000, when others have been known by a service of half or a quarter of that time, to have made a provision of ten times that amount."

From the details given below, it will be seen that he had an annual income of at least Rs. 18,000 which, over a period of five years (1809-1814), would have added up to an amount sufficiently large to meet costs and other expenses including charities. It may be profitable to study the financial position to see how Rammohun met such expenditures as purchase of house properties in Calcutta, defence in the litigations, donations, running expenses of the schools started by him, publication of books and tracts (and their free distribution) besides family expenses. A rough estimate of his income from various sources is given below :

			Annual Income
1.	Taluks of Govindapur, Rameshwarpur	purchased in 1799.....Rs.	5500/-
2.	Taluks Langurpara, Srirampur, Beerlok, Krishnagar	purchased about 1809 before going to Rangpur....Rs.	6000/-
3.	Company's bond-business and money-ending business	............Rs.	5000/-
4.	Nayebship (1795 to 1798) for 4 years at father's Estate say Rs. 50/- p.m. (average)......Rs.		600/-
5.	Service with Woodford, Digby, etc. (1801-1814) for about 10 years, at say Rs. 75/ - to 100/ - p.m......................Rs.		1000/-

This income over a number of years together with other cash accumulations from sale of the Jorasanko house etc., gave him sufficient resources to meet the following :

Capital cost of Chowringhee House ...Rs. 20,000/- (roughly)

Capital cost of Simla House ......Rs. 13,000/-(roughly)

Capital cost of Maniktala House
(now at 113 Upper Circular Road)-

cost not known but estimated at ....Rs. 13,000/-(roughly)

(Jorasanko house—a gift from his father on 1-12-1796, was evidently sold out soon after he returned to Calcutta in 1815).

Rammohun As An Integrated Personality

As well put by Miss Collet, Rammohun was essentially a religious man devoted to the general amelioration of mankind around him. Although Rammohun was a Hindu, his heart flowed to all men irrespective of religious faith and denomination; yet being a Hindu, his first concern was to put his society and men on a higher and more rational level. He wanted social improvement for all—not only in their spiritual relation with the Supreme Being but also in relation to the State in which they lived. Thus though essentially religious, he did not exhaust himself by only discussing the scriptures and pointing out the noble concepts but supplementing them in daily life. He felt that by discarding the non-essentials, either of a religious concept or a mode of worship, men might be able to live a more useful social life bringing a greater amount of joy, more institutional activities and general happiness. This emphasis on religious life will be easily seen from Rammohun's daily routine of visiting churches, in England, of all denominations even though the then English social life did not call upon him for any help. Still Rammohun not only visited churches but also carried on endless discussions with the English churchmen. All this was due to the fact that he was entirely a religious man. And yet all his efforts were motivated by social reform.

The Three Maxims Rammohun used to follow :

1. The first, he expressed in an Arabic sentence "Insanabid'-ul-ihsan" ("Man is the slave of benefits")
2. The second, a couplet from Anwar Suheili : "The enjoyment of two worlds (this and the next) rests on these two points—kindness to friends, civility to enemies".
3. The third, from the philosopher Sa'di, which he often repeated and often expressed a wish to have inscribed, as the true way of serving God, on his tomb : "The "good to man".

(Sand ford Arnot in *Atheneum Journal*, London, 1833)

REFERENCES

1. An unjustifiable pre-arranged attack of some Bengali Hindu scholars on Rammohun has been exposed in an article which is quoted in Appendix iii of this book. The eminent literary writer Parimal Goswami gives an interesting account (see *Basumati*, Calcutta, Chaitra, 1378 B.S./1972) about how a group of well-known literary men and historians planned to tarnish the image of Rammohun (Mr. Goswami confirmed this in a recent interview with the author).

2. *(i)* The first case against Rammohun was filed in 1817 by Govindaprasad (son of the deceased Jugmohan) in the Equity Court claming a share in the property and earnings of Rammohun on the ground that they were living in joint family. Although they were joint in food only in all other property matters they were separate.

   (ii) Durga Devi, the surviving widow of Jugmohun (mother of Govindaprasad) brought a suit against Rammohun claiming the taluks Govindapur and Rameshwarpur. She stated that she lent Rammohun Rs. 4540 for the purchase of the taluks. Durga Devi failed to produce a single witness to prove her case. Durgadevi lost the case (Nov., 1821).

   (iii) In 1833, Raja of Burdwan claimed from Rammohun a sum of money about Rs. 15000 on the strength of a Bond given by Ramkanta on account of arrears of land revenue which was strictly due in 1797 but the Raja of Burdwan brought the suit 26 years later. The case, barred by limitation, was forced upon Rammohun (one case dismissed in 1830, one went in favour of Rammohun in 1831 and the third dismissed in 1831).

   (iv) A few brains worked together led by a notorious anonymous letter-writer Debnarain Bose, in which ultimately Radhaparsad was implicated in an alleged embezzlement from the Burdwan Treasury which was in the charge of Digby in 1822. This case ran for a considerable time with innumerable complications in which some cunning Indians, some interested Europeans, Burdwan Raj and other were implicated. The three Judges unanimously acquitted Radhaprasad by the end of 1826.

3. "The Raja arranged my marriage in Calcutta since it was not

possible to go to the village for this purpose, as he was treated as if he lost his brahmanical caste—the "Sampradan" (handing over the bride in marriage) ceremony was done not by the Raja-not by Radhaprasad but by son's wife-Jagneswari Devi-at the time of this most touching and sacred ceremony of 'Samoradan', the Raja was standing outside-away from the marriage pandal, alone and quiet. The marriage was celebrated in the usual current Hindu rites. As a result of Shyamlal Chattopadhya marrying Raja's grand-daughter, he could not return home in Murshidabad for fear of opposition by the village. After this marriage, Raja left for England. The Raja threw away, by the marriage, the traditional rites usually performed by the family-priest (Kulaguru) of centuries past, trained and taught the womenfolk of the home the Upasana by the Brohmo-mantra, and worship of Brohmo by Gayatri. We have heard with our own ears that Drabamoyee Devi, wife of the younger son Ramaprasad, reciting the slokas of Mahanirvan-Tantra, in invocation of Brohmo from the very early hours of the morning. She used to worship in full form by the Gayatri, that Gaytri, which at one time was even forbidden for the women to hear, that Gayatri, was ushered in the home, within the daily worship, for the first time; the door was flung open for the rightful possession and privilege of women to perform religious practices in the rightful way....It is difficult to think of a man in the entire human race who is endowed with the genius to fully realise and measure the greatness of this man Raja Rammohun Roy. Words cannot measure him, his work alone can give some indication of his superhuman contribution how the world has moved in fulfillment of Rammohun's ideals."

4. Fanny Kemble (1809-93) was much impressed by Rammohun who had presented her a copy of Kalidas's *Shakuntala* (Sir William Jones' translation in 1789, which brought him praise from even Goethe). Kemble also gifted him a copy of Shakespeare's *Merchant of Venice*. She was a niece of Sarah Siddons who created a great stir in English Theatre with Garrick. She was a woman of unusual talents, intellect and versatility, being a poet, dramatist, critic, musician and actress. In March 1832 she danced at Basil Montagu's house where Rammohun was present.

5. Rammohun made forceful observations on the apathy of the people of the country to educate the womenfolk, while in contrast ordinary men folk had the privilege and organised facilities for education. He then drew attention to the inferior treatment and in some case inhuman treatment meted out to the women and then remarked as follows :

   ......How then can you accuse them with want of understanding? If after instruction in knowledge and wisdom, a person cannot comprehend or retain what has been taught him, we may consider him as deficient; but as you keep women generally void of education and acquirements you cannot, therefore, in justice pronounce on their inferiority. On the contrary, Lilavati, Bhanumati, the wife of the Prince of Karnat, and that of Kalidas, are celebrated for their thorough knowledge of all the shastras...

   Secondly, you charge them with want of resolution, at which I feel exceedingly surprised; for we constantly perceive, in country where the name of death makes the male shudder, that the female, from her firmness of mind, offers to burn with the corpse of her deceased husband; and you accuse these women of deficiency in point of resolution.

   Thirdly, with regard to their trustworthiness, let us look minutely into the conduct of both sexes, and we may be enabled to ascertain which of them is the most frequently guilty of betraying friends....

   In the fourth place, with respect to their subjection to the passions, this may be judged of by the custom of marriage as to the respective sexes, for one man may marry two or three, sometimes even ten wives and upwards; while a woman, who marries but one husband, desires at his death to follow him, forsaking all worldly enjoyments, or to remain leading the austere life as an ascetic.

6. Tracts :

   (a) *Brief Remarks Regarding Modern Encroachments on the Ancient Right of Families according to the Hindu Law of Inheritance (1822).*

   (b) Essay on the Rights of Hindus over Ancestral Property according to the Law of Bengal (1832, published in England).

(c) *With an Appendix containing letters on the Hindu Law of Inheritance—(1832, published in England).*

7. Ramsankar Bhattacharjee of Bishnupur learnt Dhrupad under a famous classical musician of northern India who stopped at bishnupur on his way to Puri. It was this Ramsankar who made his own variations and established Bishnupur Gharana (tradition) in Dhrupad which was later on strengthened by Kshetramohon Goswami, Ramkeshab Bhattacharjee, etc. Another school of Dhrupad came from Benares in the midnineteenth century through Ganganarain Chattopadhyay whose famous disciple was Jadu Bhatta (See Dilip Kumar Mukhopadhyay : "Acharya Rammohaner Sangit Prasanga" in 'Prabasi' 1369, Agrahayan on wards).

8. See Rammohun Roy : Death Centenary Commemoration Volume—Article by Dr. N.C. Sengupta.

12 TRIBUTES : PLACE IN HISTORY

SONNET ON THE MEMORY OF THE RAJAH, RAMMOHUN ROY.

When from afar we saw thy burning light
Rise gloriously o'er India's darkened shore,
In spirit we rejoiced; and then still more
Rose high our admiration and delight,
When, steadfast to pursue thy course aright,
We saw thee brave fierce persecution's power.-
As yet we knew thee not,—but that blest hour
Which first disclosed thee to our longing sight,
Awakened in us deepest Christian love,
And told us thou hadst sat at Jesus' feet.
But now a glowing halo from above
Circles our thoughts of thee, when to the seat
Of mercy, rapt in ardent prayer, we come,
"Our Father! Lead Thy wandering children home!"

M.C. Bristol,

Sunday, October 27th, 1833.

One other tribute remained to be paid to the remains of this great man. Sacred as was the spot where he was laid, and requiring to those who knew and loved him no stone to mark the spot, beneath the overhanging trees, which their hearts reverenced,—yet it was right that the public should have access to his grave, and should see a befitting monument erected over it. This could not be done at Stapleton Grove, which had now passed out of the Castle family. The Rajah's friend, the celebrated *Dwarkanath Tagore*, desired to pay this mark of respect to his memory, and it was therefore arranged that the case containing the coffin should be removed to the beautiful cemetery of Arno's Vale, near Bristol. This was suitably accomplished on the 29th of May, 1843, and a handsome monument was erected in the spring of the year following by his friend, the enlightened and celebrated Dwarkanath Tagore. A visit was afterwards paid by him to the spot, and recently by his grandson, Satyendra Nath Tagore.

Dwarkanath Tagore died also in a strange land, but he lies in a gloomy cemetery in London, Kensal Green, and no tomb befitting his rank has been eracted to mark the sport. Surely his remains will be transferred to the spot where rests his noble friend!

Many of the country men of the illustrious Brahmin have already visited the spot where reposes all of him that is mortal, and doubtless all will fell what is beautifully expressed by one of them,—"The place where lies the funeral temple of Rajah Rammohun Roy is a sacred place for Hindu Pilgrims!" May such a pilgrimage rouse and stimulate those who undertake it to fresh exertions for their country. "The memory of such a man," writes another, "Must ever be dear to the Hindus; and it is the duty of those of our countrymen who can afford to visit England, not to return without paying their tribute of respect to the spot where rest the remains of that illustrious man. To perform this duty we have visited this famous city, which has the honour of possessing the mortal remains of Rammohun Roy. It was the good name of your revered and pious father which brought the Raja here, and it is that of the later again which has attracted us here; you can therefore imagine how greatly we must feel the satisfaction of having performed this pilgrimage (if I may so call it), with your kind assistance. We hope that the performance of this duty will stimulate our exertion, and help us on in following the paths of truth the righteousness. My great ambition in life is to be useful to my country, and to do good to others; it is this strong desire that has brought me to this part of the world, in order to seek knowledge, and the acquaintance of the great and the good. Our prayer is that God may give us the power, ability and knowledge, which we may devote to the service of our country. The performance of duty is its own reward, and though our exertions may not bear any fruit in our lifetime, the thought of having done our *duty* will be the greatest happiness to us. May God hasten the day when all strifes and party feelings will subside,—when sects and castes will merge into one, that of *humanity*,—when we shall cease to regard the English, the Hindu, and the Jew, as belonging to different nations,—and when we shall all sing, the

"Fatherhood of God and Brotherhood of Man."

FUNERAL SERMONS FOR THE RAJAH, RAMMOHUN ROY, BY REV. DR. CARPENTER, REV. ROBERT ASPLAND, REV. DR. DRUMMOND. REV. J. SCOTT PORTER AND REV. W.J. FOX.

It is probable that in many pulpits there were notices of the mournful event of the Rajah's death. The Rev. Dr. Kenney, of St. Olave's, Southwark, whose, ministry Rammohun Roy had Frequently attended, preached a funeral sermon for him at the request of his parishioners; he also wrote a letter to Mr. J. Hare expressive of his warm attachment to the Rajah and high appreciation of his character. Five sermons were printed, and though now out of print, copies are before us; from these we now proceed to give such extracts as will illustrate the character of the Rajah, and show the estimation in which he was held.

The first is from Dr. Carpenter, preached in Lewin's Mead Chapel, Bristol, Oct. The 6th, 1833. It contains a full review of the labours, opinions and character of the Rajah, and was printed with a number of extracts form his writings, and with the Biographical Memoir at the commencement of this volume. From this pamphlet large extracts have been already made.

Daniel viii., 13, 14.

I saw in the night visions, and, behold, one like the Son of Man came with the clouds of heaving, and came to the Ancient of days; and they brought him near before him : and there was given him dominion, and glory, and kingdom, that all people, nations and languages, should serve him : his dominion is an everlasting dominion, which shall not pass away; and his kingdom that which shall not be destroyed.

"This sublime declaration of the prophetic spirit cannot be fulfilled till all the nations of the earth shall form a part of the kingdom of the Messiah; and it will be fulfilled in its completes extent, for it proceeded form him who is almighty, eternal, and unchangeable. The Christian believer who has cordial faith in this and other related prophecies, must have the settled unwavering conviction, that the day will come when the knowledge which is 'life eternal' shall be diffused into every region, and received into the heart of every rational being, on the face of the earth.

"No one who has just sense of the value of the Gospel, can be indifferent to the spread of its divine truths, or to the increase of their influence where they are already received. Let the question be fairly put to any who have imbibed its sacred principles; who have seen how it communicated light and guidance, how it raises and refines the purposes and desires, strengthens in weakness, supports in sorrow, heals the contrite heart, cherishes the best affection, is continually expanding, invigorating, and elevating the understanding, and directing the soul heavenward;—whether they can conceive a more inestimable treasure, or can think it a matter of no moment whether or not others share it with them. He who prays that the kingdom of God may come, and his will be done on earth as it is done in heaven, must if he pray with the spirit and with the understanding, be solicitous to promote the practical reception of the Gospel; and if, in any good degree, he bear the image of his Lord, he will decline no exertion, nor shun any difficulty or sacrifice, where he has a reasonable prospect that he may thereby promote the great end of God's moral government, the virtue and happiness of his rational offspring. From him whom he views with gratitude as his benefactor, and reverences as his sovereign and judge, he has learnt, that to know, with the knowledge of the heart, 'the only true God, and Jesus Christ whom he hath sent' 'is life eternal' : and if he have himself, as a sinful, dying, accountable creature, experienced, in godly, sorrow, its precious promises of divine mercy, its strength in temptation, its guidance in spiritual perplexity, its consolations, its warnings, and its hopes—hopes full of immortality—he will love much; and grateful to him who suffered and died to extend and assure the gracious blessings of the Gospel, and to Him from whose tender mercy they sprang, he will deem it an imperative duty to do what in him lies to enable others to share in those privileges and blessings, and to become faithful subjects of the Messiah's kingdom.

"There can be no doubt in the mind of him who has duly considered the declarations of prophecy and the genius of the Christian religion, that it is designed to be universal, both in extent and in duration. Men of the highest intellect have perceived its disclosures expanding as they have themselves advanced in comprehension of mind. As they have ascended the heights of human intelligence, they have discerned more and more of the glories of 'The light of the world'. And it is not conceivable that any period shall arrive, in this state of being, when the Gospel can be regarded, by those who possess and understand its principles and its hopes, as other than 'the pearl of great price', beyond all other gifts of our Heavenly Father of inestimable value.

"In proportion, too, as the minds of men are cultivated with sound knowledge, Christian truth is more readily discernible, and its influences are more effective. Ignorance suits not the spirit of the Gospel, which is 'the spirit of power, and love, and of a sound mind'; and where to ignorance is added the debasing influences of sordid selfishness and pollution, scarcely and thing can raise above the mire of earth. On the other hand, where the understanding is exercised, truth is found to be its best nourishment; and sound knowledge, the healthy food of the soul. The mind is thus prepared for light from heaven; and that light 'shineth more and more unto the perfect day.'

"Many parts of the prophecies are still obscure. To the eye which can only partially discern even the present, that which respects things to come must commonly have something of the darkness or the dimness of futurity. Even those portions which respect things long past, seem full of mystery to those who are little acquainted with the ancient periods of the world, and have not considered the appropriate language of prophecy. But if there is any thing clear, explicit, and certain in prophecy, it is, that the time shall come 'when the knowledge of Jehovah shall over the earth as the waters do the channels of the deep'; when, 'from the rising of the sun to the going down of the same, his name shall be exalted among the Gentiles'; when, 'in every place shall be offered to him incense and a pure offering'—the offering of the heart, the sacrifice of the life. The anticipation of this great and glorious result was one of the habitual sentiments of our Lord's prophetic spirit. He looked through darkness, and through evil, towards good unbounded, and in its influenced eternal. And this anticipation can scarcely fail to be fixed in the Christian's heart. His Lord 'must reign till all enemies are brought under his feet'. The 'Heathen have been given him for an inheritance, and the uttermost parts of the earth for a possession'. The words of the prophet in my text are singularly impressive and decisive; and they are the more important, because whenever our Saviour applies to himself the appellation 'the Son of Man', we may reasonably understand a tacit reference to them.

"While many of our Christian brethren were contemplating with intense earnestness, and cost fully promoting, the efforts made by Missionaries of their own denomination to spread the

Gospel among the Hindus—as it appeared to us with little success, or, on the system they adopted, well-grounded hope,—the attention of the Unitarians in England and America began to be arrested by the information which came to us from various quarters, that in the British capital of Hindustan a highly-gifted Brahmin had been, for some time, with little knowledge of the Gospel, preparing the way for its divine light by dispersing the debasing darkness of heathen idolatry; and that he had been endeavouring, with much success, to lead his more intelligent countryment to the ancient and purer forms of their religion. This was Rammohun Roy. We learnt that long before he had attended to the instructions of Christ, he had attained the faith of Abraham, and worshipped and served the 'one living and true likely to be his honour to contribute effectually, even if indirectly, to the diffusion of faith in Christ, partly by his personal labours, and his aid in their exertions. These labours were directed to the exposure of the evils of the prevalent faith of his countrymen; and particularly to the extension of that knowledge respecting the Supreme and Eternal Creator, which their most ancient 'scriptures' taught, in language that is not surpassed, in sublimity and truth, even by that of Moses and the Prophets;—often blended, however, with much that is mystical; and with much also that was calculated to lead away from the truth, or, at least, to furnish a pretext to the grovelling soul-in process of time abundantly and banefully employed—to direct its adorations to the manifestations of the attributes of the Supreme Being, and to worship him who is the invisible, eternal universal, and ever-present Spirit, under numberless forms of created intelligences, or of the beasts of the earth, or of things without intelligence or life.

"Several of the Brahmin's productions, with this object in view, principally designed for his own countrymen, came into my hands, now twelve years ago : but at least six or eight years before that period, he had made and extensively circulated translations of the Hindu sacred writings, and afterwards abridgements of them; and there is no doubt that great and important benefits have arisen from these publications among the cultivated and inquiring part of his countrymen, whose minds, trained by their native learning and knowledge to a great degree of acuteness and refinement, had become disgusted with the degrading nature and influences of the ceremonies and worship of their own people, yet were impressed with strong repugnance at the prevailing representations of Christian doctrine, which was increased, there is reason to believe, by the extreme absence, at that period, in British society in general, of the ordinary indications of any deep sense of religion. These publications contain numerous passages which are well fitted to elevate the sentiments, and to attract those whose hearts were already elevated; while, in their mode of expression, and in the reverence with which the Hindus are accustomed to regard these writings, as proceeding from the Deity and themselves in part possessed of deity, they are more fitted that our scriptures, *as whole,* for the *earliest* periods of departure, from the popular opinions of the Hindus.

"The absolute unity, unrivalled supremacy, sole worship, and essential mercy of the only true God, are too strongly asserted in Rammohun Roy's writings, and were too unequivocally maintained by him in conversation, to leave any doubt as to his doctrinal opinions on those points. He repeatedly told others me and that he never introduced his opinions unnecessarily; but that when the subject was introduced he never hesitated to avow them : and of his entire disbelief in the doctrine of the trinity, of the incarnation, & c., we have abundant assurance. In his replies to the Missionaries who attacked his selections from the instructions of Christ, he also develops his views respecting the person of our Lord. That he regarded him as entirely subordinate to the Supreme Being, and dependent upon HIM, for all his high powers and authority, must be obvious to every one who peruses that remarkable controversy. He dwells, with peculiar earnestness and satisfaction, on the conclusion he had attained receptions the nature of that unity which subsisted between Christ and his heavenly Father—the unity of design, of affection, of operation—such as existed between his disciples and himself. On all these points, which alone are essential to Unitarianism, he agrees with the Unitarian. In those treatises, however, he also speaks of our Saviour as pre-existent, and as employed in the creation of the natural world; in which he differs from the great bulk of contemporary Unitarians, more nearly approaching to the sentiments of the excellent Dr. Price. From the conversations which I had with him in the later part of his life, I believe that he was more disposed to regard that pre-existence as only in the divine purposes; and the creating logos, not as Christ himself, but as that divine power which wrought in and by him. But however this may be, he was undoubtedly a Unitarian; and he has repeatedly said, when not among members of the Unitarian sect, 'My heart is with the Unitarians'.

"As to his Christian belief—the only ground for uncertainty arose from the assertions, on the one hand, of those who will not allow the claims of the Unitarian to the appellation Christian, because he does not receive those doctrines which he firmly believes to be without foundation in the instructions of Christ and his Apostles; or, on the other, of those who have misunderstood the nature of the ground on which the Brahmin's convictions most rested, the manner in which he spoke of doctrines which they themselves always associated with Christian belief and deemed essential to it, and the caution with which he habitually avoided all public expression of the adoption of Christianity by those personal acts which would have been regarded by Christians in general as a renunciation of his ancient faith, and probably employed by his enemies in India to lessen his influence an to injure his interests. He never was baptized, though applied to for the purpose by the direction of some of the highest dignitaries of the Established Church : he could not have been baptized into the Trinitarian faith. He might have been baptized into Unitarian Christianity, without renouncing what he regarded as the pure doctrine of Hinduism respecting the Supreme Being; but his system prevented him from engaging in the positive rites of any sect of Christians. While he maintained his caste as a Brahmin, he had an acknowledged right to instruct his countrymen in the doctrines of their religion, which he maintained to have been, in its purest and most ancient form, monotheism in faith and in worship, and to which he laboured, in many cases effectually, to lead his fellow-Brahmins. The acknowledgements of the divine authority of Christ is, in itself, in one way inconsistent with the maintenance of their ancient faith; for as Moses and the Prophets had done, Christ and his Apostles taught the same. We have in his controversy with the Baptist Missionaries (before the attempt made to deprive him of his caste,) the clear declarations of this belief that 'Jesus of Nazareth' was 'the Christ of God', that 'he was sent with a divine law to guide mankind by his preaching and example', that he received from the Supreme Being 'a commission to come into the world for the salvation of mankind', and that he was, by him, 'empowered to perform wonderful works'. This belief, however, he rested, as we have learned from himself, less on those wonderful works, than on the internal proofs derived from the excellence of our Saviour's instructions respecting the character of God and the duty and welfare of man, and from the circumstances attending the first promulgation of the Gospel; and he laid little stress upon miracles as a means of converting his countrymen, from their being so much accustomed to miraculous relations in reference to those deities whom they were called upon to renounce. But though the elements of his faith, or the grounds on which he held it, might not agree with those of Christians in general, I am, in the recollection of several residents in this city or its neighbourhood, of the first respectability for character and intellectual attainments, and of various religious persuasions, correct when I say, that, less than a week before his last illness began, he expressed his belief in the divine origin or our Lord's instructions, in his miracles, and in his resurrecting from the dead. On this great fact, indeed, he declared that his own expectation of a resurrection rested. 'If I did not believe in the resurrection of Christ', were his emphatic words, 'I should not believe in my own'. Believing as he certain did in this essential fundamental fact of Christianity, you may term him what you please—I have no hesitation in saying that he was a Christian.

"As to his more direct services to Christianity, I view them as of vastly more importance than has yet, perhaps, been developed. It is no slight service, that he has rendered a large portion of the recorded teachings of Christ accessible to his countrymen, in their sacred language, the Sanskrit, and in the ordinary language of Bengal. Perplexed himself with the various doctrines insisted upon by the teachers of Christianity, he sought for the essential characteristics of this religion—its moral system, its sanctions, and its promises—in the words of Christ himself; and these he presented to the Hindu public in the way which he deemed most 'likely to produce the desirable effect of improving the hearts and minds of men, of different persuasions and degrees of understanding.' 'This simple code of religion and morality (he says at the end of his introduction) is so admirably calculated to elevate men's ideas to high and liberal notions of one God, who has equally subjected all living creatures, without distinction of caste, rank, or wealth, to change, disappointment, pain, and death, and has equally admitted all to be partakers of the bountiful mercies which he has lavished over nature; and is also so well fitted to regulate the conduct of the human race in the discharge of their various duties to God, to themselves, and to society; that I cannot but hope the best effects from its promulgation in the present form.'

"One would have thought that the Christian Missionaries would have hailed the learned and excellent Brahmin as their fellow-labourer, and as at least preparing the way for that knowledge of Christ which they thought essential to his Gospel. True it is that he did not introduce into the 'Precepts of Jesus' the narration of our Lord's miracles : but the purpose of the miracles was answered if anywhere led without them to the same end—the reception of Jesus Christ as a heaven-sent teacher, and the disposition to receive his words as the words of truth, and the guide of heart and life; and the Brahmin thought such narrations less likely to affect the minds of his countrymen, than the simple records of Christ's instructions. He knew that the Saviour hath declared that he that doeth the will of his Heavenly Father, was to him as a brother, or sister, or mother : and he expressed his conviction that the sayings of Christ which he had presented to his countrymen, are those 'the obedience to which is so absoletely commanded as indispensable and all-sufficient to those who desire eternal life; that they 'include every duty of man and all that is necessary to salvation', while 'they expressly exclude mere profession or belief from those circumstances which God graciously admits as giving a title to eternal happiness'; and that there is not in the New Testament, any commandment 'similarly enjoining a knowledge of the mysteries of historical relations contained I those books'. But it is an immer.se advance when any are led from the degrading forms and disgusting and cure God, and to seek for the words of the only true God, and to seek for the words of eternal life in the instruction of Jesus Christ. Even if they were only brought near to the kingdom of God, he who presented the means of this progress, and in a way that he deemed more likely than others to affect their minds, should surely have been received with conciliatory encouragement; and perceiving—as his previous writings showed—that he had a mind open to truth, it would have been wise calmly to present to him the means of greater light, and to await its effects, without attempting to thwart or to oppose his progress. But his reception by the Missionaries 'surprised and disappointed" him; and he appears to have had some reason to complain of a want of candour and liberality towards him. The attack had, however, a highly beneficial effect : it led him to mature his view of Christian truth; and to discern, by close examination of the Scriptures, what are the real doctrines of Christ and his Apostles. His First and Second Appeals especially (and also, though more directly critical, and more influenced by English controversial works, his Final Appeal,) present the extraordinary efforts, and most important researches, of a mind faithfully seeking for light, and coming to the Scriptures with no other prepossessions than these which arose from views respecting the Supreme Being which Christianity had only to extend and establish. In addition to a remarkable critical skill, they display the sagacity of a clear and acute understanding, guided by the love of truth and duty, and illuminated by devotion, and dispensations of the supreme and universal Parent which perfectly harmonized with all the spontaneous dictates of his pious and benevolent spirit. I persuade myself that the reasonings and representation of the Brahmin will yet lead many Christians to review their own conclusions; and assist them to discern that the faith required for the benefits of the Gospel, is perfectly accordant with the dictates of a sound understanding : while, at the same time, the beautiful manifestations of his charity, humility, and benevolence, may contribute to improve them in the spirit which the Gospel require.

"His enlarged and benignant spirit, the tenderness and purity of his own heart, the maternal love which he had experienced, and the influences of that soothing kindness which he had received from the women of Thibet when he was separated from the endearments of home, aided (I repeat it) to produce in has mind those sentiments of respect for women in her domestic and social and moral relations, which entirely raised his above the narrow and degrading views entertained of the female sex by his countrymen in general; and which led him to contribute, in various ways, to the just appreciation of them, and to their protection from the sordid purposes and superstitious zeal of those who degraded them by debasing rites and practices, and condemned them to self-immolation. He regarded woman, whether considered as an intellectual or as a spiritual being, as fitted, by natural powers and capabilities, to be the companion, the friend, and the helper of man. In all this his sentiments admirably coincided with the genius of the Gospel, and with the spirit and conduct of its benevolent Author; and it is no unreasonable supposition, that the perception of this characteristic of the Christian system contributed to his interest in our Scriptures, which record the most affecting instances of the reverential attachment of devout women to the Saviour, and their devoted faithfulness when even his disciples deserted him; and which present various indications of the readiness of the female sex to receive his heavenly truths, and to labour for the diffusion of them among mankind.

"Such was the illustrious person whose removal from an extensive field of usefulness we feel to be a call for trust and submission; and such the nature and extent of his labours in it. Premature we might be tempted to think his summons from life, while the powers of his mind were in their vigour, and while his sources of enjoyment and of self-improvement were so great, in the intercourses of friendship and affection in the honour and attachment of wise and good men of all ranks and of all persuasions, in the engagements of kindness and benevolence, in the perception of the effects of his labours of patriotism and philanthropy, in the pursuit of truth, the study of scripture, and the exercise of piety : but the future is unknown; and God's time is best. Protracted life might have displayed, in languor and exhaustion, if not a long course of that arduous toil and often severe conflict, which had been occasioned by his own beneficient purposes, or by the harassing opposition and even hostility of others. He might have had unlocked for trails of faith and patience, in the slow and sometimes interrupted operation of those causes of good to his country which his comprehensive and ardent mind must have viewed as now effectually commenced. At any rate, he has sunk to rest in the midst of affection and respect, with all those purposes carried into effect which had been his object through life : and could we have known the thoughts of his heart, when he believed the hour of his departure approaching, I am persuaded that we should have found, blended with them, the emotions of devout thankfulness—which now fill our hearts—that he had lived so long, and that his toils and his conflicts had not been in vain.

"They have not been in vain; and the tomb does not terminate their efficacy. The influence of his personal example and of his instructions will be felt impressively among many who have witnessed and received them. His writings will be more read and appreciated. Those who have been already acquainted with them, will review them with that new interest which the mournful thought produced, that he whose intelligence and benevolence dictated them, is now among the dead. The purposes of his exertions will, in the heart of many a one, receive an new impulse from the consideration that all who valued him for them and are able to promote them, are bound to do what they can to supply the loss of his efforts and his counsels. In many and various ways his great objects may be carried into effect, with an influence derived from the termination of his course, which the misinterpretation of his motives, or a wrong estimate of his mode of accomplishing them, or the belief that it peculiarly rested with him to effect them, might have contributed to prevent. The spirit under which he obviously laboured will transfuse itself into the hearts of other who have those objects in view; and his writings will aid the wise and benevolent in promoting them. 'Though dead he yet speaketh'; and the voice will be heard impressively from the tomb, which, in his life, may have excited only the passing emotions of admiration or respect.

"That voice may be heard by his intelligent Hindu friends and other enlightened Brahmins. It may excite them to renewed and increased efforts of carry on the work of intellectual and moral improvement among their countrymen : to diffuse the purer light of religion which his writings contain, among those who are yet debased and superstitious : to give the advantages of a wise education to the young and uninformed : to rise themselves, and teach others to rise, above the narrow prejudices of caste and sect; and thereby weaken that thraldom which so much interrupts the progress of truth and virtue; and elevate, by knowledge and a just appreciation, those who may thus be the friends and companions of the present generation, and whose early instruction and training will so much promote the welfare of the next : to cooperate with the benevolent efforts of the British Government for the welfare of their country; and by giving the system adopted the aids they may effectually afford it, prepare for the extension and increase of the advantages which benevolent wisdom has in view. May we not hope, too, that his example will lead the best and most enlightened among the Hindu to study, and thence to value, those Scriptures which he habitually studied and valued? And, perceiving, as he has practically shown them, that the religion of Christ requires no renunciation, in faith and worship, of the purest and most ancient principles of their own, to follow him in this respect also, and to receive themselves, and lead others to receive, the instructions of Jesus as the guide to peace and happiness? If such should be the results; his death will be blessed to their highest interests, and to those of their countryman at large.

"To all of us, the rapid progress of fatal disease, by which he has unexpectedly been called from life to whose intercourse we had here looked forwards with so much earnestness and hope, presents a fresh warning as to the uncertainty of life. The voice speaketh from his tomb, and urges us to work the work of life while it is day. His example, too, may well strengthen our desire to work that work faithfully, and as those who are to give an account. A strong sense of responsibility influenced him in the course which Providence marked out for him. The spirit of benevolence, of humility, and of piety, dwelt in his heart. You learned not from himself, except by casual expressions, or in reply to direct inquiries, what he had done for mankind, in respect to their temporal and spiritual well-being; but on reviewing it for ourselves, we see that it claims our admiration and our deep respect. He sought the blessing of God on his work, and pursued this as an accountable being; and we may well say that the blessing of God has rested upon if for great and important good.

" 'Servant of God! farewell! work is o'er'. Thou has been summoned to that rest which remained for the people of God, and we shall soon commit thee to the silent tomb; but it will be with the hope of meeting thee again, when this mortal shall put on immortality, and that which is sown in weakness, shall be raised in power and glory. Thy honoured remains will not repose in ground that has been consecrated by human ceremonial, or even by the exclusive employment of it as the abode of the dead; but they will themselves hallow the spot where they rest, and it will be endeared by the remembrance of thy benignity, thins affection, and thy friendship. Never will be effaced from our memory the beamings of thy countenance, and the mild accents of thy voice; and by all who knew thee, will thy name be loved and revered.—'Blessed are the dead which die in the Lord; they rest from their labours; and their works follow them'. The influences of thy labours, thine instructions, thy example, are still with us; and these will render thee still the guide and the benefactor of thy race. As respects others, thy labour will not be in vain; and as respects thyself, thou art awaiting thy reward. The day will come when the Lord of Christians will call thee from the tomb; and then, I doubt not, wilt thou hear the approving words addressed to thee, 'Well done, good and faithful servant, enter thou into the joy of thy Lord!'

"God grant, my hearers, that a like blessedness may be our lot; that we may faithfully improve our talents for usefulness to other and our own spiritual well-being; and that, when the Lord of Christians shall call us and all men from the tomb, we may receive the blessed welcome, and be admitted into the joy of our Lord."

On the same Sunday, the Rev. R. Aspland preached a funeral sermon in the New Gravel Pit Meeting, Hackney, where the Rajah had not unfrequently been a listener. A large portion of the sermon consists of biographical notices of the Rajah, and extracts from his writings, which had been already presented to the public by Dr. Carpenter. Is was therefore, not intended for publication. Mr. Aspland states in the preface that "he considered the sermon preached upon the occasion by his respected friend Dr. Carpenter, of Bristol, to be the proper funereal tribute to the memory of the Rajah; and this he hoped, and still hopes, the see published, especially as Dr. Carpenter was in frequent intercourse with the illustrious deceased, during his last days, and enjoyed, besides, peculiar opportunities of acquiring an exact knowledge of his life and opinions. But an edition of the sermon having made its appearance (printed, it is supposed, from notes taken at the time of delivery), without the sanction of the author, no alternative is left to him, unless he could consent to bear the imputation of putting out a mean and illiterate publication, in reference to a name entitled to every outward mark of respect." On the title page of the sermon are the appropriate lines of the poet of paradise Lost and Regained :

"One man except, the only son of light,

In a dark age, against example good,

Against allurement, custom and a world
Offended."

The subject of the sermon is "The future accession of good men of all climes to Christianity, and their final congregation in heaven." Mr. Aspland thus prefaced it,-

"Judging that it would not be uncongenial with the feelings of the congregation, nor presumptuous on my part, nor, perhaps, wholly unserviceable to the cause of Christian truth, I ventured last Sunday morning to announce that I should adapt the present discourse to the melancholy event of the somewhat sudden and, according to the course of nature, premature decease of our distinguished oriental visitor, Rajah Rammohun Roy; the rather, as he was an occasional worshipper in this House of Prayer, and repeatedly expressed that he felt a deep interest in this congregation. On that occasion, I stated that I did not meditate a mere eulogy upon the departed Brahmin. My object is to represent him as, with my means of knowledge, I consider him to have been, and to describe his religious character and profession as it appeared to myself, and to others that had still better means of forming a correct opinion. His condition in relation to Christianity was so peculiar; his rank and acquirements and labours justly attracted to him so much public attention; and so many contradictory statements have been made of his religious views, that it cannot be regarded as an indelicate or uninteresting inquiry, whether he embraced the gospel entirely and unreservedly, and what was his decision amidst the conflicting theories of Christian sects upon the true scheme of doctrine propounded in the Christian Scriptures. My answer to this inquiry will be anticipated from the words which I shall now read as a text,—the groundwork of some observations not, I trust, foreign from the subject. You will find the words in.

Matthew viii., 11.

And I say unto you, that many shall come from the east and west, and shall sit down with Abraham, and Isaac, and Jacob, in the kingdom of heaven.

"The speaker is our Lord. He was now acting in his great and delightful character of a Comforter and a Saviour, and his gracious prediction was uttered upon the contemplation of an extraordinary degree of faith and piety in one from whom they might have been least expected, a Roman centurion or captain, who improved the opportunity of his military employment in the Holy Land to inquire after true religion, and whose inquiry terminated in his abandonment of the idolatry of his fathers and his adoption of the pure Jewish worship.

"It would seem to follow of necessity from the admission of the gospel as the power of God and the wisdom of God, that the more earnestly and diligently it is studies, the better it will be understood and the more highly valued; that the pleasure derived from it will be in proportion to the love of it, from a knowledge of its fitness and excellence : that oneness with its spirit and obedience to its requirements will always go together; and that the union of faith and virtue is the only qualification for the perfect enjoyment of its promised blessings in that world where faith will be turned into sight, but where charity never faileth.

"These are solemnly important conclusions. They should impel us, on the one hand, to inquire seriously into the truth of God by Christ, lest by our own indolence and worldly-mindedness we fail of discovering the pearl of great price; and on the other hand, to take a willing part in all wise and sincere efforts for the promotion of the moral and spiritual improvement of the world, and to hail with disinterested fervour, and to embrace with fraternal love, all the wise and good, whether from the east or the west, from the north or the south, who enter into the church of Christ with minds enlightened by the wisdom from above, and hearts purified by the influence of divine truth, praying and seeking only for glory to God in the highest, peace on earth, good-will to men.

"We shall thus, my Christian friends, be prepared to unite with the multitude that no man can number, out of every kindred, tribe, tongue and people, and from every dispensation of light,—with patriarchs and prophets, apostles and martyrs, who, their warfare accomplished, their affections wholly sanctified and their spirits perfected, will sit down in heavenly places with Him after whom the whole family in heaven and earth is named, to pursue divine knowledge, to exercise universal love, to taste pure bliss, and to proclaim eternally growning gratitude to the Almighty Father, blessed in himself and blessed, too, in all his creatures for evermore.

"To apply the subject to the occasion. There has been recently taken from the earth one to whom many of our humble observation, to whom I solemnly believe the sublime words of our Lord, apply a rare, perhaps an unparalleled instance of a man who, by the virtuous use of great talents and splendid acquirements, under the divine providence and grace, delivered his own spirit from the enthralment of idolatry, and entered by degrees into the glorious liberty of the sons of God.

"None can deny that our departed Christian Brother was an extraordinary man, whether we consider his intellectual energies, his moral qualities, or his theological attainments. Centuries may intervene before his equal in all respects shall rise up in Hindustan, so bright a light shining in so dark a place. He is a memorable example to the world of what an individual may accomplish by firmness of purpose, diligence, perseverance, fortitude, disinterestedness and candour, in the acquirement of truth, amidst the greatest disadvantages, and the diffusion of truth, amidst opposition and reproach. Would that they could be warned by his example, who, with all the opportunities of improvement around them, neither inquire nor think, neither instruct nor are instructed, lay down no error and acquire no truth, and, except as far as self-interest prompts, meditate no one good service to their fellow creature.

"The name of Rammohun Roy will endure as long as the history of religious truth. It is already, in part, and will hereafter be generally cherished in both hemispheres, in that which is distinguished by his birth, and in this, which will, it is now probable, have the boast of keeping his honoured relics : *here*, he will be celebrated for breaking the first link of the long chain which has pressed down the heart of his country to the dust; *at home*, when India shall stretch out her hands to the true God, he will be revered as the fist of her reformers and philanthropists. And more than this, and above all earthly fame, may we not gather from the promises of the gospel, this morning imperfectly expounded, that when the Throne shall be set, and the books shall be opened, and the dead, from both sea and land, shall be judged out of those things that are written in the books, according to their works, his name will be found in the Book of Life, and the Son of Man will welcome his, with all the righteous, into his Heavenly Father's kingdom! Even so. Amen."

Mr. Aspland gives in notes to his sermon the following statements, which were probably derived from the article in the "Athenaeum" :

"Mr. Arnot says, that during the greater part of the period of Rammohun Roy's residence at Calcutta, 'the whole powers of his mind were directed to the vindication of the doctrine of the unity of God. In this, he maintained the sacred books of Hindus and Mussulmans, Jews and Christians, agreed; and that all apparent deviations from it were modern corruptions. He propagated it day and night, by word and writing, with the Zeal of an apostle and the self devotion of a martyr. He was ever ready to maintain it against all gainsayers, from the believer in thirty-three millions of gods to the denier of one : for both extremes are common in the East. The writer remembers finding him at his Garden house, near Calcutta, one evening, about seven o'clock, closing a dispute with one of the followers of Budh, who denied the existence of a Deity. The Rajah had spent the whole day in the controversy, without stopping for food, rest or refreshment, and rejoicing more in confusing one atheist than in triumphing over a hundred idolaters : the credulity of the one he despised; the scepticism of the other he though pernicious; for he was deeply impressed with the importance of religion to the virtue and happiness of mankind'."

" 'There were,' says Mr. Arnott, in the 'Athenaeum', 'There maxims in politics, in ethics, and in religion, which he often repeated; with these I shall sum up this brief sketch of his life and character. The first he expressed in an Arabic sentences, Insan abid ul ihasn : 'Man is the slave of benefits.' The second, a couplet from the Anwari Soheili, which will be found in many a fair lady's album : 'The enjoyment of the two worlds (this and the next) rests on these two points; kindness to friends, civility to enemies'. And the third, from the philosophic Sadi—which he often repeated, and often expressed a wish to have inscribed on his tomb :

'the true way of serving god is to do good to man.'

"Amen : so let it be : the religious reformer of the Hindus could not have a more appropriate epitaph."

Though the Rajah had not been able to visit Ireland yet the Sister Isle was not uninterested in the visit of the Hindu Reformer, and on October 27th, 1833, a sermon was preached in the Presbyterian Church of Strand Street, Dublin, on occasion of his death, by the Rev. William Hamilton Drummond, D.D., which was published by special request. "The Rajah received addresses," Dr. Drummond states, "from Ireland, particularly from Belfast and Cork, and a gentleman of this city was commissioned by the Irish Unitarian Society to invite him to a public entertainment. It was accordingly his intention to pay this country a visit. He seemed to take a deep interest in the affairs of Ireland, and I can state on the unquestionable authority of a friend, who was frequently in his society in London, that in the course of a month after his arrival, he had acquired such an intimated knowledge of its statistics, politics and religion, as might almost justify the belief that he had long been directing his exclusive attention to these subjects of enquiry." The following are extracts from Dr. Drummond's sermon, which was entitled 'A learned Indian search of religion" :

Psalm lxxxvi., 8,9,10.

Among the gods there is none like unto thee, O Lord! Neither are there any works like thy works. All nations whom thouhast made shall come and worship before thee, O Lord; and shall glorify thy name—for thou art great, and doest wondrous things : thou art God alone.

"Yes-Je... is God alone, and all attempts to raise up any god beside G... he Father, are as impotent as would be the attempt to sap the foundations of the earth, or pluck the sun from his orbit. His works, through all their boundless variety and amplitude, declare him, by the unity of their design, to be One, The voice of Revelation, through all the rich diversity of her communications, declares him to be One. The great legislator of the Jews, their king, their prophets, the inspired apostles; the blessed Savior himself, he who was filled with the Spirit of the Most High-all declare him to be One. This is the conclusion at which the wisest and best of men, in all ages and countries, who have faithfully followed the twin lights of nature and revelation, have arrived. The light of nature and the light of revelation flow in parallel lines from the same great foundation of everlasting truth. The latter shines with a brighter and more intense ray than the former—but they never cross each other's path, not stream in opposite directions; nay, they may be said to blend and mingle together, as the rays of heat, and of colour, in the solar beam, as the rays of heat, and of colour, in the solar beam, to produce one white and brilliant illumination. The God of nature is the God of revelation; and it is impossible that by the voice of the one he can contradict what he has uttered by the voice of the other. What nature has spoken, revelation has repeated in more audible sounds. The aspirations of nature in the soul of man after a holier, happier, state of being, are re-echoed by revelation; and nature's 'longings after immortality,' are cherished and exalted into a lively faith in the resurrection from the dead, by that 'gospel, which hath brought life and immortality to light.'

"Of the character of the excellent Rajah, intellectual, moral religious, there seems to be only one opinion. As for what may be thought or said of him by those, and such no doubt there are, who because he could not embrace their peculiar doctrines, would still denominate him a heathen, it is unworthy of a moment's notice. Would that but one little shred of his Christianity were shared among them, it would make them better Christians than ever they are likely to become with their ignorant and malevolent bigotry! We have the testimony, not only of friends to his religious views, but of some who were opposed to them, that he was pious, and good, and learned, and wise, and patriotic, and generous, and disinterested. In fact, I cannot at this moment recollect the name of any individual, since the days of the apostles, that has so pre-eminent a claim to the title of Christian.

"The accession of such a convert as the Rajah to the truth of Christianity, should, we might suppose, be hailed with exultation by all his friends, and especially by those employed in missionary labours, though his opinions did not altogether harmonize with theirs. But no, such is the spirit of bigotry—such the effect of entertaining narrow views of Christianity, and making it consist, not in 'meat and drink' indeed, but in something still worse, in the belief of doctrines which shock reason, and impeach the justice and mercy of the Father of all-that it would rather such coverts as he had remained still immersed in the idolatries, and abominations, from which he had escaped! That a Brahmin of such high character, so distinguished for strong intellectual powers-for superior mental cultivation—for such patient and persevering industry in the study of languages to aid him in the search after truth—that such a man should strip off the prejudices of education, should renounce the popular superstitions of his country, under the severe penalty of incurring the hostility of his relatives and friends, and at the no small risk of losing his paternal property, and most dreadful of all, of losing *caste*, which, as you well know, is to the Hindu a grievance more terrible than ex-communication in the Roman Catholic Church—that such a man, under such circumstances, should come forward to avow his belief in Christianity at all, ought surely to be a subject of rejoicing to every one who feels a real interest in the extension of the Saviour's kingdom.

"Such was the learned Indian's high veneration for the sacred Scriptures, that he refused to receive any doctrine, as a doctrine of religion, which they have not revealed. He gave the decrees of Council and Fathers to the winds, and taking the word of God as his only true guide and instructor, asserted with it, the divine unity, in opposition to all Tritheism and Polytheism.

" 'It is my reverence for Christianity', says he, in his second Appeal (p. 304), 'and for the author of this religion, that has induced me to endeavour to vindicate it from the charge of Polytheism, as far as my limited capacity and knowledge extend. It is indeed mortifying to my feelings, to find a religion that from its sublime doctrines and pure morality should be respected above all other systems, reduced almost to a level with Hindu theology, merely by human creeds and prejudices; and from this cause brought to a comparison with the paganism of ancient Greece, which while it included a plurality of Gods, yet maintained that Qeoc eci eic, or 'God is one', and that their numerous divine *persons* were all comprehended in that one Deity.'

" 'Having derived my own opinions on this subject entirely form the Scriptures themselves, I may perhaps be excused for the confidence with which I maintain them against these of so great a majority, who appeal to the same authority for theirs; inasmuch as I attribute the different views, not to any inferiority of judgment compared with my own limited ability, but to the powerful effect of early religious impression; for when these are deep, reason is seldom allowed its natural scope in examining them to the bottom. Were it a practice among Christians to study first the books of the Old Testament as found arranged in order, and to acquire a knowledge of the true force of scriptural phrases and expressions, without attending to interpretations given by any sect; and then to study the New Testament, comparing the one with the other, Christianity would not any longer be liable to be encroached on by human opinions.' (304,305.)

"Again he observes, in his Final Appeal, 'The doctrine of the Trinity appears to me so obviously unscriptural, that I am pretty sure, from my own experience and that of others, that no one possessed of merely common sense, will fail to find its unscripturality, after a methodical study of the Old and New Testaments, unless previously impressed in the early part of his life with creeds and forms of speech preparing the way to the doctrine.'

"The Rajah attributes that prevalence of belief in the Trinity, which exists in Christendom, to the same causes as those which perpetuate and establish Hinduism in the East,—the force of early impression.

" 'The minds of youths, and even infants, being once thoroughly impressed with the name of the Trinity in Unity and unity in Trinity, long before they can think for themselves, must be always inclined, even after their reason has become matured, to interpret the sacred books, even those texts which are evidently inconsistent with this doctrine, in a manner favourable to their prepossessed opinion, whether their study be continued for three, or thirty, or twice thirty years. Could Hinduism continue after the present generation, or bear the studious examination of a single year, if the belief of their idols being endued with animation were not carefully impressed on the young before they come to years of understanding?'(355.)

"Having in another place noticed some facts in Mosheim, ad shown how some nominal converts to Christianity came to pass a decree constituting Christ one of the persons of the Godhead, he says,

"These facts coincide entirely with my own term persuasion of the impossibility, that a doctrine so inconsistent with the evidence of the senses as that of three persons in one being, should ever gain the sincere assent of any one, into whose mind it has not been instilled in early education. Early impressions along can induce a Christian to believe that three are one and one is three; just as by the same means a Hindu is made to believe that millions are one, and one is millions; and to imagine that an inanimate idol is a living substance, and capable of assuming various forms. As I have sought to attain the truths of Christianity from the words of the author of this religion, and from the undisputed instructions of his holy apostles, and not from a parent or tutor. I cannot help refusing my assent to any doctrine which I do not find scriptural.'

"Noble, magnanimous declaration! Would that these who pride themselves on there exclusive right to the name of Christian, were to profit by this example!

"Having, during the progress of this discourse, been under the painful necessity of animadverting on the illiberality of some of the Rajah's opponents, it is with no small satisfaction that I turn to the agreeable takes of showing that his character and views were highly appreciated, not only by that denomination of Christians who claim and him as their own, but by liberal and enlightened members of other denominations. A striking instance of this occurs in the dedication to him of a sermon entitled 'Charity, the greatest of the Christian graces,' by the Rev. RICHARD WARNER, Rector of Great Chalfied, Wilts, 1832. The letter dedicatory runs thus,-

"Rajah!—Allow me to introduce the following sermon to the notice of the public under the auspices of 'your respected and respectable name.'

'The epithets are appropriate, not so much on account of the condition, fortune, or talent (distinguished as they may be) of the person to whom they are applied, as for the deep interest which he takes in the happiness of his fellow creatures, and for the labours in which he exercises himself or the diffusion of the Light of Christianity, and the promotion of EVANGELICAL LOVE among an hundred millions of his countrymen, immersed in spiritual darkness, or drunken with intolerant superstions!

'Rajah! Never shall I forget the long and profoundly interesting conversation which passed between us a few days ago, on subjects the most important to the comfort and peace of mankind here, and their felicity hereafter;—nor will the noble declaration fade from my recollection—that 'you were not only ready to sacrifice station, property, and even life itself, to the advancement of a religion which (in its genuine purity and simplicity) proved its descent from the *God of Love,* by its direct tendency to render mankind happy, in both a present and a future world; but that you should consider the abstaining from such a course, as the non-performance of one of the *highest duties* imposed upon rational social and accountable man!

'Rajah! a 'door' of the most extensive usefulness is 'opened' to you by Divine Providence, *macte virtute esto.* Go on as you have begun! And may God prosper your benevolent endeavors to spread through the fairest, but most benighted portion of the earth's surface, the knowledge to Christ and the practice of Christian charity.

" 'I am, Rajah,

" 'Your friend and brother in Christ,

" 'RICHARD WARNER.'

"This, I doubt not, you will affirm to be a truly Christian letter, as worthy of its writer as of him to whom it is addressed; such sentiments, from a Rector of the Church of England, is a sign of the approach of favorable times-of 'times of restitution' to the knowledge and the worship of the only living and true God. On the sure word of prophecy we found our belief, that the time is approaching when 'all nations whom Jehovah hath made, shall come and worship before thee, O Lord, and shall glorify thy name, for Thou art great, and doest wondrous things, 'Thou art God alone' 'They shall come from the south, and shall sit down in the kingdom of God.' We may wish to see that day at hand, and we should do all in our power to expedite its approach.

"The illustrious Rajah is among the first and choicest fruits of Indian conversion, and his conversion is remarkable in this, that it was effected in opposition to difficulties and discouragements which, to any mind of ordinary stamp, must have proved insuperable, solely by his superior knowledge of Scripture, combined with an invincible love of truth. It is well known that Mr. William Adam, a Baptist Missionary of Serampore, who endeavored to make him a convert to orthodoxy, concluded his task by acknowledging himself a convert t the true evangelical opinions of the Rajah! By him has the great, the everlasting truth, 'Jehovah our God IS ONE,' been proclaimed to the nations of the East. It has been attested to those of the West by his appearance among them, by his character, by his writings. May his great and good example be followed by thousands and millions of his countrymen, and may we lend our strenuous efforts to promote a cause, which has for its objects the glory of God, the honour of Christ, and the felicity of man. Amen."

A funeral sermon on the death of the Rajah Rammohun Roy, was also reached in the Meeting House of the first Presbyterian Congregation, Belfast on Nov. the 10th, 1833, by the Rev. J. Scott Porter. This gentleman was associated with Mr. Davison, when the Rajah confided to him the care of his adopted son, and there, he states, he had the high gratification and honour of forming the acquaintance of that illustrious man." Mr. Porter had the privilege of being admitted to some degree of intimacy with the Rajah, who seldom failed to call at least once a week to inquire respecting his son's progress. He had thus peculiar opportunities of acquiring a knowledge of the Rajah's manner and mind, as developed in ordinary intercourse. To these he bears strong testimony in the discourse, from which we give the following extracts :

Matthew xiii., 31,32.

The kingdom of Heaven is like to a grain of mustard seed; which a man took and sowed in his field : which indeed is the least of all seeds; but when it is grown, it is the greatest among herbs, and becometh a tree : so that the birds of the air come and lodge in the branches thereof.

"There are men who have achieved, in their own breasts, victories over self, over passion, appetite and desire, compared with which the conquests of Alexander or Napoleon were but the amusements of children. Such characters, God has from time raised up to adorn and dignify the race of mankind; to spread around them the lights of science and philosophy; to kindle the torch of philanthropy; to fan the genial flame of benevolence; and to teach the base, the grovelling, and the low in soul,—the little vulgar, and the great,—what human nature is, and to what an elevation it may soar. In my mind, the accession of one of these, confers more glory on Christianity, than would accrue from the homage of a host of kings. Were I called on to point out the person whose testimony I considered as of the greatest importance to the Gospel, I should direct my finger, not to the wealthy, the dignified, the powerful;—not to the warrior, the statesman, or the sovereign;—but to some patient persevering votary of truth and righteousness. I should select someone who lived in calm seclusion from the turmoil of business, and the pomps of greatness, devoting all the energies of a mighty spirit to the discovery and diffusion of sound principles; little regardful whether his doctrines might be popular, or the reverse, provided only they commended themselves to his own reason; and who practiced what he taught.

"And, my friends, I could point out, not one, but many such examples. I could select those whose vigorous minds have run the most excursive career into the realms of science and fancy,—but who returned to take their rest in the branches of the Christian Revelation; and who valued far more than those intellectual qualities and attainments, in which they outstripped all their comtemporaries, the possession of that invaluable treasure, the truth as it is in Jesus. I could point to his who sung in sublime accents the fall and the recovery of man,—the strife of angels, and the overthrow of fiends; the glorious majesty of heaven, and the gloomy horrors the infernal abyss;-Milton! He was a Christian;—a zealous, a conscientious Christian;—a Christian upon ration and deliberate conviction;—a Christian who spent much of his time, and employed much of his talent, in elucidating the sense of these venerable writings in which the principles of the faith are recorded; and who esteemed this the noblest occupation of his mental energies. And so was Newton : he whose comprehensive soul grasped the huge machinery of the universe in its embrace; and reduced to order the fragments of a mighty plan, before but imperfectly understood. So, too, was Locke; who led the way to the knowledge of the human mind; teaching the student of nature to look inwards; and revealing to him a world there, not less interesting nor less important in its relations, than the world without. And such was Lardner, the close, accurate, patient investigator of antiquity;—whose assiduity never tired; whose inquiring spirit was never satisfied while any fact relating to the early history of the faith was unexplored; and whose can dour in stating the result of his inquiries, has never been impeached, even by those whose judgment he controverted, and whose arguments he exposed. Such, too, was Sir William Jones, whose researches into the language, history, and records of the oriental nations, have never been equalled by the labours of any other scholar, before or since his dav; and who undertook these inquiries for this among other important purposes,—that he might determine whether or not there existed in the literature of the East any authentic history irreconcilable with the Christian Scriptures. The result of his search was his confirmation in the faith of Jesus : a conclusion the more important,—because, as he himself declares, he would not have hesitated to avow, and had no motive to conceal the contrary inference, if fit had appeared to be supported by the facts of the case, and sound argument. And,—not to trouble you be enumerating others whom it would be easy to add to the list,—such was one, whose name I do not hesitate to introduce in connection with those just mentioned, because I conceive him to have been in many respects the equal, and in some the superior, of the greatest among them;—I mean the late illustrious Christian Brahmin,—the Rajah Rammohun Roy. These and such as these are the great men whose names add weight and value to their testimony. These were the truly great;—great not by the accident of birth,—not by the circumstances of fortune,—not by the chances of conquest, nor by the apportionment of worldly dominion; but great in genius, learning, and virtue. The dominion they have exercised, is over the spirit of man, the immortal soul,—not the gross material frame. Their patent of nobility bears the stamp and seal of the celestial chancery. When I contemplate the conduct and history of these illustrious sages; when I witness their ardour in promoting the knowledge of divine truth; when I see them exerting, in this holiest and best of causes, the transcendant abilities with which they were gifted by their Creator; I am struck with the fulfilment of my Saviour's prophetic similitude : *'The kingdom of Heaven is like unto a grain of seed, which a man took and sowed in his field;—which is indeed the least of all seeds; but when it is sprung up, it becometh a tree',* in whose branches the high soaring birds of heaven take refuge. My faith is strengthened, when I witness the accomplishment of this seemingly most improbable prediction. I am made to feel that though heaven and earth may pass away, the words of Jesus shall not pass away. And I revere that Gospel, which though first preached to the poor, and, more than any other religion, adapted to the wants of persons in humble life, is not less suited to the requirements of the most refined and enlightened minds.

"I have mentioned the lately deceased Rajah Rammohun Roy, as one whose talents and history entitle him to be ranked among these men of illustrious soul, to whom, as it appears to me, the phrase in the parable of our Saviour may be most expressively referred : and a brief survey of the leading facts in his eventful life, will be sufficient to justify the estimate I have formed."

The substance of the biographical sketch of the Rajah here given has appeared in a former part of this volume. Mr. Porter thus speaks of the publication of the "Precepts of Jesus" :

"The conduct of Rammohun Roy in presenting to his countrymen the didactic and moral parts of the Gospel, at first, in a detached form, was evidently prompted by reflection on the experience of his own conversion. These were the passages which first attracted his own attention, interested his feelings, and allured his mind; he naturally concluded they were the most likely to engage the souls of other persons similar in faith and habits. His procedure was warranted by reason; for there is nothing in the nature of things, or in the laws of morality, that requires any advocate to bring forward, at the very outset, those part of his case, which, as he well known, may and must prevent him from obtaining a hearing in urging what farther he has to advance. It was demanded by policy; for had

Rammohun Roy insisted upon the doctrinal and miraculous portions of the New Testament, in addressing persons unprepared to receive them, he would only have confirmed them in their prejudices, and strengthened them in their obstinate rejection of Christianity altogether. Whereas, by presenting to them those section whose truth, beauty, benevolence, and utility, could not but be apparent to every can did observer, he took the most promising means of securing their attention and favour, when he should afterwards have occasion to introduce the other portions of the sacred volume to their notice. His conduct was sanctioned by the example of the apostles of Christ. In this sense, Paul openly avowed to some of his converts, that he '*fed them with milk and not with meat, because they were not able to bear it*; and even Christ himself spoke the word unto the multitudes who frequented his preaching, '*as they were able*' to receive it. For the same purpose, he spoke much to them in parables, '*that seeing they might see and not perceive; that hearing they might hear and not understand*;—that is, that they might attain to some impressions of the truth without their knowledge, unaware of the process by which it was acquired."

With respect to the Rajah's character, Mr. Porter says :

"I believe I only speak the general sentiment of all who knew him, when I declare, that the extent, vigour, and profundity of his mind were much more evident to those who conversed with him personally, than to those who only knew him in his works. Never have I known a person who brought a greater variety of knowledge to bear upon almost every topic on which he conversed;—never one whose own remarks were more original ingenious, solid, and useful. Yet, with all his great attainments, he was a modest seeker after knowledge. He did not disdain to ask information from the youngest person in company, if he seemed disposed and qualified to afford it : for he was far removed from the puerile ambition of wishing to appear a universal genius. But he chiefly addressed himself to the old, to whom he always paid remarkable deference and respect. He frequently questioned the respecting their recollection of the state of moral and political knowledge in their youthful days, and as compared with the present time. He loved to hear of the progress of society in philanthropy, virtue, and religion; and to discuss the means by which that progress might be accelerated.

"It occurred to me, that, even while discussing the affairs of England, his beloved India was uppermost in his thoughts. Often, after conversing on the means adopted for the support and education of the poor,—upon the industrial and commercial system, and upon the social machinery of Britain, some expression would escape him which impressed the attentive observer with the conviction that the Rajah was treasuring up in his mind, facts and suggestions that might be of service on his return to that country, for which his bosom never ceased to beat with a son's affectionate solicitude. It was for India, that he left his native land;—it was for India, that he sojourned among strangers; subjecting himself to the thousand in-conveniences of a residence amidst a people differing totally in manners and customs from those which he was obliged to maintain;—it was for India, that he exposed a delicate constitution to the vicissitudes of a strange climate, and risked the loss of health and ease, and endangered life itself.

"The purity no less than the benevolence of his mind, was conspicuous in all the acts and words, and even the tones and looks of the Rajah Rammohun Roy. Offences against the laws of morality, which are too often passed over as trivial transgressions in European society, excited the deepest horror in him. His whole manner and appearance discovered how much he shrunk from the very though of them, when associated with the names of any for whom he had formerly felt respect. The admonitions which he addressed to his son, upon such subjects, were among the most impressive that I ever heard. They have left upon my mind the sentiment of a holy sublimity. It was an elevating thing to hear the mild, solemn and affectionate tones of the voice, inculcating the practice of whatsoever things are pure, lovely, and of good report; and to behold the eye and the whole expressive countenance of the

Rajah beaming with benevolence and piety. Never will the impression of those moments be effaced from the recollection of those who witnessed them. Nor was it for those only with whom he was closely connected, that the Rajah felt and expressed such sympathy. I can tell my countrymen, that for Ireland's welfare, he felt all the interest of a philanthropist. I remember well, that, on the first and only occasion when he attended divine worship in Carterlane Chapel, during my ministry, my flock were engaged in making a collection for the relief of the suffering poor in the West of Ireland, then in a state of lamentable distress; and when I read a letter from a clergyman in that quarter, giving an account of the state of things in his neighbourhood, the tears which feel from his eyes declared how deeply he was moved by the recital. I have reason to think that the liberal contribution which we were enabled to transmit to the general Committee, was materially aided by his generosity. The Rajah was habitually serious, pious, and even devout. He was in the daily habit of perusing, in a very thoughtful manner, some portion or portions of the word of God; and prayer, both public and private, was an ordinance which he never neglected. This practice he observed, no matter what might be his avocations; even when they were of such a nature that most Christians would hold them a plausible excuse for omitting the duty. He was, as his writings testify. A Unitarian Christian. Such he frequently avowed himself, both on the title page of his works, where the name appears; and by his attendance upon the anniversaries of the Unitarian Association, in London. On one of these occasions, I heard him deliver his sentiments at considerable length, with great force and correctness; although the weak state of his health, at the time, rendered it impossible for him to make himself heard at a distance, and the speech consequently could not be reported. It chiefly dwelt upon the importance of practical principles, as compared with mere articles of faith; and more especially those which are called mysteries.

"One defect in his character, of perhaps I should say in his manner, the partiality of friendship would have led me to pass over in silence, or under a general admission of imperfection :

but it has been publicly mentioned, and need not now be concealed; but it has especially, as I am persuaded that the more it is examined, the more will it appear to admit of extenuation. It is this : that either a personal disposition to acquiescence, or compliance with the laws of oriental politeness, sometimes induced him to act in such a way as allowed strangers of leave him with incorrect impressions of his opinions and view. With those whom he knew and love, he conversed most freely an unreservedly upon all topics : and by them his sincerity and candour were most highly appreciated. But, in conversing with strangers,-and more especially those who called upon him out of mere curiosity, without any introduction or business of any kind, as multitudes did, he would not enter into controversy; even though in shunning it he yielded seeming assent to principles most opposite to his know opinion, and which he would rather have laid his head upon the block than have published to the world as his own. This has been set down as insincerity; but, however contrary to our better regulated judgment, I am informed that it is no more than is required of every person who aspires of the character of a well-bred man among the natives of India. It would be judging too harshly to condemn him, an Oriental and a Hindu, for non-conformity to a European standard. After all, it would be difficult to assign a motive for the deception, if he has wished to deceive : and it is universally allowed, that few have sacrificed more to he cause of truth and sincerity than he.

"Another point which has been sometimes objected to in his conduct, is, in my mind, capable of a very easy defense : I allude to his anxiety to avoid every act by which he might forfeit the privileges of *caste*. It has been held that this anxiety showed him to be wavering in his profession of Christianity. But, never was objection more futile. Even if the distinction of caste were founded on religious considerations, the Rajah might be defended on the same principles with the apostle Paul; who, with the Jews lived as a Jew, that he might gain the Jews, though he himself strenuously maintained, that those restrictions to which he subjected himself, were abolished. But the best authorities are agreed that caste is a civil, not a religious institution. Adherence to it, therefore, is no more a proof of insincerity in the profession of Christianity than the retention of a title of nobility would have been. And when it is considered, that without caste he would have been cut off from intercourse with all the enlightened and learned among his countrymen,- and, at the same time, would have been deprived of his landed property sufficient reason will be seen for the conduct which he pursued. This view of the origin of caste was not peculiar to Rammohun Roy. It has been taken up by other competent and strictly impartial authorities, including the Abbe Dubois; the Danish Missionaries at Travancore, the most successful of all the teachers of Christianity in India, who freely permit their converts of retain the distinction of *caste*; and, finally, by the Supreme Court of Hindu law at Calcutta, which, by its decision already mentioned, may be considered as having finally settled the question.

"Thus departed one of the most extraordinary men whom the world have witnessed for centuries : one, whose freedom, vigour, and independence of thought, commanded the admiration even of adversaries; and whose amiable disposition, purity of mind, and benevolence of heart, attached to him, by indissoluble ties, the souls of all who were admitted within the circle of his friends : one whose ardent love of truth, and indefatigable search after it, led him to renounce prejudices the most dear, and connections the most beloved; to embrace opinions once the most obnoxious, and to submit to losses and deprivations the most painful and severe. He was a man who left all and followed Christ : and closely did he tread in his master's footsteps. His integrity and philanthropy were never questioned, and could not be called in question. He fell in a land of strangers, surrounded by countenances of which his eye had never till a few days before; where feature, complexion, language, manners, all told him that he was dying in a foreign soil; from his beloved India, for whose good his heart beat unceasingly. He was carried off in the midst of his days, she much of active usefulness might have been expected in the course of nature. But now,—all his benevolent plans are suddenly cut short, and all his high thoughts are perished. Alas!

How many hopes has this mysterious dispensation brought at once to a close! We trusted,—we fondly trusted,—that it was he who should have redeemed unto Christ the Israel of the East; but it has otherwise pleased God, and our duty is resignation. Let us hope that He will, in His own good providence, raise up other reformers, to finish the work so nobly begun; and to complete that which is now left unfinished for lack of time. Let us pray the Lord of the harvest, that he may send forth other labourers into this field, men like-minded with the Rajah Rammohun Ray.

"In conclusion.—Let us bless God, for the progress of the Gospel throughout the world, up to the present period. Let us glorify him for the illustrious men whom He has raised up to adorn its profession. Let us rejoice in the labours of those who have devoted their lives to the illustration and spread of its pure doctrines. Let us pray, that a succession of such laborers may be raised up to purify it still farther from these corruptions which yet obscure its native beauty. Let us trustfully anticipate the time, when, in its divine and simple majesty, it will be acknowledged and obeyed from the rising to the setting sun; the day, when 'Jehovah *shall be King over all the earth; when there shall be One Lord, and his name One.'* "

The last sermon is by the Rev. W.J. Fox. He prefaces it by saying,—"The following discourse was delivered of Finsbury Chapel, South Place, on Sunday, October 14, 1833, and is published at he request of the congregation, and in testimony of the feelings of the congregation, and in testimony of the feelings by which both preacher and hearers were influenced towards the extraordinary man whom it commemorates."

Genesis, xii., 1.

Now the Lord had said unto Abram, get thee out of thy country, and from thy kindred, and from thy father's house, unto a land that I will show thee.

Hebrews, xi, 8.

And he went out, not knowing whither he went.

"Abraham was an Oriental; and whatever the nation of the individual, I apprehend that an Orientalism of nature and mental character belong to this class of reformers. I mean by Orientalism, a tendency towards the spiritual, the remote, the vast, the undefined, as distinguished from the microscopic and grovelling intellect, which looks only upon earth, sees only in detail, and comprises all philosophy in the calculations which most directly solve the questions, 'What shall we eat, what shall we drink, and wherewithal shall we be clothed?' the men whose monuments rise on the ascending path of human impotents, like 'towers along the steep,' beneath which the tide of time has hitherto beaten in vain, have always had loftier and wider views than these. They have seen, and foreseen, what to others was only a shadowy distance; and even Socrates, who brought down philosophy from the clouds to the business of mankind—the Utilitarian of antiquity—had his inspiring demon; and mode, perhaps, of admonishing his disciples that there are impulses and influences of higher origin than *they* perceive, whose spirits are incarcerated I the gross material world. Of Christian reformers and philanthropists most evident is it, that this Oriental spirit is upon their spirits, for they imbibe it in the religion itself. Our bible is Eastern; it finds or creates an affinity in these whom it vests with a power and a commission to enlighten, exalt, and bless the should of their contemporaries.

"Another mark of this type is, the departing, always figuratively, and often in a literal sense, from the paternal home, and the shrines in which worship the family, or the countrymen of him to whom, in his youth, God speaks, that he my benefit mankind. For such light springs up in the darkness. It implies a conscientious originality of thought. There must be the clearness and the boldness which consanguinity is not likely to have anticipated—which society is not likely to recognise, and which as, in the first instance they display the mental strength of the individual, next subject his moral strength to a severe and painful trial. Parent, child, friend, countrymen, all clinging to the superstitions against which the reformer bears his testimony, become instruments of torture, agonizing in proportion to the superior susceptibilities of his nature. Perhaps, by the very operation of trying and wounding him through his sympathies, expanding an refining those sympathies, so as to contribute to his better qualification for the work of generous, but ill-required beneficence, which he was created to accomplish.

"Such men make their pilgrimage as did the patriarch, in one sense, 'not knowing whiter.' It often leads them to lands they little though to visit-to mental path they little expected to trace-to exertions and associations they little thought to make or form—to conclusions which once their minds would have deemed appalling—to some unexpected rest of faith from their spirits, and perhaps an unexpected grave for their mortal bodies. They know, as Abraham knew, whiter they go, in this particular, that it is where truth, and conscience, an benevolence shall lead; they have the faith which, knowing this, deems it knowledge enough, a sufficient revelation of futurity, such as the Saviour used not only for his won strength, but for his disciples' consolation, 'whither I go ye know, and the way ye know:' and that way known, that path illumined, they are content it should lead through unknown regions, covered with clouds and darkness.

"I will only mention more, that in such men's views, if chiefly directed to scientific and social improvement, there has usually been involved a recurrence to some sublime simplicity of principle, from the forgetfulness of which, error and injury had been occasioned. In theology, the reformation has generally related to the divine nature and character, and has been a protest against some modification of polytheism or idolatry. All great eras of religious improvement have been a return towards the simplicity of that faith in one infinite spirit, of which Abraham was the patriarchal confessor. The losing sight doctrinally or practically, of the Divine Unity, has been the source of almost all corruptions and debasement of religion, whether among Jews or Gentiles, in ancient or mediaeval times. That 'there is one God,' truism as the assertion may seem to us, is, in reality, a proposition so full of truth, and so exclusive under some modification or other, is some application or other of it to the details of faith and practice, it has always been deeply enshrined in the should of spiritual reformers. Whenever and wherever such men arise, their lives, characters, and influence are deserving of our earnest study—whenever and wherever they did, their loss is to be lamented, and their memories cherished; and so be it with him, the unexpected termination of whose career has occasioned the feeling which pervades this assembly, and in whom was visible the image and superscription of that excellence which I have been describing, and which, first in distant report and then personal observation, our hearts recognized in the Rajah Rammohun Roy.

"Strange in it that such a man should have been given by India to the world. * * Strange, that in the proudest and most selfish tribe of the land of caste, which arrogates a diviner origin than the rest of the community, and unscrupulously makes the rest subsidiary to its pleasures, its cupidity, and its arrogance legislating for the Brahmin with recklessness of all inferiors' rights, to which there is nothing comparable even in the worst insolence of feudality—should have been born one, in whose heart men's common nature and equal rights seem ever to have been recognized; whose own soul was such a revelation to him of the universal brotherhood of humanity, that he read it everywhere, even in the reveries of Brahminical theology, and became its advocated and missionary before the chief of the Apostle had told him it was the word of God. Strange, that from that exclusive an restricted land, where the selfish interest alike of the native priesthood, and of the foreign conqueror, obstruct free communication with the world at large; where the invisible wall of superstition guarded by temporal, even more than by spiritual terrors, has hitherto confined all, except the very outcasts of the people, within its magic circle-should have come one who was already, in principle and feeling, a citizen of the world, a member of he great fraternity of enlarged and liberal minds, in whom the foremost men of all free and civilized nationwide welcome a congenial visitant, and whom one country after another was anxiously waiting to tell, upon its own shores, how he was already new and hunoured there. Strange is it—but he was not *of* India, so much as *for* India;

and the influences of race and of country that were over him, only so far tinged the universality of his spirit, as to give it that colouring in which the best of his countrymen would delight, and which would more completely qualify him to be (as in the, perhaps, remote agency of his character and instructions I think he will yet be) the moral and spiritual reformer of his people, the Apostle of Hindustan, the patriarch there of a purer faith, worship, and morality.

"The remarkable faculties and operations of his intellect,—the readiness with it received new impression, and the tenacity with which it retained whatever had once been made;—the wide field over which his acquirements spread, comprising sciences and languages, which individual knowledge rarely associates together;—the caution with which he arranged facts, and the acuteness with which he detected sophism,—the minuteness of detail to which his investigations descended, and the broad principles which he so early adopted, and so extensively applied : these qualities, remarkable as the were, and remarkable as they would have made him, even amongst the literary men of the most enlightened countries,—owed their highest worth to that pure and beautiful moral constitution which was the real glory of his character. Facility and kindness are the common qualities of his countrymen, so far as priest craft and subjugation allow us to discern the native qualities of that gentle but perverted race. Not only were these, in him, sublimed into virtues, by their combination with his intelligence and his principle, but he was born to that expansiveness of sympathy and feeling which, when feeling is also strong, present the germ of the noblest philanthropy—of that which will love man, and toil for man, and suffer for man, and eventually bless man; while yet not the most exclusive fabricator of a family-interest can have more of tenderness and fondness to all who dwell within the circle of his domestic affections. And there was yet more than this in him; there was a tendency, which took the happiest direction, towards what we may call natural religion, or more properly, veneration; I mean the ready recognition, the deep appreciation, of "whatever is morally superior. Real greatness, which is moral greatness, he felt, he love, he venerated, wherever it existed. Hence the beautiful humility of his character; its freedom from the restlessness of the mere innovator, from the pragmaticalness of the mere controversialist, from the nationality of the narrow-minded patriot, and from the hard ambition of the sectarian leader and religious despot. It was this which made him turn with disgust from the gross mythology of his county; it was this which made him rejoice in every beam of the true light which he found glimmering among the dark pages of their Shasters; it was this which guided his unerring selection of those wise and holy fragments, which have floated down from the remote antiquity of their theological books, intermingled with wild dreams, and prescriptions of foolish or pernicious ceremony; it was this which made him so promptly perceive, that, whether his mission were natural, or supernatural , the 'precepts of Jesus' were the 'guide to happiness :' and if we may advert to a lower, though not less striking operation of the same faculty, it was this which overcame his young hostility towards the English name and people, his aversion from the conquerors and despoilers of his country-making him comprehend to what a superior race and nation they belonged, and arms, and literature, and polity, and even in religion; it was this which made him neither the indiscriminating admirer, nor the indiscriminating associate of European residents; but attracted him towards, as they were attracted towards him, the most distinguished for the best qualities of head and heart; the most able, the most honourable, the most upright, though not always the most influential, of all that sojourned there. It was this which made him select, when he came to the daring resolution of passing abroad to other nations, the countries most worthy of such visitation; and dictated alike the purposes which he should, in each pursue, and the association he should form with kindred spirits, to whom, in the simplicity of his own worth, he did homage, because he reverenced in them, that which made them his moral kindred, his spiritual brethren. Such a disposition is of itself a preparation for, and pledge of, final beatitude in heaven; it ripened him to feel blessedness in sitting down with patriarchs in the kingdom of heaven, and in joining the society of the spirits of just men made perfect.

"His adoption afterwards of Christianity, I can scarcely call a conversion; for it no more wrought an essential change in him, than it would have done on the patriarchs and holy men of the Jewish nation, who live before the coming of the Saviour, but in whom was the spirit of Christ. It was not a *change*, but an enlargement, and new modification of his religion. It affected rather the evidence of his principles, than the principles themselves; for the unity, spirituality, and perfection of the Deity, and moral government, and a future life, with the summary of duty in love to God and our neighbour, had long constituted his religion. And these are the substance of Christianity; the peculiarity of which, as distinguished from the pure theism of the Hindu Reformer, consists rather in evidence and application, in the bearing upon these truths of a supernatural system, and in the resurrection of Christ, than in the truths themselves. He had previously that faith, that enlightened and filial confidence in God, which the writer to the Hebrews has so distinctly characterized as the life of all pure religion, most acceptable to God-most sage and hourable for men. 'He that cometh unto God, must believe that he is, and that he is the rewarder of them that diligently seek him.' So came the inquiring philosopher; and what bigot shall say that, so coming, he was not accepted? Like another character in this same record, 'he walked with God,' he already manifested that spirit of devotion which permanently possessed him; which was neither weak originally, through the imperfection of his knowledge, nor polluted afterwards by the false of controversy in which he was compelled to engage; but ever strong,—shining steadily even through the last days of silence and darkness, when his life ebbed away. This is religion : this is Christianity in spirit and in substance, whatever its appellation. Nor is it improbable, that, by a direct influence, as well as a native affinity, his faith was linked to that of the patriarch, in the words of whose history we have ventured to desirable his character and destiny. Through the traditions, both of India and of Arabia, might something of the spirit of the Father of the faithful descend upon the Indian Reformer; like the mantle of the ascending Elijah, borne hither and thither on the whirlwind, but resting at length on the meek and expecteant disciple who knelt upon the earth. Strong as must generally be the prejudices of the Hindu against the gospel : strong, from the interweaving of idolatry with all the dictates of education and the concerns of life; strong, from its remote antiquity and unquestioned reception by the many millions around them; strong, from the connection of the Christian name with those whom they fear and hate, while they obey, and who exhibit little of his bening spirit to mitigate their prejudice; strong in all the arts employed to uphold idolatry by a shrewd, unprincipled, ambitious, and rapacious priesthood, possession the hereditary reverence of the community; we may yet well believe that his mind, which had vanquished these prejudices in itself, and long struggled with them in others, was neither unprepared nor indisposed for the reception of Christianity. He must have felt congeniality with the sacred writers, as soon as their pages were fairly open before him. The simplicity of their narrative, the fervour of their devotion, the depth of their philosophy, the purity of their precepts, the boundlessness of their benevolence, the splendour of their hopes-all must have touched corresponding chords in his bosom-must have made him feel that his was what he wanted-must have led him to the Lord of all, not like John's disciples, *questioning*, but affirming, thou art he that should come; I look not for another.

"Yet his reception of Christianity was no act of impulse, of gratified curiosity, or accordant feeling, but of investigation as patient and perfect as if it had been to him, of ass systems of religion, the most incredible or uncongenial. He acquired both the Hebrew and Greek languages, that he might study the Scriptures in their originals. He called in the aid of a Jewish Rabbi, for the one, and of a Christian missionary, for the other; the singular circumstance having occurred, as you know, of the Missionary, who thus aided his labours, being himself converted from the Trinitarian opinions which he was sent thither to promulgate. This investigation, and the doctrinal controversies which ensued, occupied at least three years : he looked back on them with complacency: he had found in Christianity his own pure theism and morality, not overturned, but gloriously strengthened and had been to him a stumbling block, at the portal of the Christian temple, The angel of inquiry rolled away the stone, and told him of the resurrection of the man Christ Jesus. But while he was more and more appreciating Christianity, many Christians were lest and less appreciating him, because it was not their dogmatized and sectarianized Christianity. He sat at Jesus' feet, with listening ears, and loving and obedient heart; while they were pointing to church and to chapel, and saying, 'Lo! here is Christ,' or, 'Lo, Christ is there!' it better became him, than it would become us, to forget the insults and vexations to which he was subjected, by that spirit of sectarian bigotry which dwells in the nominally Christian body, the worst of demoniacal possessions. Not for such man should there be that poor and pitiful, that blind and bitter conflict, to make a party trophy of that which could not, from its very nature, become the prize or the possession of a party. The factions of Jerusalem might as reasonably have battled for the light that used to irradiate their temple. What can matter, whether he said Shabboleth or Sibboleth, or neither? He space with the tongues of men and angels; for his speech was charity, the true language of heaven, to which the noise of creeds and their partizans is but as the sounding brass, or the tinkling cymbol.

"The Unitarians, who expected (if such there were) that he should only worship in their chapels, and be identified with their affairs—and the Trinitarians, who because he went about the walls of their Zion, to mark its towers and palaces, would incarcerate him within its gates, and claim him for their own,—alike mistook that which became such a man on such a mission. It was in his own free and Catholic spirit, ever ready to ask 'Are ye not all brethren? Why fall ye our by the way?' that he wended his way, in charity, awhile with each; nay, that sometimes, with a literal on observance of the precept, when some partizan, with rude hand, constrained him to go a mile with him on his rough roads, he would, in his oriental courtesy, 'go with him twain'. But the affectation of a doubt on the doctrinal opinions of a man who his illustrated them with unsurpassed acuteness of criticism, variety of information, and conclusiveness of argument, through a succession of publication, is scarcely more endurable than the bigotry which would append everlasting damnation to his known continued belief in the doctrines so defended, of the proper unity of God, and the forgiveness of sinners, by his unpercased mercy.

"The testimony which he thus bore against the departure from the worship of the one only God, both by Hindus and by Christians, has not been borne in vain. Its useful influence has already been made apparent, although it will probably be long before the full extent and power of that influence will be manifested. Thousands of his countrymen have followed his example in the renunciation of idolatry. The philosophical theists of India now comprise on inconsiderable portion of whatever is eminent amongst the natives for intelligence and character. In their temple at Calcutta, where his voice has been often heard, and at the mention of which his countenance would glow with devout and benevolent pleasure, no exclusive worship is offered to the Deity, but homage in which the Hindu and the European, the rationalist and the supernaturalist, the Jew, the Mahommed, and the Christian may and do unite. Where the votaries of so many creeds must continue to meet and mingle in the midst of an idolatrous multitude, may there long remain, though he shall never return to it, that one spot in which man, unquestioned, may offer the universal prayer to the universal Father. And the flame which he had kindled continued to burn and brighten in his absence! The liberal Hindus, notwithstanding the power and wrath of the idolatrous priesthood, are growing in strength and influence. To them, apparently, we must look for the carrying on of his work, and the continuation of the process whose consummation will be the disuse of idolatrous ceremony, the extinction of caste, the enlightenment of the people and improvement of their condition, the reception of pure Christianity, and the attainment of political existence and freedom. Then will his name receive its rightful honours, and his country know its benefactor.

"We shall see his face no more! His presence has passed away as a poetic image fades from the brain! But it has left impressions which will long endure; influences of good, wide and deep, here; yet wider and deeper in the distant land of his nativity. And, 'being dead, be yet speaketh' with a voice to which not only India but Europe and America will listen for generations. A few days of fever have made him dust. It appears that no skill could have saved a life which, as he was probably but in about the fifty-fifth year of his age, seems to us prematurely terminated. Subsequent to all other sings of consciousness, he indicated the yet surviving sense of the kindness of his friends, and, by silent devotion, of the presence of his God. His body will be silently committed to its rest in ground only hallowed by its reception-the noblest of all consecrations. Many will there be whom personal attachment will draw towards that spot, and it should draw them thither; for it is good to weep over the grave of such a man, and makes the heart better. Good will it be for them, there, to adopt as the rule of their own conduct his favorite quotation from the Persian poet, which he often wished should be inscribed on his tomb- 'the true way of serving God, is to do good to man.'

"And if we shed at his death 'no faithless tears', such is the service which the contemplation of his life will stimulate us to render. God is not served by our forms and ceremonies, our creeds and anathemas, our wild emotions, or our bustling zeal. He will have mercy, and not sacrifice. The garland with which the Hindu decks his idol is not less worthy heaven than the useless observances and mysterious dogmas, by the faith and practice of which many who are called Christians, have thought to propitiate God. The dissemination of knowledge, the mitigation of suffering, the prevention of oppression, the promotion of improvement, the diffusion of a beneficent piety,—these are God's work, for us, towards others; and they are all reflected upon ourselves in the building up of our own characters to intellectual and moral excellence. 'Speaking the truth in love', we shall best bear our own testimony, and prolong theirs who have joined the 'cloud of witnesses' that compass us about, as we 'run the race set before us, looking unto Jesus.' The voice of duty may not call us to quit either county or kindred; but our souls have their pilgrimage of faith to pursue, through varied trials, to our Father's house, in which there are many mansions, wherein ultimately shall be gathered together the whole family of heaven and earth. Already should our hearts feel the bond of that holy fraternity,—the love which never faileth, which never shall fail, in time or in eternity; for it is the essence and the influence of God, and 'he that loveth dwelleth in God, and God in him.'

"Thus may we anticipate, according to our usefulness and progress, acceptance in degree like that which awaited our departed visitant and friend. For may we not devoutly trust that the Great Master has received him with—'Well done, good and faithful servant, enter thou into the joy of the Lord;' and that patriarchs and prophets, apostles and confessors, philosophers and reformers, the holy and illustrious of all times and countries, gathering round to greet a brother, have responded in gratulation, 'Amen, even so, Lord Jesus!' "

Here we bring to a conclusion the notices we have been able to collect of the last days in England of the illustrious Hindu Reformer, the Rajah Rammohun Roy,—a man who, though he was greatly admired and appreciated during his life by those who could discern even a small portion of his greatness, will perhaps be far better comprehended, and there fore exert a far wider influence over his countrymen, now that time has removed some of the barriers which separated him from them during his lifetime. India will doubtless not much longer delay to prepare for him an enduring tribute of reverence and respect, as well as to perpetuate the history of his life for future generations. It is probable that the painting from which the frontispiece is copied is the best representation of his living form that exists;—while the bust taken after death preserves his actual form. Will the capital of his country long remain without the honour of possessing such a statue of him as may show to future generations the noble benefactor of his country? Ere all have passed away who personally knew him in India, will not efforts be made to collect all that can be known respecting him into a complete and permanent Memoir?

There is, however, one further mark of respect due to this illustrious reformer, which he would value more highly than any other.

We have seen how earnestly he laboured to disseminate the great truths which he had devoted his whole life to discover, and to present them to his countrymen for their serious consideration in a simple and popular form. To accomplish this he spared no expense, no time, no personal exertion. His unexpected, and, to our narrow view, premature summons to the other world, prevented his accomplishing all he had purposed in this respect. His works were never given to his countrymen and to the world in a connected series :— many of the books which he published are now out of print, and it is probable that manuscripts of his may yet be discovered which he intended for publication, had not death arrested his hand.

Let his countrymen undertake the sacred task of collecting and publishing in a complete and permanent form all his works, and of rendering those of them to which he attached the greatest importance acceptable to the public generally by being printed in a cheap and popular edition. Thus will the most enduring monument be raised to his memory! Thus may his high and excellent aspirations be enabled to kindly the hearts of generation after generation of his countrymen, and through them of countless multitudes. Listening with reverence to his voice, now speaking to them from the World of Spirits, may his countrymen be led on by him to a pure and holy religion, which will guide them in peace and happiness through this world, and prepare them for another and a better. And thus, without distinction of county of clime, shall myriads bless the name of the first Hindu Reformer the Rajah Rammohun Roy.

RAMMOHUN ROY : A REPUBLICAN IN POLITICS

The distinguished Brahmin, Rammohun Roy was a native of the province of Bengal, properly so called and born in the district of Burdwan, the most fertile and the most populous of all British India. He was about 60 years of age; and as the district in question was ceded to the British government as early as

1760, Rammohun was of course born a subject of the British government. Considerable pains appear to have been taken with the early education of Rammohun, long before he had formed any acquaintance with Europeans; for, in his own district he was instructed in all the learning usually bestowed upon a Brahmin, and was afterwards sent to the celebrated seminary of Benaras, where he remained for several years engaged in studying the Sanskrit language. His first acquaintance with the English language he owed to the care and patronage of the late Mr. John Digby, collector of the land tax in the district of Rungpore, one of the most easterly portions of Bengal. His merit soon raised him to the highest office which a native can hold, that of Dewan, or chief native superintendent. It was in this office that he acquired the little fortune which enabled him to become a zeminder or proprietor in the district of Hooghly, to no larger extent however, than an income of 1000 a year. Earlier portion of his life he has left an interesting account published in the Literary Gazette.

"My ancestors were Brahmins of a high order and from time immemorial were devoted to the religious duties of the race, down to my fifth progenitor, who about 140 years ago gave up spiritual excise for worldly pursuits and aggrandisement. His descendents eversince have followed his example according to the usual fate of courtiers, with various success, sometimes rising to honour, and sometimes falling in success, sometimes miser able through disappointment. But my maternal ancestors being of sacredotal order by profession, as well as by birth and of a family and which none holds a higher rank in that profession, have, upto the present day, uniformly adhered to a life of religious observance and devotion, preferring peace and tranquility of mind to the excitement of worldly grandeur.

In conformity with the usage of my paternal race, and the wish of my father, I studied the Persian and Arabic languages, these being accomplishments indispensable to those who attached themselves to the courts of the Mohammedan princes; and agreeable to the usage of my maternal relation, I devoted myself to the study of Sanskrit and the theological works written in it, which contain the body of Hindu literature, law and religion.

When about the age of 16, I composed a manuscript calling in question the validity of the idolatorous system of the Hindus. This together with my known sentiments on the subject having produced a coolness between me and my immediate kindred. I proceeded on my travels and passed through different countries, chiefly within but some beyond the bounds of Hindustan, with a feeling of great aversion to the establishment of British power in India.

When I had reached the age of 20, my father recalled and restored me to his favour; after which I saw and began to associate with Europeans and son after made myself tolerable acquainted with their laws and form of government. Finding them generally more intelligent, more steady and moderate in their conduct I gave up my prejudices against them, and became inclined in their favour, feeling persuaded that their rule, though foreign yoke, would lead out speedily and surely to the amelioration of the native inhabitants. I enjoyed the confidence of several of them even in their public capacity.

My continued controversies with the Brahmins on the subject of their idolatry and superstition, and my influence with their custom of burning widows, and other pernicious practice received an increased their animosity against me, with renewed force and through their influence with my family, my father was again obliged to withdraw his countenance openly, though his limited pecuniary support was still continued to me.

After my father's death, I opposed the advocates of idolatry, with, still greater boldness : availing myself of the art of printing, now established in India. I published various works and pamphlets against their errors in native and foreign languages. This raised such a feeling against me that I was at last deserted by every person, except two or three Scotch friends, to whom, and the nation to which except two or three Scotch friends, to who, and the nation to which they belong, I always feel grateful. The ground which I took in all my controversies was not that of opposition to Brahmanism but to a perversion of it; and I endeavoured to show that idolatory of the Brahmins was contrary to the practice of ancestors and the principles of the ancient books and authorities which they profess to revere and obey. Notwithstanding the violence of the opposition and resistance to my opinions, several highly respectably persons, both among my own relations and others began to adopt the same sentiments.

Now I felt a strong wish to visit Europe and obtain, by personal observation a more thorough insight into its manners, customs, religion and political institutions. I refrained however from carrying this intention into effect until my friends who conceded in my sentiments should be increased in number and strength. My expectations having at length been realized in November 1830, I embarked for England as the discussion of the East India Company's Charter was expected to come on, by which the treatment of the natives of India and its future government would be determined for many years to come; and an Appeal to the King in Council against the abolition of the practice of burning Hindu widow was to be heard before the Privy Council and His Majesty the Emperor of Delhi had likewise commissioned me to bring before the authorities in England certain encroachments on his rights by the East India Company, I accordingly arrived in England in April 1831."

In politics, Rammohun Roy was a republican. At Calcutta he seldom or ever visited the Government house and kept at a distance from all the chief functionaries of Government. Among Europeans he associated chiefly with the ultra liberal party. In 1820, on the breaking out of the Spanish, Neapolitan, and Sardinian revolutions, Rammohun gave a public entertainment in honour of them. He was master of the Sanskrit language, and also of the Arabic, he was exceedingly good Persian scholar and quoted Persian poets liberally, appropriately and gracefully, of course he understood thoroughly the Hindu and Beangalee. He had read a great deal of English literature, chiefly historical and, considering the late period of life at which he made this acquisition, the precision and grammatical accuracy which he had attained were remarkable. He wrote much better than he spoke. With a view of being able to read the Jewish scriptures without the medium of a translation, Rammohun entered upon the study of the Hebrew, his progress in which was facilitated by the previous acquaintance with the cognate Arabic.

He was about six feet high and large in proportion, but his person though not wanting in apparent symmetry was unwieldy and without activity.

The Annual Register, London 1833,

RAMMOHUN ROY : PATRIOT WITH UNSURPASSED INDEPENDENCE OF CHARACTER

The public career of this distinguished and lamented individual has been that of a true patriot and genuine philanthropist, and his name will go down to posterity as one of the most extraordinary men of the age in which he lived. Many native gentlemen have indeed within a few years past, cast off the prejudices of education and habit and united in the task of promoting the moral and political elevation of their countrymen : but it was the glorious distinction of Rammohun Roy, to take the lead in this great work of reformation and to stand forth pre-eminent above all the rest, one of the shining lights of the age. He had made himself conversant with the Greek and Hebrew languages with a view of studying in their original the sacred weeks of the Christian faith; he was a Sanskrit and Arabic scholar, he spoke and wrote English with elegance and fluency; he had studied the American and English Constitutions, and in short his attain ments were only surpassed, by his high sense of honour and morality and his ardour in the noble cause, to which his fortune and life were devoted.

In independence of character he was unsurpassed by any of our countrymen, and equally despised in theory and eschewed in practice, the servility of the Asiatic. If he was too plaint in conversation, if his politeness and a 'bienseance', the kindness and mildness of his disposition led him to concede too much, as we think they did, in principle he yielding nothing. His enthusiasm carried him too far, perhaps, but it that be wrong, it is indeed, a glorious error. We have seen in him here foremost on every occasion in promoting the success of great public objects. Who can forget his eloquent Memorial to the King in council for the liberty of free printing worthy in some respects to be ranked with Milton's defence of the English people and perhaps considering the circumstances of its author, a still more extraordinary production? That powerful appeal which Mr. Cutlar Fergusson pledged himself to deliver to Mr. Canning and to support with all his talent and influence, but which he consigned in so far as he was concerned oblivion, bore the signatures of Dwarkanath Tagore, Prussonoo Comar Tagore, Radhapreshad Roy and some other natives of distinction who were a little hand of patriotic members of our community, of which Rammohun Roy was the respected and distinguished leader. In appeals against illegal taxation, in petitions for the extension of civil rights and commercial privileges of this country, these gentlemen were even found zealously cooperating with their European brethren, incurring and enduring with a philosophy worthy of the course, the hatred and persecution of the bigotted and all the penalties to which reformers in all ages and countries have subjected themselves. In all these cases the zeal and perseverance of this lamented patriot shone conspicuous, but honourable as his exertions were in these case, they are thrown into the shade, but that which is without a parallel perhaps in the annals of mankind his proceeding to England—he who had never perhaps half a dozen times in his life put himself in a boat, to undertake a voyage of 15000 miles to a new and rigorous climate so repugnant to his habits, involving so much privation and suffering for a Hindu still preserving the customs of his caste-so opposed to the feelings of his relatives, and demanding such a sacrifice e of his own—in a separation from them for the first time at his advanced age when it seemed too probable that separation would be for ever; but all these considerations were absorbed in the desire to benefit his country which burned with an ardour that could only be extinguished in death, in the breast this enlightend and virtuous man; and regardless of all difficulties which only acted indeed, like oil poured upon the flame of his patriotic zeal, he encountered them all with cheerfulness and landed safe in England, destined alas! Never to return.

While there; where he was received by the first men in the Kingdom, in point of talent and worth, with a homage, perhaps beyond any example, all his energies were devoted to the great object, which led him into that distant land. He visited all our public institutions, our Legislative Chambers, our Courts of Justice, our Churches; he cultivated acquaintance of statesmen, and philosophers; examined for himself the progresses of the arts and sciences and aided in his investigation by the great men, whose names are for ever associated with them he furnished new and valuable information on the state of his county to our statesmen; he fought the battle of his country to them and there is no doubt that however defective the Indian Charter may be, to his suggestions some of the wisest provisions as respects of the natives of his country, are to be ascribed. We know that he shared the esteem and confidence in a very high degree, of one of the greatest men of our day-Lord Brougham, and we have reason to believe that his influence, over that gigantic intellect was exerted for good of his countrymen. It might be supposed that when the Charter was passed his labours and the necessity of his further stay in England would have ceased, but he felt that in many arrangements consequent on that measure which to originate in England, his presence and his advice might be useful to India and he deferred his return here where his arrival would have been hailed as a glorious triumph and an epoch in the history of the country; but alas! Instead of having to welcome his return we are left we are left to mourn for his death, a public and irreparable loss to British India-consoled however by the reflection that his name and his fame as a patriot and philanthropist will live for ever.

It is well known to man who read this hurried tribute to the memory of a distinguished man, that we who write it were honoured with his friendship; but witnesses of his exertions during so many years in this country, the companion of his voyage to our native land and informed of his zealous effort here; we do not fear that our partiality has led us into any exaggerations of his merits or his claims to public admiration-on the contrary writing from the impulse of the moment midst all the hustle of getting up a daily paper, we have endeavoured to estimate and feel that we owe some apology to the friends of this eminent man and to the public for the imperfections of this hasty sketch literally written against time and doing therefore no justice to the subject.

It will be universally conceded however by all but the few bigotted enemies of this lamented man that his death is as we have stated a great public loss to the native of this country and we trust that no time will be lost in preparing to do honour to his memory by some much worthier and more enduring tribute to his memory than any mere sketch of his character in any epheral publication could confer, however well executed. Some of the leading members of this community will no doubt get up a requisition for a meeting to commemorate the "Benefactor of British India" they will confer honour on themselves in so doing and as we feel assured we only imitating the example of some of the most eminent men in Great Britain.

THE BENGAL HURKARU.

The India Gazette, Calcutta

February 10, 1834.

RAMMOUHUN ROY :
A CITIZEN OF THE WORLD.
Joachim Stocqueler :

1

Self-freed and self-erect-thy ardent mind
Sought, found the light, where all around were blind,
Burst the strong chains man's heaven-ward flight control
And rent the gloomy fetters of the soul.

2

The world's true citizen, of man's whole race,
How varied e'er by manners, form or face,
In all, thy heart an equal kindred owned
In each of all mankind, a brother found.

3

Pride's lordly bounds, or bigot priesthood's ban,
Which dare proscribe inferior-man to man,
Alike unknown, alike despised by thee,
Thy true benevolence knew no boundary.

4

"Oh shame to pride, to bigot priesthood shame,
Which scorns a brother, though his creed the same!"
Accept this tribute as thy worth-sincere.
Dissembling never was thine-nor mingles here.

5

And let not flattery's hand the tribute pay,
Nor fulsome praises derogate the lay-
Let truth itself thy worth severely scan,
And say to all the world "This was a MAN".

The *Englishman*,
Calcutta, Friday, February 14, 1834.

RAMMOHUN ROY : A BENEFACTOR OF INDIA

If it is a merit of have first thrown off
The shackles of Indian superstition and to
Have attacked it in its stronghold, to have
Commenced the twilight of intelligence? Which has now dawned among us after ages of darkest ignorance, to have give the first
Impulse to the dormant energies of native
Intellect to have set an example of patriotism
In this land of cold blood, to have been one
Of the principal means of redeeming one's own
Country from the character of barbarism?
Such merit Rammohun Roy possessed in abundance
to say he had no fault would be saying he was
more than a man. He had his errors as every

human being has and nevertheless future ages
will remember him as a benefactor of the nation

The Englishman, Calcutta,
Wednesday, February 12, 1834.

RAMMOHUN ROY :
THE CELEBRATED BRAHMIN, WITH HIGH MORAL QUALITIES

James Sutherland

The public career of Rammohun Roy in Calcutta must be familiar to most of my readers; but although he was generally known, and esteemed by the European community, I doubt if he was properly appreciated. These people, accustomed to hear other natives speak English perhaps even more fluently, and who met them only in that sort of mixed society in which there is little scope for the display of mind, wondered what other saw in him so astonishing. Of his various acquirements, and the immense obstacles over which he had triumphed in shaking off the prejudices of habit and creed, born as he was, a high caste Brahmin, they could form no adequate estimate; for it is wonderful how little the generality of our countrymen, especially of those located at the Presidencies, know of these matters. They heard something a Rammohun Roy's numerous writings, but they read them not, and fancied, if they ever thought about them at all, that they probably related to the feats of Brahma, or the incarnation of Vishnu; they confounded of his own countrymen, and the more intellectual of ours, however, he was better appreciated, and especially by those who approached to a closer intimacy with him, and met him in the case and freedom of familiar intercourse.

The writer of this article had shared the friendship and confidence of Rommohun Roy for several years, and was early after his acquaintance with him imbued with a profound veneration for his character, which displayed qualities extremely rare in An Asiatic. Although he had adjured the prejudices of caste, he still abstained from the food forbidden by it, in order that his reasons for departing from the faith of his ancestors might not be mistaken; and that he might still pressure his influence over his country. That he did to a certain degree; but to such an extent was he persecuted by the more bigotted Hindus, that his life was actually in danger from them, and at one time Dwarkanath Tagore and a few faithful friends only adhered to him; while his aged mother is said to have gone to Juggernaut, and died of grief and vexation at his apostasy, as she probably called it. He never could go to a party at any European gentleman's, but he was watched by *hurkaurs* and bearers till a late hour at night, peeping though the *jhilmils* to detect him in any violation of the rules of caste, so that he has been known to suffer severely from thirst, being afraid to take even a glass of water. The civilians of the old school too, by no means approved of any indication of the march of mind among the native : they infinitely preferred the sleek and servile Baboo who threw off his shoes at the foot of the stairs and hoped "master was well"; and some of them treated him with indignity. It is said that he once fought a duel with someone who had presumed to do so, and I know that he had a very high and delicate sense of honour. One of his relatives also was shamefully persecuted in those days when it was too much the principle of our government to support power at the expense of justice. It will be admitted that these were trials, which it required no common fortitude to sustain : but they were borne with a dignity and firmness that has seldom been surpassed.

Rammohun Roy was great friend of Mr. Buckingham's, and it was highly honourable to the former that at a time when party-spirit ran very high here, and Mr. Buckingham was held up to the world by the Government and its adherents as a sort of political bugbear and his house *tabooed* as they say in the Pacific that this enlightened active advocate of freedom made a point of being more frequent in his visits to him, and they discussed with zeal and animation the great questions of Indian polity.

The first striking indication of deep reflection and earnestness on subjects of political importance I met with in Rammohun Roy, was shortly after his memorable appeal to the King in Council, for the liberty of free printing in India, was ready for the press. We had conversed about it frequently, but it had been said that it had been written for him, and not knowing him so well, I thought it not unlikely; but while talking it over one evening with him, he observed suddenly, "That another argument or rather illustration might still be introduced which would give additional force to the memorial. Urge, said he, that in Canada where free institutions have long prevailed, notwithstanding its proximity to the United States, that even during the war the loyalty of the subjects there has never been shaken or suspected; but that on the contrary, these privileges have increased their attachment to the British throne. I wrote the clause down nearly in his own words, and they are printed in the memorial. At that time, I believe, he was in the habit of getting his English compositions looked over by some of his European friends, from his anxiety to be correct, though he wrote the language with considerable fluency and elegance; and even in his latter days, though his knowledge of it was of course improved, he would frequently get an acquaintance who might be near him to write a note for him; but then he was most fastidious and difficult to please as to the style, and no one better understood how to adapt his expressions with the greatest exactness to the condition of the party addressed and the circumstances of the case.

His philanthropy was unbounded, and generally took a wise direction it is known that he maintained a school here for many years, and in printing books and contributing to useful institutions and objects benevolence, he expended large sums of money. Some of these publications, perhaps-too much devoted to speculative theology. I should rather have seen his energies directed to subjects less sacred and abstruse than disputations with Missionaries on the divine incarnation—a question of faith rather than of reason and logical inquiry.

He was not always judicious in the choice of friends. His generosity and unsuspecting nature were sometimes abused; and he was too apt to be misled by high-sounding professions. One instance of the kind, he and reason bitterly to repent; for the individual alluded to, a European, on whom he and his friend Dwarkanath had heaped kindnesses in overflowing measure, disappointed in his hopes of accomplishing by means of Rammohun Rou, other objects of ambition, turned round upon him and assailed him with the most atrocious calumny, in which he was to a certain degree abetted, by a journal here that too eagerly lent itself to the propagation of any base slander against a political rival. The offender in this case, however, afterwards begged pardon on his knees, and successfully solicited a pecuniary favour from the man he had reviled!

Speaking of his eldest son, who is still living in Calcutta, he told me that he never attempted by direct efforts of argument, still less by ridicule or sarcasm, to bring him round to his own opinions, and that he was still, when he had nearly attained to the age of manhood, worshipping his images of wood and stone but, said he, I invited him to study with me, and as his mind became enlarged, he gradually forsook these prejudices of ignorance and superstition.

Persons who first met him in company, where political and literary subjects came under discussion, were astonished at the acquaintance he displayed, with our institutions, our public men, and our literature; they were surprised to hear a native talking of the *Quarterly*, the *Edinburgh*—of Whigs and Tories—of Lord Liverpool and of Mr. Canning. There was something in the sparkling oratory of the latter that had a peculiar charm for him, and indeed that statesman's advocacy of the Catholic claims touched him nearly, for their was no subject on which he felt more keenly than on one which involved the great question of religious liberty; he always reflected on the possibility of this county being made, like Ireland, another arena for the fierce contention of rival sects, owing to the adoption here of those principles against which Mr. Canning so successfully contended at home.

In short, he was the enthusiastic advocate of liberty, civil and religious, all over the world, and watched with intense anxiety every indication its advance or retrogradation; When the Spanish constitution was established, he and his enlightened friend Dwarkanath Tagore, who were regarded as the leaders of the Liberal party of the natives in India, gave a grand dinner in honour of the event. It was at one of these parties, indeed, given by these distinguished natives, that Mr. Fergussion made one of those eloquent speeches which, alas! Were all sound and fury, signifying nothing : for he went to England, and so entirely forgot his native friends and all his pledges to them that he never attempted even to present their powerful appeal in behalf of the liberty of the press. But with Rammohun Roy the love of freedom was not a mere matter of impulse or momentary excitement, subsiding with the occasion that called it forth. I had sunk deeply into his heart, and so completely carried him away at times, that his own interests were entirely absorbed in it. When he heard the news of the French Revolution-the glorious Three Days, so great was his enthusiasm that he could think and talk of nothing else, thought it was the period, as it has actually fallen out, for ever.

He did not, however, in his interest in European politics forget those of his own country, and as the period for the renewal of his charter approached, he made up his mind to undertake that voyage over so many thousand miles of ocean, so arduous to a native, who had scarcely ever even crossed the sacred Gunga in a boat, and who had still new prejudices to over-come, new privations to suffer, new trials to undergo, in making it, to which the Anglo-Indian is of course not subjected; but his devotion to the cause triumphed over all obstacles, and has conquered all but death, to whose stern fiat we must all alike submit.

On ship-board Rammohun Roy took his meals in his own cabin, and at first suffered considerable inconvenience from the want of a separate fireplace; having nothing but a common earthen *choola* on board. His servants too, fell desperately sea-sick (though, as if his ardour supported him against it, he himself never felt this malady at all), and took possession of his cabin, never moving from it, and making it, as may be easily conceived, no enviable domicile; in fact, they compelled him to retreat to the lockers : but still the kindness of his nature would not allow him to remove them. The greater part of the day he read, chiefly, believe, Sanskrit and Hebrew. In the forenoon and the evening he took and airing on deck, an always got involved in an animated discussion. After dinner, when the cloth was removed, and the desert on table, he would come out of his cabin also, and join in the conversation and take a glass of wine. He was always cheerful, and so won upon the esteem of all on board, that there was quite a competition who should pay him the most attention, and even the sailors seemed anxious to render him any little service in their power. In a gale of wind he would be upon deck, gazing at the foam-crested surges as they roared by the vessel, and admiring the sublimity of the scene. On one occasion I brought on deck the "Ocean Sketches", and read to him the first piece, entailed "*The Breeze*", which though I am writing for the editor of the Literary Gazette, and the author of he poem, he must permit me to quote-

> The distant haze, like clouds of silvery dust.
> Now sparkles in the sun. The freshening breeze
> Whitens the liquid plain; and like a steed
> With proud impatience fired, the glorious ship
> Quick bounds exultant, and with rampant prow
> Off flings the glittering foam. Around her wake,
> A radiant milky way, the sea-birds weave
> Their circling flight, or slowly seeping wide
> O'er boundless ocean, graze with drooping wing
> The brightly-crested waves. Each sudden surge,
> Up-dashed, appears a momentary tree.
> Fringed with the hoar-frost of a wintry morn;
> And then, like blossoms from a breeze-stirred bough,
> The light spray strews the deep.
> How fitfully the feeble day-beams pierce
> The veil of heaven!-On you far line of light,
> That like a range of breakers, streaks the mian,
> The ocean swan-the snow-white Albatross,
> Gleams like a dazzling foam-flake in the sun!
> Gaze upward-and behold, where parted clouds
> Disclose ethereal depths, its dark-hued mate
> Hangs motionless on arch-resembling wings,

As thought were painted on the sky's blue vault.

Sprinkling the air, the speek-like petrels from
A living shower! Awhile their pinions gray
Mingle scarce-seen among the misty clouds,
Till suddenly their white breasts catch the light,
And flash like silver stars!

He recognized at once the fidelity of this picture; although not given to poetical reading.

His equanimity was quite surprising. In more than one case the thing in his cabin was quite afloat, owing to the sea washing into the gallery window-but it never disturbed his serenity. If any thing threw him off his equilibrium of temperament, it was the prevalence of contrary winds; because of his great anxiety to get on, and his alarm lest the great question of the Company's Charter should come on before he arrived in England.

At the Cape he did not go ashore, except for an hour or two, and then only at the particular request of a friend-at first owing to the sickness of his adopted son (who accompanied him to England, and who is still there), and afterwards to an accident he met with himself in returning on boards the vessel, when in consequence of the carelessness of the officer on deck in not securing the gangway ladder, he got a fall, from which he was lame for eighteen months afterwards. Indeed he never entirely recovered from it I believe, and it frequently gave him great pain. But no bodily suffering could repress his mental ardour. Two France frigates, under the revolutionary flag, the glorious tricolour, were lying in Table Bay; and lame as he was, he would insist upon visiting them; the sight of those colours, indeed, seemed to kindle the flame of his enthusiasm and to render him insensible to pain. He would listen to no remonstrance, and accordingly went. His reception of course was worthy of the French Characther and of him, though he gave no time for any preparation. He was conducted over the vessels and endeavoured to convey by the aid of interpreters how much he was delighted to be under the banner that waved over their decks, an evidence of the glorious triumph of right over might : and as he left the vessels he repeated emphatically "Glory, glory, glory to France!"

Some of the most distinguished people at the Cape left their cards for him at the hotel, and some called on board, but not the Governor. Perhaps it was contrary to etiquette; but yet how insignificant in point of rank and influence was this Colonel Governor, compared with some of the great men of England and France, who afterwards crowded to pay homage to Rammohun Roy. And though the honour all on their side.

As we approached England, his anxiety to know what was passing there became most urgent, and he implored the captain to lose no opportunity to speaking any vessel outward-bound. At length, near the Equator, about a fortnight after we had passed St. Helena (Where we did not touch), we fell in with a vessel which supplied us with papers announcing the change of ministry, and his exultation at that intelligence may be easily conceived. We talked of nothing else for days : but his was not the triumph of party or of a sectarian spirit-it was in its probably beneficial effects on the fate of India, that he regarded the event as a subject of triumph. When we got within a few day's sail of the channel we fell in with a vessel only four days out, that brought us intelligence of the extraordinary circumstances of the second reading of the Reform Bill being carried in the House to which the Tories had so long commanded majorities, by a single vote! It was evident, that the cause of Reform was progressing, and that a dissolution would insure the ultimate success of a measure which from its unexpected comprehensiveness seemed to have united the suffrages of the whole country in favour of the Whig administration. Rammohun Roy was again elated with the prospects of the success of the great objects of his mission to England, indeed of the general advance of the cause of liberty, which these events promised. A few days afterwards, at that eventful crisis of our history when the whole nation was in a state of excitement and the topic of conversation in every drawing-room, in every club, and at every tea-table-the all-absorbing topic, was-Reform, and the great question was fixed for a second reading-at that important and deeply interesting crisis, Rammohun Roy first landed in Great Britain. The effect of this contagious enthusiasm of a whole people in favour of a grand political change, upon such a mind, was of course electrifying, and he caught up the tone of the new society in which he found himself with so much ardour that at one time I had fears that this fever of excitement, which led him to neglect all precautions, would prove too much for him and that he would fall a victim to his zeal in noble cause, ere he could strike a blow for it, in the very fields in which the great battle was to be fought and won.

His arrival was no sooner known in Liverpool, than every man of any distinction in the place hastened to call upon him; and he got into inextricable confusion with all his engagements, making half a dozen sometimes for the same evening, inspite of very attempt to keep him right by entering them in tablets presented to him for the purpose, until at last people understood him so well that they never invited him until they had consulted his visiting list and of course no one took offence at breaches of etiquette which were occasioned not so much by his ignorance of its laws, to which they were ascribed, as to the kindness of his nature, which made it painful to him to refuse any one. He was out morning, noon, and night, though the change of climate (we reached Liverpool in April, in a rather backward spring), had brought on a slight cough, and he suffered much from his lameness, owing to the accident at the Caps, in ascending and descending stairs. Of course on all occasions whether at breakfast or dinner, a number of persons were assembled to meet him, and he was constantly involved in animated discussions on politics on theology, which made him forgetful of time and fatigue.

The first public place we attended was Dr. Grandy's Unitarian Chapel. I endeavoured, as the day was raw and chilly, to dissuade him from going, knowing that in a large lofty building, sitting for several hours, he would aggravate his cold, and perhaps suffer severely; but all remonstrance was vain, and accordingly we went to this place of worship with an amiable family of the name of Yates, who brought their carriages for us. The chapel was crowded. The sermon was judiciously adapted to the occasion, in exposition of the duty of unlimited charity in our judgments of the creeds of other men and of the principles of belief; I think, if I have not forgotten it, seemed to me on the whole, rather too metaphysical; but not the less approved apparently by Rammohun Roy, who listened to it with the most profound attention, and afterwards expressed himself very much pleased with it. When the sermon was over, the scene that ensued was curious; instead of dispersing as usual, the congregation thronged up every avenue I crowding to get a near view of him as he passed out; indeed his own attention was arrested by an object which deeply affected him : a nural tablet to the memory of Mr. Tait, an amiable member of this community, who died here some years ago, was pointed out to him, and he was unable for some moments to recover the shock which it occasioned him by vividly re-calling the loss of dear and intimate friend. When he did, he attempted to express his feelings, and as he did so with propriety, though with hesitation, the surprise and excitement of the crowd at hearing a native of India address them in their native tongue, was extreme, and it was near an hour after the service terminated ere we could make our way out of the church, thought this dense throng; indeed, we should have been detained longer if one of the Mr. Yates's had not got upon a seat and addressed the people, explaining that their distinguished visitor was in delicate health and lame from an accident. All this time he was standing and suffering much pain; and at length, as we made our way out of the chapel, he had to shake hands with many who had waited for that purpose. To some his adopted son was scarcely less an object of curiosity, and to him it was fine fun; he seemed to enjoy being stared at, amazingly.

In the evening he went to hear the Reverend Mr. Scoresby, the son of the celebrated artie navigator, who was also a sailor himself at one time, and is a man of great scientific reputation, though now of the Established Church and of the evangelical sect. As a preacher, I believe this gentleman is chiefly remarkable for his earnestness, thought the experience of his early life in some of the sublimest scenes of nature, and his adventures in the frozen seas in whaling, as well as his scientific researches, supply him with varied and striking illustrations, in the application of which I am told he exhibits much skill and judgment. Rammohun Roy spoke in terms of admiration of his preaching.

Among the first to pay their respects to my lamented friend were three of the sons of the celebrated William Roscoe, the elegant historian of the Medici, of whom Washington Irving says in his brief but beautiful sketch of him, that "Wherever you go in Liverpool, you perceive traces of his footsteps in all that is elegant and liberal." They came not merely on their own account, but charged with an affectionate greeting from their eminent and amiable parent, who had already the very day of our arrival sent a note to Rammohun Roy at the hotel, acquainting him of the interesting fact that he (Mr. R.) had some time previously written him a letter, addressed to Calcutta (which had crossed him in the voyage), accompanied by a copy of all his works, in token of his admiration of the zeal, and worth, and talent, of his Hindu collaborateur, in the great cause of reform and philanthropy. The note was a very touching and characteristic communication, and was immediately acknowledged by the warmest expressions of admiration and regard for its gifted and amiable author. Mr. Roscoe had not I think for years quitted his apartment being troubled with a paralytic affection, which confined him to the recumbent posture; and latterly he had not been in the habit of seeing any but his most intimate friends.

The interview, I learned, at which none but the two distinguished individuals, and one of Mr. Roscoe's sons, were present, was deeply affecting, and indeed Rammohun Roy felt it so much, that he could not speak about it. I believe they both wept with mingled emotions of joy and sorrow, which will be appreciated only by those who can understand how much there was in the circumstances of the case, touch the hearts of two men of such ardent and enthusiastic minds. Mr. Roscoe had looked forward to this event as one of these contingencies which was scarcely within the range of probability, and when it came to pass, he was scarcely prepared for it. He had long been acquainted with Rammohun Roy's reputation, with his writings and his patriotic and philanthropic views, which found and echo in his own enlightened mind and generous heart, and perhaps even magnifying all the obstacles which a Hindu has to surmount ere he can present such claims to our admiration, the great Roscoe considered his native friend a being to whom even he should look up with the sort of reverence which extraordinary talent, worth and devotedness ever command. Then again the reflection could not escape them both, that this delightful interchange of ennobling sentiment must soon be terminated by the relentless decree of the grim tyrant who seemed already to have visibly asserted his power over one of them. In short, they felt that in all probability this was their first and last interview on this side of eternity, and so it proved; for Rammohun Roy remained only a few days in Liverpool, leaving it with the avowed intention of speedily returning to it. He heard of Mr. Roscoe's death while residing in London.

His introduction to the celebrated Roscoe took place, as I have mentioned, up-stairs (at the well-known house in Lodge Lane), but the room below was crowded with all the most distinguished persons in Liverpool, of almost every creed and profession. A great many ladies were present, and among these was Miss Roscoe, who appeared to inherit much of her father's enthusiasm and elevation of mind. All were eager in their inquires, about his title, his opinions, his habits, his objects in visiting England, & c. until he returned into the lower room, when, after recovering from the effects of his interview with the great and good man above, he immediately got into a very animated discussion with Miss Roscoe and some other ladies. In general, these friendly colloquies took a political or a religious turn. To hear a Brahmin zealously advocating Reform, and with an earnestness and emphasis that bespoke his sincerity, expatiating on the blessings of civil and religious liberty, of course, amazed our countrymen, and perhaps they were not less surprised if the discussion took a religious direction, to find him quoting text upon text, with the utmost facility, and proving himself more familiar with their sacred book than themselves : while the suavity of his manners delighted a much as his acuteness and acquirements surprised his auditors.

The wealthy and esteemed Quakers, the Croppers and Bensons, paid him a great deal of attention, and at their hospitable mansions, where there was a display of elegance and a luxury of living, that seemed scarcely accordant with the simplicity of their peculiar sect. He met with persons of all faiths. Indeed, it is a fact honorable to the inhabitants of Liverpool that there is a greater absence of the sectarian spirit, than I have witnessed in any other town in England.

At one of these Quaker's parties, there were present high churchmen, Baptists, Unitarians, and Deists, all mingling in perfect harmony and Christian charity. On one of these occasions, Rammohun Roy, with a *naivete*, which particularly amused the Reverend Mr. Scoresby I recollect, attacked the Quaker practice of not paying their ministers. "The labourer," said he, "is worthy of his hire; if you preachers do their duty, why not remunerate them?" "Because," he was answered, "they are sufficiently rewarded in discharging it, seeing that none enter on that holy vocation, without they have a call to this labour of love to bring souls to Christ. If they are in want, we relieve them as we do all worthy brethren in thee faith : but we hold it to be inconsistent with the gospel to hold out the temptation of lucre to the ministers of religion." It seemed to that my friend had rather the worst of the argument; though he still continued it. Mr. Scoresby, on the contrary, fancied him triumphant, I believe; at least as soon as he heard him quote "the labourer is worthy of his hire," he exclaimed, "Good, very true"; and abruptly terminating an interesting conversation in which I had been engaged with him, he rose and approached the disputants at the other end of the room, so eagerly, that I thought he was going to take part in the discussion; but he had the good taste to remain merely an attentive auditor.

On questions of religious faith Rammohun Roy was in general too pliant, perhaps from his excessive fear of giving offence or wounding the feelings of any body, which accounts for the controversy which has arisen about his religious opinions. In fact, no matter what the creed of the parties with whom he converted on such subjects, he was sure to impress them with an idea either that he was of their peculiar faith, or that they had converted him to it. A lady once observed to me, that she was rejoiced to find that he was a sincere Trinitarian and that he had merely gone to Unitarian meetings, the Jewish Synagogue, & c.

On one occasion, a gentleman in Liverpool Mr. William Rathbone (there is no reason, I think, for concealing his name), expressed a very great anxiety to hear his real opinions on religion, and invited him for that purpose to a quiet family tea-party. Mr. Rathbone is a Unitarian Christian, and very sincere in his own creed; but at the same time very tolerant of all other creeds, and of this he emphatically assured Rammohun Roy, that no one in Mr. Rathbone's, we found that there was, as he had promised, no one present but his family, save Spurzheim, the celebrated phrenologist, who was living in the house; and there seemed no reason for any disguise of my friend's views, nor did he I believe intend any. He entered freely into conversation with Spurzheim, until all of a sudden he seemed to fancy that Mr. R. s mother, a very elderly lady, might perhaps be of a different persuasion from the rest of the family, and less tolerant, and he drew in, and expressed some opinion at variance with the views he was supposed to entertain; when Spurzheim, with that quickness and good humour for which he is remarkable, immediately replied, "I shall not ask you, my friend, to yield to my arguments, but an authority for which in this house we have very high respect," and rising, he brought from another table Rammohun Roy's "Precepts of Jesus", and read a passage that directly contradicted the opinion the author of the book had the moment before expressed! The conversation afterwards took a general turn, and Mr. R.S. curiosity was disappointed.

Spurzheim and Rammohun Roy met very often, and as another example of the frankness with which he expressed his opinions on all subjects except religion, I may mention, that he never hesitated to laugh at the science of the great phrenologist, who parried his thrusts with infinite skill and good nature, always assuring him that it he would only study the fact on which it rested, he would change his opinion. He was very anxious to get a cast of the head of Rammohun Roy, but felt delicate in asking him to bare his cranium for the purpose, having been informed of the strong prejudice natives of India had to uncover their heads in the presence of strangers : he was at least promised, however, that he should be permitted to take one; but the promise was not fulfilled.

While he was at Liverpool he received a call from a gentleman with whom he was much amused; his visitor, a retired Indian officer, of the old school, with a squat figure, a jolly face, and a conscious smile of self-satisfaction playing on his features, was much more gifted with good nature than good sense or good taste. As soon as he saw the Hindu philosopher, he began addressing him in that elegant dialect in which European in this country make their *coup d' essai* in Easten languages. *Ucha, toom Bengali, hum Bengali, toom Bengali-well, Kysahy Sahib?"* Then turning to the young Raja, who was present. *"Ah! Chuckera (Chokera), well, kitna burras?"* (Or rather brass, as he made it), *Kysa mulk (Mooluq), Utcha hy*? And so on; to all which Rammohun gracefully bowed. At length, the gallant officer was informed, that the gentleman he was addressing, spoke English as well as he did (in truth he spoke it much more correctly). It appeared, that he came as a delegate from no less a potentate than the Mayor, who fearful of compromising his dignity by calling himself, had deputed his friend to suggest the propriety of the distinguished stranger's calling upon this high civil functionary, and to hint that if he did, the honour would be acknowledged by an *invite* to Lord Mayor's dinner; and the intimation was delivered with an air of importance, which seemed to imply, 'Think of that, Master Brooke!" it happened however, that the party he addressed, had not formed exactly the same lofty estimate of its importance as his visitor, and therefore declined the intimation with cold ingratitude, and when the Mayor was gone, he vowed, using an emphatic English expression, that if the Mayor wanted to see him, he might call upon him, as his superiors had done, and as it seemed to me, that hospitality, propriety, and good feeling demanded; but mayors are not always, it must be confessed, possessed of taste,

"unless it be

for calipash or calipee,"

And so our friend lost the opportunity of making his bow to the Mayor of Liverpool!

Rammohun Roy's stay in Liverpool was purposely shortened, in order that he might be present in the house of Commons on the second reading of the Reform Bill, about which he was deeply anxious. His enthusiasm on that subject, however, did not prevent him from observing the evidences of wealth and high civilization which the country presented, as he travelled up to London, and especially the contrast to India it exhibited, in the enclosure of every meadow and every field of cultivated land. The country seats, the beautiful prospects, the roads, the bridges, the canals, the innumerable public vehicles, we passed, all attracted his attention and admiration, and were eagerly pointed out by him to his adopted son, as the fruits of knowledge, industry, and public spirit, to which England owed her proud pre-eminence among the nations of the earth, and as objects which ought to excite in him a noble emulation. His journey by the steam trains from Liverpool has been described in a letter published here two years ago, and need not be repeated.

The scene at Manchester, when he visited the great manufactures, was very amusing. All the workmen, I believe, struck work, and men, women and children rushed in crowds to see the *King of Ingee*! Many of the "great unwashed" insisted upon shaking hands with him : some of the ladies, who had not stayed to make their toilets vary carefully, whished to embrace him, and he with difficulty escaped an honour which he by no means desiderated. The aid of the police was required to make way for him to the factories, and when he had entered, it was necessary to close and bolt the gate to keep out the mob. On one occasion, they had nearly succeeded in following him in. After shaking hands with hundreds of them, he turned round and addressed them, hoping they would all support the King and his Ministers in obtaining Reform; so happily had he caught the spirit of the people. He was answered with loud shouts, "The King and Reform forever."

On the road to London, wherever he stopped, the inn was surrounded; and at one place, the John Bull landlord, who had picked up a few words of French, which he pronounced vilely of course, would persist in attempting to speak to him in that language, though he soon found there was no necessity for it. "*Mounseer je parli Franchay, common voo portee voo*?" The landlord being such a linguist was the oracle of the place, I suppose, and he explained to the gaping auditors that "*Tippoo Sabe*" had come to England for to visit King William."

He arrived in London at night, and was, set down at some filthy inn near Newgate Street, where he intended to remain till morning : but going up to his allotted bedroom, the closeness and abominable that saluted his sense of smelling, induced him instantly to order a coach and set off to the Adelphi Hotel, where he arrived at 10 o' clock at night. He could not prevailed on to write to his friends in London to apprise them of the day in which he should reach it, but some gentlemen of the East India Committee had done that for him; still no one knew where to meet him, and Mr. Crawford had prepared rooms for him at Long's Hotel in Bandstreet : yet, strange to say, long after he had retired to rest, the venerable Bentham, who had not for many years called on any one, or left his house, I believe, except to take his habitual walk in his garden, found his way to the hotel, and left a characteristic note for him, "Jeremey Bentham to his friend Rommohun Roy", Alas! He also is now-gone to that bourne whence no traveller returns. Bentham, Roscoe, Rammohun Roy-these are names that will go down to posterity as those of the benefactors of the human race, and the most extraordinary men of their age.

As soon as it was known in London, that the great Brahmin

philosopher had arrived; the most distinguished men in the country crowded to pay their respects to him : and he had scarcely got into his lodgings in Regent Street when his door was besieged with carriages from 11 in the morning till 4 in the afternoon, until this constant state of excitement (for he caught the tone of the day, and vehemently discussed politics with everyone), actually made him ill, and confined him to his room, indeed to his bed almost, when his physicians gave positive orders to his footman not to admit visitors; of course not a few of these appreciated his character and attainments : but there were too many who sought only to *lionize* him, and turn him to account as an attraction to fill their rooms at their routes or *soress*. The old Dowager Countess of Cork, who assembles the literary, the scientific, the religious, and all sorts of characters of distinction, by turns, was among the earliest of his pressing invitors.

The Directors, the King of the East, who had countenanced the persecution of a near relative of his by their servants, eagerly paid their court to him, and laboured very anxiously to convince him how earnest they were to promote the good of the people of India. It was curious to witness also the sycophant adulation he received from some of those retired Indians, who, when here, had spoken of him contempt, and who would have felt their dignity offended if he had ventured to ascend their stairs without taking off his shoes. Ex-councillors and judges, even ex-governors were all forward to claim the honour of his acquaintance! In fact, the scene was strange and ludicrous, like some of these changes which the Harlequin in the Pantomime effects by a touch of his wand.

Among the distinguished visitors who really sought his acquaintance with a view to acquire information for an important purpose was Sir Wilmot Horton, then appointed to the situation of Governor of Ceylon, on which he has since conferred so much advantage and done so much honour to himself. Sir Wilmot was introduced to him I think by Sir Henry Strachey, a name that now belongs to Indian history.

It is curious fact that my lamented friends was for a

considerable time much more in Tory than in Whig circles; because, I suppose, that party, with its usual alertness and activity, had been the first to pay court to him; but I confess I could scarcely forgive his being introduced into the House of Lords by the Duke of Cumberland. In politics, however, he never disguised his opinions, but attacked his Tory friends with great vehemence, without and hesitation. I was present one day when he had a long controversy with the honourable Stuart Wortley on the Reform Bill, in which his opponent, a handsome and most gentlemanly young man, by the way, and of most pleasing manners, insisted upon it, that no man could be a judge of the question who had not studied the *practical working* of our glorious theory, and made himself master not only of the principles of the Bill, but of every item of it from the preamble to the last borough in schedule F.

The next amusing instance I remember of his extraordinary bluntness with his Tory friends occurred at an interview with Sir Edward Hyde East, whose name appeared on one of the minorities on the great question. "Indeed, I am very much shocked," said he, "to see your name on the list of those-vagabonds", (I think he said; but he used a coarse word, which of course he immediately recalled) who voted against the Bill last night. Wool-rich Whitmore, who was present, enjoyed the Honourable Baronet's confusion, but his courtier habit soon enabled him to recover from it, and parry the thrust with a card of invitation.

The influence which Rammohun Roy obtained over the first men in the kingdom, of all parties, was extraordinary. An urgent letter of his prevented the Tory Peers from opposing the Indian Jury Bill, and indeed on all questions of Indian policy he was regarded as quite an authority : though the Company's influence or the weakness of the ministry must finally have prevailed against him. With Lord Brougham he was on terms of the closest and most confidential intimacy; and, in short, he was honored and esteemed by men of the most opposite opinions.

It is stated in London paper, in an article published since

his death, that he was a republican in politics. I believe this to be a mistake, if it respected England. He admired republicanism in the abstract, and thought that in America it worked well. He had a great partiality for that country where he had many friends, and which he certainly intended to visit; and I have been informed, that it was resolved to receive him throughout the Union as a national visitor.

Of his religious opinions all can say with confidence is, that he certainly was not an "Atheistical Brahmin," but a devout believer in Divine Providence, and assuredly a most devoted advocated of Christian morality. He was a member of a Unitarian Society here, and appears from the last accounts to have died in that faith.

His style of living in general was perfectly unostentatious; except for a short time, about three months, when he had yielded to advice, that was any thing but disinterested, and taken up his residence in a most magnificent abode in Cumberland Terrace, Regent's Park, where he live extravagantly; but his good sense soon prevailed over this folly : he reflected that men whose good opinions was worth having, who could appreciate his higher claims to esteem, would not respect him the more for this display and lavish expenditure, which indeed, his means were not adequate to maintain for a long period : and he abandoned this splendid mansion, and went to live with Mr. Hare, the brother of Mr. David Hare of Calcutta, in Bedford Square, where he continued while he was in London. He kept a plain chariot with a coach-man and footmen in neat liveries; in fact, adopted and adhered to the style of a private gentleman, of moderated fortune; though still courted by the first men in the Kingdom. It has been said, that he had never enjoyed health in the country. This is a mistake : he had suffered occasionally from illness, but I often heard him declare that he was surprised to find the climate agree with him so well, and that he felt better and stronger than when in India.

Rammohun Roy surpassed the generality of his countrymen in his personal appearance, almost as much as in his mental powers, in his prime of manhood his figure was beyond the common height, and was stout and muscular in proportion. His countenace wore an expression of blended dignity and benevolence, that charmed at first sight, and put his visitors at their ease while it checked an irreverent familiarity. In the latter part of his life, which closed in his sixtieth year, his manly figure began to droop, perhaps not so much from age as the weight of thought and the toil of study. But his fine dark eye, though it lost something of its fire, retained its intelligence and amenity to the last.

It is time to close this communication, for I have already occupied too large a space with these imperfect reminiscences and hasty remarks, and I will only add, therefore, that whatever and have been his errors, he displayed high moral qualities, extraordinary intellectual attainments, and a zeal and enthusiasms in a noble cause that has never been surpassed in short, that his death has been justly described as a public calamity,—an irreparable loss to the people of India.

The Calcutta Literary Gazette, Calcutta,
February 15, 1834
March 4, 1834.

CHRONOLOGY

May 22, 1772 : Rammohun Roy's birth at Radhanagar, near Krishnanagar, Hugli.

1787 : Rammohun Roy leaves for Tibet to study Buddhism.

1790 : Rammohun Roy returns from Tibet and leaves for Benaras for the study of Sanskrit literature.

1800 : Birth of Radhaprasad Roy, the eldest son of Rammohun Roy.

1801 : John Digby of the Bengal Civil Service meets Rammohun Roy.

1803 : Rammohun Roy publishes his first work *'Tuhfatul Muwah-Hidin' or Gift to Monotheists,* in Persian with a preface in Arabic.

1803 : Death of Rammohun Roy's father, Ramakant Roy.

1811 : Death of Rammohun Roy's eldest brother, Jagmohan Roy Rammohun Roy tries to present Jagmohan's wife from self-immolation, but fails. He takes up a vow to uproot the custom of widow-burning.

August 3, 1812 : Birth of Rammohun Roy's second son, Ramaprasad Roy.

1812 : The Model Constitution of Spain is dedicated to Rammohun Roy, the most liberal, noble, wise and virtuous Brahmo.

February 1, 1814 : Rammohun Roy makes Calcutta the permanent centre of his activities.

1815 : Rammohun Roy publishes his translation to he *Vedanta Sutra,* from Sanskrit; to Bengali. It was republished in 1815 itself in Hindi, Bengali and English. The *Abridgement of the Vedanta.*

October 25, 1815 : William Yates meets Rammohun Roy.

1815 : Rammohun Roy visits the Baptists Mission at Serampore and meets William Carey.

1816 : Rammohun Roy publishes an *Abridgement of the Vedanta* in Bengali, Hindi and English. *The Government Gazette,* Calcutta hails it as a phenomenon in the literary world on February 1, 1816.

1816 : Rammohun Roy translates the *Kena and Isha Upanishads* into Bengali and English.

1817 : Rammohun Roy publishes *A Defence of Hindu Theism* and translates *Mandukya Upanished and Katha Upanishad into* Bengali and English.

1817 : Rammohun Roy's nephew, Govind Prasad Roy, files a suit in the Supreme Court, Calcutta, laying claim to the movable and immovable properties held by Rammohun Roy.

August 20, 1818 : Rammohun Roy lays the foundation of the 'Brahmo Samaj' at Calcutta.

November 30, 1818 : Rammohun Roy publishes the English edition of his tract on sati, *The practice of Burning Widows Alive.*

1819 : Rammohun Roy holds discussions with Subramanya Sastri on religion at the meeting of he Atmiya Sabha in Calcutta.

December 4, 1819 : Rammohun Roy establishes a Bengali Journal, the *Sambad Kaumudi* at Calcutta.

December 1819 : Rammohun Roy wins the legal suit against his nephew, Govind Prasad Roy regarding movable and immovable properties.

February 26, 1820 : Rammohun Roy *publishes the English version of his second tract on Sati The Practice of Burning Windows Alive.*

1820 : Rammohun Roy publishes his *Precepts of Jesus, and Appeal to the Christian Public* at Calcutta.

May 7, 1821 : Rev. William Adam writes to N. Wright' regarding Rammohun Roy's views on Christianity.

August 11, 1821 : Rammohun Roy writes to James Buckingham, editor of the *Calcutta Journal*, Calcutta regarding liberty of European nations and other colonies.

September 1821 : Rammohun Roy and Rev. William Adamestablish 'the Unitarian Committee, at Calcutta.

December 1821 : Dr. Josua Marshman publishes his comments in the *Friends of India*, Serampore on Rammohun Roy's *Second Appeal to the Christian Public.*

1822 : Rammohun Roy publishes his Encroachments on the Ancient *Rights of Females according to the Hindu Law of Inheritance.*

1822 : Rammohun Roy establishes an English school at Calcutta.

1822 : Rammohun Roy establishes the *Miratul Akhbar at* Calcutta.

1823 : Rev. Henry Ware, Unitarian Minister of Harvard College, Cambridge, United States, addresses a number of questions to Rammohun Roy on " *The Prospects of Christianity and the means of Promoting its Reception in India.*

January 12, 1823 : Rammohun Roy published his *Pathya Pradena,* In Bengali from Calcutta.

January 30,1823 : Rammohun Roy publishes his *Final Appeal to the Christian Public in defense of the Precepts of Jesus,* Calcutta.

May 3, 1823 : Dr. John Tytler comments on Rammohun Roy's concept of Divinity of the Christ in the *Bengal Harkaru,* Calcutta.

June 16, 1823 : Maharajah of Burdwan sues Rammohun Roy for the non-payment of Rs. 15002 towards land-revenue.

July 2, 1823 : Rammohun Roy writes to Samuel Smith Regarding promotion of Unitarianism.

December 11, 1823 : Rammohun Roy writes to Lord Amherst regarding English Education in India.

1823 : Rammohun Roy publishes his *Humble Suggestions for his countrymen, who believe in one God,* at Calcutta.

1823 : Rammohun Roy stops the publications of the *Miratul Akhbar* as a protest against the Government's Press Ordinance of March 14, 1823.

February 2, 1824 : Rammohun Roy writes t Rev. Henry Ware on the *Prospects* ‹.*f Christianity*.

June 4, 1824 : Rammohun Roy writes to Dr. T. Rees of the Unitarian Committee in London regarding the State of Unitarian Society in Calcutta.

1824 : Rammohun Roy and Members of the Presbyterian Church of Scotland submit a memorial to the General Assembly of the Church of Scotland, Calcutta regarding the missionary work in India.

1824 : Rammohun Roy and Rev. William Adam organize a Unitarian Mission in Calcutta and to which Rammohun Roy contributes Rs. 5000.

1825 : Rammohun Roy, Dwarkanath Tagore, Prassannakumar Tagore and others submit a petition to the Government for the freedom of the Press in India.

January 18, 1825 : Rammohun Roy publishes his tract on *Different Modes of Worship, at* Calcutta.

1826 : Rammohun Roy establishes the Vedanta College in House No. 74, Monictolla Street, Calcutta.

1826 : Rammohun Roy publishes his *Bengali Grammar* in English at Calcutta.

1827 : Rammohun Roy translates a Sanskrit tract on Divine Worship.

December 30, 1827 : Rammohun Roy establishes the British Indian Unitarian Association at Calcutta.

February 5, 1828 : Rammohun Roy writes to John *Bowring*. London regarding his endeavours to unite the Hindu Unitarians of Calcutta into an Association of Worshippers of One God.

August 18, 1828 : Rammohun Roy writes to John Crawford against the Jury Act, enclosing petitions signed by Hindus and Muslims, for submission to the British Parliament.

August 20, 1828 : Rammohun Roy lays the foundation of the Brahmo Sabha at Calcutta.

September 30, 1828 : Colonel J. Young wites to Jeremy Bentham from Calcutta regarding the Brahmo Sabha and the religious ideas of Rammohun Roy.

January 22, 1829 : Rammohun Roy writes to John Tuckerman regarding the British Indian Unitarian Association.

August 27, 1829 : Rammohun Roy and others submit a petition against the Jury Act.

December 4, 1829 : Lord William Bentinck abolishes *Sati* through a Regulation, issued from Calcutta.

December 17, 1829 : 116 persons "representing the entire wealth and intelligence of Calcutta", hold a public meeting at the Town Hall demanding the right of the Europeans to settle in India.

December 15, 1829 : Rammohun Roy attends a public meeting at the Town Hall, Calcutta, for throwing open China and India Trade through British Parliamentary intervention.

December 19, 1829, 800 Hindus submit a petition to the Governor General against the regulation of December 4, 1829.

January 16, 1830 : Rammohun Roy and his followers present an address to Lord William Bentinck, congratulating him for the abolition of sati.

January 17, 1830 : Rammohun Roy's opponents : Raja Radhakant Dev, Maharaja Kalikrishna Bahadur, Nimaichand Siromani, Harnath Turkbhushan, Bhawani Charan Banerji, Gopi Mohan Dev, Nimoni De and Gokul Nath Mallick collect Rs. 11260 for appealing to the authorities in England the prohibition of Sati. They form themselves into a religious society, the Dharma Sabha.

July 13, 1830 : Rammohun Roy permits Alexander Duff to run his English School at the Brahmo Samaj establishment.

November. 14, 1830 : J. Young writes to Jeremy Bentham regarding Rammohun Roy's profound knowledge of the sacred books.

November 19, 1830 : Rammohun Roy sails from Calcutta to Liverpool in the *Albion*, with his adopted son Raja Ram Roy, Ramratan Mukherjee, the cook Ramhari Das, the attendant, and James Sutherland.

April 8, 1831 : Rammohun Roy lands in Liverpool

May 1831 : Rammohun Roy addresses the Unitarian Association in London.

June 28, 1831 : Miss Lucy Aikin describes Rammohun Roy as a person of extraordinary merit, with great intelligence and ability, uniting modesty with simplicity and well-versed in the political state of Europe and an ardent well-wisher to the cause of freedom.

September 19, 1831 : Rammohun Roy publishes his *Questions and Answers on the Judicial System of India* and pleads for the substitution of English for Persian in the Courts of Law, trial by jury, separation of judiciary and the executive, and the codification of the criminal and civil laws of India.

June 1832 : The British Parliament passes the Reform Bill.

September 13, 1832 : Rammohun Roy Sails for Paris.

1832 : Rammohun Roy meets the French Emperor Louis Philippe.

November 10, 1832 : The Brahmo Samaj organises a public meeting in Calcutta to congratulate the King of England for the abolition of sati.

January 1833 : Ram Mohun Roy returns to England from France.

January 11, 1833 : The British Parliament rejects an appeal against the abolition of sati.

September 2, 1833 : Rammohun Roy leaves London for Bristol.

September 11, 1823 : Bristol Unitarians arrange a party in honour of Rammohun Roy at Stapleton Grove.

September 12, 1833 : The British Parliament renews the East India Co.'s charter for another 20 year.

September 19, 1833 : Rammohan Roy stricken with fever and his pulse gows weak. He develops spasms and headache and later he was paralysed on his left side.

September 27, 1833 : Rammohun Roy dies of billous fever at Stapleton Grove, Bristol.

Index

U

V

W

Z